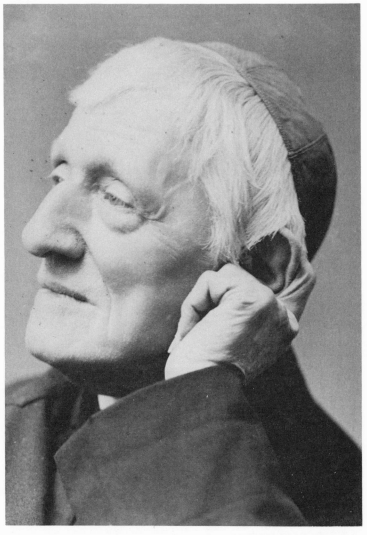

(photo by Barraud)

John Henry Newman

ON THE IDEA OF CHURCH

John Henry Newman
ON THE IDEA OF CHURCH

by EDWARD JEREMY MILLER

With a Foreword by
JAN WALGRAVE

THE PATMOS PRESS
SHEPHERDSTOWN, WEST VIRGINIA
1987

Dedicated to

KATHLEEN
BRIAN
KEVIN

Contents

Foreword

To a Victorian like John Henry Cardinal Newman, writing letters was an important part of daily life and of literary self-expression. Newman did it very carefully, as if with a consciousness that the letters might someday be published. His own saying that a person can best be known from his correspondence probably had one of its roots in his own practice and actually finds in his case an eminent exemplification.

Moreover, Newman's psychological attitude toward friends and close acquaintances was significantly different from his attitude toward the human world at large and the anonymous circle of possible hearers and readers to whom he addressed himself in his discourses and his many controversial and other writings. Whereas toward the latter he skillfully observed the claims of adaptation, reserve, "economical" limitation, and rhetorical fitness, he felt with the former a greater freedom and ease to speak his mind and to express his convictions and opinions without restraint. To be sure, being perhaps the most consulted Catholic personality of his time and knowing the weight of his utterances with those who consulted him, he never failed strictly to adapt and limit his counsels and arguments to the needs and capacities of his correspondents. He could be very aloof and buttoned up with unknown or unfriendly persons who put to him indelicate or insidious questions or pressed upon him unsympathizing criticisms or irrelevant objections. Some of his letters are masterpieces of cunning circumspection and subtle irony. But with his friends, his next of kin, and familiars, his behavior and conversation were—according to this testimony—easy, tender, pleasant, and openhearted. Thus does he reveal *himself* in his private correspondence.

There were many subjects of the day that Newman could not deal with in public as outspokenly as it was his natural tendency to do. On ecclesiastical matters especially, he had to be very prudent under the watching eye of Propaganda and the English ultramontanists. His sense of obedience to church authority and of respect for his superiors often prevented him from exercising in public that freedom of thought and speech which in his view was as basic a principle in the church as that of authority itself. He boldly asserted his principles on certain occasions, such as the writing of the *Apologia* and the public letters to Edward Pusey and to the duke of Norfolk; yet even for such general statements he had to suffer contradiction and suspicion on the part of ultraconservative theologians and churchmen. Were it not for the general applause of the Catholic laity, for the efficiency of his explanations and arguments with the British intelligentsia, and for the rapid increase of understanding and sympathy he won in England for the Roman Catholic religion, he would probably have met with more serious difficulties. In the time of Pio Nono, however, and the atmosphere created by the predominance of an intolerant ultramontane party, Newman could not take the risk openly to criticize concrete actions, decisions, counsels, and rules emanating from leading ecclesiastical powers or inspired and encouraged by them. How often he did not agree, yet kept silent and advised patience! There was in Newman a combination of historical insight and prophetical lucidity, a deep conviction that important, comprehensive changes simply were a matter of time, prudent preparations, and confident forbearance. These qualities perfectly fitted within his encompassing providential system.

To friends, however, and people he knew he could trust, Newman often confided candidly his judgment on current affairs and did not mince his words, and this particularly on ecclesiastical topics of the day. Those judgments and confidences are indispensable materials for a full and correct knowledge and appreciation of Newman's theological views on the church. To be sure, by reason of the comprehensiveness and consistency of his Christian view of things, his personal utterings were not inspired by passing moods but by his general principles and in keeping with the idea of the church. The church was perhaps the main idea that in his dealings with the problems of the Anglican church and later of the Catholic church—the main concern of his life and thought—had taken possession of his mind, in a process of slow and gradual development led on by ever-fresh experiences and constant reflection. Therefore we may expect that the idea of the church reflected in his writings and the idea of the church exhibited in his letters are substantially the same and that they mutually complete one the other, the former explaining Newman's general principles and views, while the latter showing his application of them in practical issues.

The idea of a reality, somewhere defined by Newman as the "sum total of its possible aspects" gradually clarified through the ages by historically conditioned reflection, may be more or less complex. In the case of the church as a visible, historical world-institution, the idea is particularly rich, multifarious, and complex. So many functions and offices, each with its own special concerns and interests, enter into its essential constitution; from their very nature they give rise in their functional togetherness to all kinds of tensions and conflicts. In his last major contribution to ecclesiology, the preface to the third edition of the *Prophetical Office,* Newman not only attempted to describe and analyze this inner and essentially conflictual structure but also tried to make it acceptable and illuminating as necessary and fruitful for the life of such an institution as the church in such an ecological medium as the historical human world. This synthesis is his final conclusion from his experiences in the church and is meant to be a hypothesis that most adequately accounts for the facts and justifies the otherwise disquieting phenomena that could be brought up against the church.

Edward Jeremy Miller's treatment of Newman's idea of the church, although particularly based on a careful and exhaustive study of all the relevant remarks, judgments, and arguments, spread through the twenty-one volumes of Newman's recently published Roman Catholic correspondence—his knowledge on this point is really complete—gives no less attention to Newman's occasional and systematic writings. Miller particularly gives full attention to the final synthesis of the preface to the *Prophetical Office,* keeping constantly in view the ideas developed in it in order retrospectively to understand the hundreds of scattered remarks and partial treatments on this topic in the letters and earlier essays. Hence it may be said that Miller's work is, to date, the only complete study of Newman's idea of the church. This judgment holds good also for Miller's integration in the idea of the church of its more secret spiritual dimensions that are the proper object of a theology of the church: the invisible world that is the kingdom of God in which the risen Lord has been enthroned as the governing head, bestowing grace and eternal life on those who have faith in him as the God of love who became human and suffered the death on a cross "for us and our salvation." This invisible Christ is the church in which the dispensation of forgiveness and eternal life is worked by the sacramental mediation of grace through the visible actions of preaching and theology, sacramental ministry and pastoral care, government and authority, accepted in a spirit of faith and obedience.

The articulated richness of illustrations and applications, picturing in actual detail this essential image of the church, is the unique merit of Miller's book. It fills a gap in the already immense output of Newman literature.

J. H. Walgrave

Prologue

Two decades have passed since the Second Vatican Council unleashed a renewal movement in the Roman Catholic church. The early days were euphoric for many church-minded Catholics, and one heard enthusiastic predictions for an invigorated Catholic Christianity. Protestant church leaders were also excited by the surge of ideas and hopes coming from the council halls, especially those setting the Catholic church on a new and encouraging ecumenical path. There were at the same time, however, wary onlookers. Some Protestants were suspicious of the ecumenical overtures, thinking that Rome could not be other than its long history of triumphalism. Some Roman Catholics became so-called prophets of gloom, predicting that the council's directions would lead to the destruction of that unity and stability which they reckoned as hallmarks of the true church.

Neither the euphoric visions nor the dire predictions came to pass. The post–Vatican II church presents a mixed picture. It has undertaken renewal but not with the speed and thoroughness its "progressives" had envisioned; it experienced destabilization but not to the extent the "traditionalists" predicted. On one matter all parties agree: Catholicism became an "opened church." The phrase is suggested by Henri Bergson's distinction between an open and closed society. Closed societies are agents of strong group cohesion and uniformity; outsiders are held suspect or scorned. Open societies are filled with currents and movements somewhat in tension; furthermore, the group's activities reach out to persons and ideas beyond its pale.[1] Roman Catholicism was "opened up," in this latter sense, by the Second Vatican Council.

Some features of this postconciliar period suggest why a book on John Henry Newman's ecclesiology may be pertinent. The conciliar renewal surfaced many tensions and reminded people how large and diversified the church actually is. The laity, for example, assumed greater prominence. Laity were indeed active before the council, but their contributions usually were under strict clerical control. In new movements, however, and even in many parishes laity have begun to exercise greater autonomy and self-determination, or at least to demand them. This activity has caused tensions between laypersons and clerical authorities. Some laity feel that their gains have been too modest or too controlled. Some pastors and bishops, on the other hand, think that the laity are becoming too critical and aggressive, and these ecclesiastics long for the more docile attitude of yesteryear.

Another tension is felt in the relationship between the teaching role of theologians and that of the hierarchy. Immediately after the council theologians enjoyed "smooth sailing." They traveled the lecture circuit and explained to eager audiences, including bishops and parish pastors, the new theological orientations. Publishing houses turned out all sorts of books whose authors became well known and respected. But the flow of ideas was moving too quickly and unchecked. The Vatican began to exercise censoring muscle; charges of unsound doctrine, theological excesses, and disloyalty to the Catholic tradition were made. More recently the Vatican has removed from some theologians the title of teacher of Catholic doctrine and has prohibited others from publishing. Tensions led to questions: What are the responsibilities of one group to the other? How are they to complement each other? What are the range and limits of academic freedom for professor-theologians? Such questions had simpler answers in preconciliar days.

In a survey of postconciliar tensions, one cannot avoid mentioning the *Humanae Vitae* encyclical. This papal teaching condemning certain methods of birth control has had a very mixed response from Catholics, both priests and laity. Surveys conducted in the United States indicate that the majority of married Catholics do not agree with the teaching and do not follow it. These are not people with so-called bad will; they are committed and earnest Catholic Christians. They simply do not "buy the teaching." A deeper issue is involved that goes by the technical theological phrase, the 'reception of an authentic teaching.'

What is to be concluded when a teaching from the desk of the pope is, apparently, not 'received' by large numbers of the faithful? Are they disobedient and in the wrong? Or are their conscientious instincts truer? In whatever event, laity and episcopacy are not together on this issue, and the disjunction is symptomatic of a new questioning mentality toward the teaching office. The same conflict resulted from the Vatican Declaration against the possibility of ordaining women. It, too, has met with public dissent in some quarters.[2] Papal noninfallible teachings are being examined with critical eyes, and adherence is no longer assured by the weight of authority alone.

The final tension to be noted is more fundamental than the others, yet it is somewhat confined to the professional ranks of theologians. I refer to the pluralism characterizing contemporary theology. For a very long period prior to the Second Vatican Council, Catholic theology was based on certain shared convictions found in scholastic philosophy. While there were always isolated exceptions to this "theology of the schools," such as the Tübingen theologians and J. H. Newman himself, and while there were subtleties of scholasticism under heated debate, a common *world view* was shared that at least allowed the scholastic theologians to understand what each was claiming. This situation has changed. Today's Catholic theologians base their research on different and often conflicting philosophical foundations. There is no single world view allowing shared basic assumptions on which all agree. Some very respected theologians, such as Karl Rahner and Edward Schillebeeckx, have maintained that a single world view, integrating the claims of philosophy, the findings of natural and human sciences, and the experiences of individuals, is no longer possible. The resulting pluralism is intensified further when one takes account of current biblical exegesis. Theology uses exegesis as one of its sources for reflection, yet there are strong differences of opinion among biblical scholars on the meaning of scriptural texts. What exegetical position is one to adopt, and on what criteria?

This fundamental pluralism, which amounts to different ways of sizing up the world and interpreting our experiences, is also at play in the tensions of the birth control teaching. Many married Catholics disagree with Pope John Paul II, and disagreed with Paul VI at the time of the encyclical, because of a different world view. They responded from their experience as married persons and parents, and they concluded that the pope viewed certain aspects of sexual love differently from the way they did or could. While no attempt is made to discriminate world views as theologians must do, many laity are in a situation of pluralism *vis-à-vis* the hierarchy, are following their consciences, and in effect are contributing to the social tension. In this study of Newman we shall be meeting the themes of experience-as-teacher, the following of conscience's voice, and the place of tension within the social fabric of the church.

These few samplings from the postconciliar situation coalesce around a common motif: authority in the Roman Catholic church. Some have termed the current situation a crisis of authority. Such tensions about authority may be an oversimplification of the social complexities, but they are surely ingredient to any transition from a more tightly controlled church to an "opened church," and it is in that direction Vatican II pushed the Catholic church. So why consider Newman's ecclesiology, since he is remembered as the great apologist of the authority-heavy Catholicism of a century ago? Does not that Catholicism represent the "closed society" which Vatican II opened? Would not his ecclesiology be a Victorian period piece?

Newman worked out his views on the church during a highly authoritarian period of Roman Catholicism, and it is true he defended Rome's claims for possessing doctrinal authority. But in many ways his full view was very much out of step with the prevailing mentality of his times. I have used the distinction between an opened and a closed society. Newman struggled for an opened church. He was constantly under fire from "closed society" folk, those whose mentality historians term *ultramontane*. Many people today are unaware of Newman's struggle with church authorities and with ultramontanism. Ironically the title of cardinal has tamed him in twentieth-century eyes. John Henry Cardinal Newman was the great upholder of things Catholic, the great polemicist against the church's detractors. These things he surely was, but there was another side to him too little known and appreciated. He was the great defender of the rights of the laity. He was a staunch advocate of freedom of thought. He was a critic of authoritarianism in the church. In these re-

gards I like to think of him as Fr. John Newman of the Birmingham Oratory, not as Cardinal Newman. And Fr. John Newman
was his title through three decades of battles he waged for a
more opened church. He was seventy-eight years old, with the
struggles behind him, when a new pope came along and named
him a cardinal in 1879. Sometimes I wonder how even this happened, because Fr. Newman of Birmingham was such a maver-
ick to the ultramontanists. But Leo XIII, who honored Newman, was a different cut from Pius IX and the theologians he
gathered about himself.

Part of Newman's genius lies in what the cardinalate represented. I do not refer to the power of the position but to the
legitimacy it gave to the kind of ministry and influence he exercised in the years before the Red Hat. Newman integrated an
ability to love the church and to criticize its defects at the same
time. He was both loyal and questioning. He respected authority
and challenged its misuse. We are tempted to think that future
cardinals are those who have avoided controversy and have
never "rocked the boat." Newman was always in a controversy,
and more than once he upset the people in high ecclesiastical
office. In 1859, for example, one of his articles on the rights of
the laity was sent to Rome for censure. Yet it was this Fr. Newman who received the title by which we know him today, the
cardinal.

At the very least Newman's battle scars give him some claim to
speak to our situation. Both his personal life and his theology—
and these can never be fully separated—illustrate the tensions
and polarities of the last twenty years. In life he was constantly
dealing with misunderstanding and suspicion. Although he converted to Roman Catholicism because he saw it as the true
church, he did not believe it was a perfect church. He pushed to
reform many areas, most of them relating to the use of ecclesiastical authority: preemptory decisions, overcentralization, controls on theological reflection by a single and quasi-official school
of thought, a clericalism that paid little heed to the experiences
of the laity. When he pushed in these areas, he met suspicions
and secret countermeasures from highly placed Catholic
sources. From another direction he heard allegations from Anglicans and evangelical Protestants that his conversion was insin-

cere, that he was on the verge of returning to the Church of England after having made a bad mistake. He seemed caught in the middle.

Newman's conversion was sincere, firm, and unshakable; thus he did not want to undermine the witness it gave to wavering Anglicans of the rightness of Catholicism. Yet in conscience he could not remain silent about certain needed reforms. How was he to balance the witness of loyalty and love with the witness of reforming critic? We must remember that Newman was a very public figure; whatever position he espoused would be widely reported. The tension of being both a committed Roman Catholic and a reforming voice was intensified by this public stature. It is especially in his private correspondence that one senses his strategy in dealing with the tension.

Newman's theology also illustrates current polarities and tensions. He was a strenuous champion of freedom of thought for doing theological work. But he recognized and supported the legitimate claims of hierarchical authority over the theological task. We must see what he meant by *legitimate*. Regarding the laity, he supported and worked for a vision of lay ministry that many have seen the Vatican II documents to mandate; yet laity had limits to which they were accountable, just as theologians had. Furthermore, he was concerned with the *process* of church teaching—how it came about and how it was assimilated. For the former he described the *sensus fidelium* (the consultation process) and for the latter the *consensus fidelium* (the reception process).

I note one final polarity: The church is holy; the church is sinful. Newman was convinced beyond a doubt that the church shares in the holiness of Christ, and it was for him the community in which he met saving grace. Yet as a keen student of history he knew more about ecclesiastical faults than most Protestant polemicists. How is one to affirm its holiness and recognize its faults? I have called these dual aims Newman's "theology of abuses" since both aims ought to be part of a more embracing vision. Because practicing Christians meet the church's wheat and chaff and must deal with this duality, Newman's vision should be instructive.

With these various aspects of his theology, Newman speaks essentially to the issues that exist as tensions in the post–Vatican II church. The questions will not go away, for they are fundamental. Freedom/authority, laity/clergy, the teachers/the taught, grace/sin, etc., involve such subtle relationships that they can never have a settled and final answer. As life itself, the tensions ebb and flow. They move first in one direction, then another; one pole balances the other. Newman was well aware of this curious dynamism in the fundamental issues of ecclesiology. One never feels he offers finished answers but rather a strategy of action. Living, for Newman, concerns right actions more than getting the answers straight. In the ecclesiology that follows I have termed the strategy *dialectics*. The term comes from a philosophy with which Newman was unfamiliar, and although the word was not his own, the idea was. The church is a living organism. It is composed of forces: clergy/laity, the freedom of the inquiring mind/authority, etc. These forces seek aims proper to themselves, yet for the well-being of the whole organism the forces must interact, must at times clash, and eventually they balance each other. This process is a simplified description of the dialectical strategy I perceive to be a motif in Newman's vision of the church.

Some observations need to be directed to the structure and then to the sources of the study that follows. Newman never wrote a systematically organized text on the church. He never, in fact, wrote any systematic texts; it was not his style of "doing theology." He preferred essays for reasons to which I shall return. As a result, his thoughts on the church are scattered throughout the nearly forty volumes of the Uniform Edition (the collected publications through which most readers know Newman) and the projected thirty-one volumes of private correspondence (materials through which he is scarcely known).[3] From this mass of material an arrangement emerged that reflects what I believe to be Newman's instincts about the church, his three basic orientations to it. He was continually concerned to relate people's more detailed thoughts to certain fundamental and deeply rooted convictions, which practically defined the *types* of persons they were. He called these convictions the "first principles" of thinking. Second, he was interested in *processes*. "Life is for action," was the way he put it.[4] Activity reveals theory, and theory should lead back to actions. Consequently, Newman's theology arose from what had in fact happened in the church, and his ideas were directed to what ought to happen.

The church *in process* absorbed him. Finally, certain dimensions of it were credible only if grace were present. Were God's grace not believed to be the primary cause and ultimate explanation of certain features of the church, such features would be nonsense and impossible to accept.

These orientations of Newman's thinking suggest three visions of the church. I term them a foundational, a pastoral, and a theological viewpoint. As such they are similar though not identical to the threefold distinction: fundamental theology, praxis theology, and dogmatic theology. Newman's threefold orientation responds to three different kinds of basic questions: (1) Why does someone practice religion in a church? (2) How ought that church to behave? (3) Is that church expressing more than the native abilities of its members? The questions remain both current and vexing.

In this study the three fundamental visions of the church are preceded by an initial chapter on Newman's personal style. A simple explanation governs this choice. One cannot separate what Newman thought from the kind of person he was. He admirably fulfilled his own dictum that the whole person thinks. Intellect alone does not explain thinking; memory, feelings, moral conscience, personal biography, etc. are necessary components also. There is need, consequently, to examine Newman himself, to assess his style, and to relate some of his story because his theology, between the lines, is autobiographical. It arose from the pastoral situations in which he found himself. He never wrote disembodied theology, as if he could retire to the quiet of his room and theorize over some distant issue. He reflected on his personal experiences, on the experiences of the church at that moment, and on the its past experiences as recorded in history.

I now turn to the textual sources. The Uniform Edition of Newman's books and essays has been in print for more than a century. It has been the main source for scholarship on Newman, and there has been a great deal of that.[5] One can readily get the impression that "Newman"as a subject is overworked. Curiously, however, even though the church figured so pivotally in Newman's life and thought, there are very few studies of his ecclesiology.[6] To this curiosity a second must be added. Newman's letters and diaries contain materials nearly as abundant as the Uniform Edition, yet they rarely informed Newman scholarship. Save for a few published selections,[7] the great bulk of his letters remained relatively inaccessible to the public and to most scholars until their recent publication. Thirty-one volumes are nearly completed, containing more than twenty thousand pieces. The sheer amount of letter writing boggles the mind! But the collection is both large and rich. The letters reveal aspects of Newman's thought hitherto unsuspected, or if suspected from the traditional sources, at least difficult to corroborate.[8]

The correspondence is particularly instructive for Newman's ecclesiology. In his books he rarely criticized the faults of Roman Catholicism since he was the great defender of its claims against Protestants. His letters do not gainsay this defense as if he had fabricated it all along, but they do show the other side of the issues, the darker side, as Newman assessed them. One finds unaccustomed candor in the letters. In writing to friends Newman could afford to express himself bluntly and unguardedly. He criticized the misuse of authority; he deplored the treatment of individuals. We find appeals for reform and renewal expressing themselves with a clarity and bluntness not to be found in his published books and essays. For Catholics of the post–Vatican II church, interested in the ongoing renewal, the Newman of the letters and diaries will seem a supportive colleague and timely commentator.

When Newman did write lengthy studies, he opted for the essay genre in preference to systematic tomes. A pastoral objective lay behind this choice. He wrote in order to help people to *decide*, to come to a concrete choice of action, especially to decide upon the identity of Christ's church and to act accordingly as he in midlife had done. Newman wanted his readers to be led to a "real apprehension" of an issue rather than to what he termed "notional [i.e., abstract] apprehension." One meets images, concrete examples, affective phraseology, all of which were calculated to stir the imagination to such a vivid apprehension of an issue that choice (the power of will) was invited. Newman's essays, even those of book length, moved in the direction of real apprehensions; systematic textbooks fed notional apprehension and served technical purposes, and these purposes he left to others.

In his essays, consequently, and more clearly in his private letters, Newman operated pastorally. He wished people to think clearly, but, more than that, he wanted them to come to conscientious decisions on those major questions of religious living: Is there a God? Has there been a revelation that provides an intimate knowledge of God? Is there a religious community (church) continuing God's purposes? Where is it to be found? How ought it to behave? Because these are questions of great urgency, Newman threw himself into them with an energy reflecting the difficult choices he had to make, and with the tender sympathy a pastor should bring to others who struggle with choices. He has helped me face such questions, and I hope that other readers find in him a pastoral companion who speaks to some of the real questions they carry.

John Henry Newman
ON THE IDEA OF CHURCH

CHAPTER ONE

Life and Style

*T*o understand Newman's theology and especially his ecclesiology requires one to understand a good deal about his temperament and the pivotal experiences of his life. Unlike many other major thinkers who fall within a school of thought or under the influence of an intellectual mentor, Newman lacks clear parentage. Although he himself mentioned influences in his autobiographical *Apologia pro Vita Sua* and others have correctly identified tendencies in which he shared, as John Coulson has done with the Anglican sacramental tradition of S. T. Coleridge and F. D. Maurice,[1] nevertheless these are people with whom Newman saw things similarly rather than mentors to whom he was indebted. In large measure Newman's seminal instincts came from within himself. They were rooted in certain personal tendencies—what I am calling his *style*—and they were fed by his experiences of people and events.

Style and story are causes in everyone's thinking surely, but with Newman they are paramount. He excelled in being able to plumb his experience thoroughly and to unravel it clearly. The intellectual mentor was within himself and extremely keen. Consequently, this study of Newman's ecclesiology begins with life and style rather than with his historical antecedents. Of the two, style in the sense of temperament and character is for present purposes more necessary to describe than is the story of his life. Biographies abound, most notably the 1912 classic by Wilfrid Ward and the definitive study by Meriol Trevor appearing in 1962.[2] I intend only a brief sketch of Newman's life, selecting those more salient features that provide context and backdrop to issues of his ecclesiology and that offer to readers unfamiliar with Newman a broad sense of his story. This sketch will make possible fuller attention to Newman's personal style.

John Henry Newman's life (February 21, 1801–August 11, 1890) spanned practically the entire nineteenth century. He was the oldest of six children, whose father was a London banker and whose mother had French Huguenot roots. She gave her son a religious orientation toward her own mild Calvinism and to her evangelicalism centered around family bible reading. When fifteen, Newman experienced a five-month illness he later described as a conversion period that gave him an intense and enduring sense of God's presence; it also led to his decision to remain a celibate. At this time he was introduced to the writings of the fathers of the church, and he became convinced that religion needed to be grounded in definite creeds.

Newman matriculated at Trinity College, Oxford, in 1817, but the college exerted little influence on his religious or intellectual life. His 1822 fellowship to Oriel College, then at the apex of its scholastic fame, was to change him profoundly and set the stage for his life of controversy and influence. In the Oriel common rooms Richard Whately taught Newman that the church was divinely founded and hence independent from the state. Edward Hawkins convinced him of the doctrine of baptismal regeneration, causing Newman to abandon the evangelical dicotomy between the 'converted' and the 'nonconverted.' Most important, Oriel introduced Newman to Edward Pusey and Richard Hurrell Froude, a disciple of John Keble. They brought Newman into contact with the High Church Anglican tradition and sensitized him to the common ground between Rome and Anglicanism, i.e., the continuity with early Christianity, particularly as regards the episcopacy and the sacraments. In 1825 Newman was ordained priest, the act a sign that he would never do theological work apart from its pastoral implications.

While traveling alone in Sicily in 1833, Newman was beset by another serious illness, this time typhoid, and during the long recovery he became convinced that God had a mission for him in England. His famous poem, "Lead, Kindly Light," was composed on the ship going home. Less than a week after Newman arrived, Keble preached the famous Assize Sermon attacking Parliament's interference in internal church affairs. Thus began the Oxford movement, which defended the divinely established prerogatives of the church and sought to renew the established church according to the pattern of the early centuries. Newman,

Keble, Pusey, and others authored the *Tracts for the Times,* thereby becoming known as Tractarians. Newman emerged as the movement's intellectual leader, a position testified to by his publications: *Lectures on the Prophetical Office of the Church* (1837) concerning authority; *University Sermons* (eventually published 1843) concerning religious belief; and above all the *Parochical and Plain Sermons* (1834–43), which translated the principles of the movement into a spirituality for Christian living and spread them over the nation.

After the publication of his Tract 90, which offered a Catholic interpretation (i.e., one consonant with the nature of the earliest church) of the Church of England's Thirty-nine Articles, Newman was censured by the bishops in 1841 and forced to leave Oxford; he and several companions (including his lifelong friend and confidant, Ambrose St. John) set up a quasi-monastic life-style at nearby Littlemore. For the next few years Newman sought to clarify his thoughts on the nature of the church and whether Roman Catholicism could be the legitimate evolution of the ancient and true church. Eventually coming to the conviction it was, he was received into Catholicism on October 9, 1845, and a few weeks later he published the justification for his conversion in *An Essay on the Development of Christian Doctrine.* Forty-five years of life remained, and Newman was at midlife in many senses.

Ordination to priesthood in Rome followed a year of study there, and Newman returned to England to establish the Oratory of St. Philip Neri—a group of secular priests, living in community together but without religious vows—in Birmingham. Here Newman lived the rest of his life among fellow Oratorians, ministering to the parish's mostly poor and uneducated members, many of them refugees from Ireland's crop famine. His pastoral activities have been overshadowed by the more famous controversies involving theological disputes. Nicholas Wiseman, his Birmingham district bishop, soon after left for assignment in London, and William Bernard Ullathorne was to be the Birmingham bishop under whom Newman worked.

During a "no-popery" period in the early 1850s, Newman delivered his famous lectures on prejudice, published as *Lectures on the Present Position of Catholics.* His attacks on the vile allegations of an Italian ex-Dominican, Giovanni Achilli, led to a long and costly libel trial brought by Achilli's sponsors, the Protestant Alliance. During the next few years Newman was involved in establishing a Catholic university in Ireland and was invited by Archbishop Paul Cullen to be its first rector. Frustrated by hierarchical interference, Newman resigned the rectorship after three years, but his lectures on *The Idea of a University* became a lasting monument to the ideals of Catholic higher education.

Other Oxford people who had followed Newman into the Roman church were to affect his later life. Frederick W. Faber joined the Birmingham Oratory but soon after founded another in London; he displayed a convert's enthusiasm in importing Italianate devotions into British Catholic life and proved to be a constant thorn for Newman. Edward Manning, who was to succeed Wiseman as cardinal archbishop of Westminster, and W. G. Ward, who was to edit the *Dublin Review,* represented ultramontane Catholicism, which stressed church authority, especially papal prerogatives, and opposed anything that implied Catholicism underwent development or was in need of reform. In 1859 Newman took over editorship of the *Rambler* in order to preserve an alternative Catholic voice to ultramontanism; his article on the right of the laity to be consulted about doctrine was sent to Rome as suspect of heresy. Furthermore, in the aftermath of the Dublin university failure, Manning thwarted Newman's attempts, all through the 1860s, to establish a Catholic foundation at Oxford that would afford high-quality education to the laity.

In 1864 Newman was unexpectedly delivered from these institutional frustrations by a public attack on his honesty from Charles Kingsley. All along Newman had had to deal with rumors that he was unhappy in Catholicism and was on the verge of reverting. Kingsley's assault led to Newman's account of the history of his religious thinking, the *Apologia pro Vita Sua,* which was read far and wide and has become a classic statement of personal faith alongside of St. Augustine's *Confessions;* it also returned Newman to national status.

Two significant writings mark the last years of the decade. Pusey, with whom a friendship was renewed when Newman needed letters for the Kingsley affair, had written about Roman abuses in Mariology; he afforded Newman occasion to write his *Letter to Pusey* describing a Catholic devotion to Mary much more moderate than Faber and the ultramontanists liked. Years of reflection on the nature of faith and certitude led to *An Essay in Aid of a Grammar of Assent,* Newman's most significant contribution to the philosophy of religion and also destined to become a classic.

The Vatican Council that convened on December 8, 1869, shaped Newman's life during the next decade. He was decidedly against the ultramontane push for a definition of papal infallibility, although he himself believed in the doctrine. Defining it, Newman thought, served no purpose; most Catholics already believed it, and Protestants would be angered by a formal definition. Papal infallibility was defined, however, and its interpretation was pushed to extremes by the ultramontanists, especially by Cardinal Manning in England. Many moderate-thinking Catholics urged Newman to come forward, but he could not provide his own interpretation without seeming to attack the cardinal. On Guy Fawkes Day, 1874, William Gladstone, the politician, launched a fierce attack, claiming that Catholics could not be loyal citizens to the Crown as long as they were under the decrees of the Vatican Council. This attack enabled Newman to respond indirectly to ultramontane exaggerations by ostensibly answering Gladstone. His *Letter to the Duke of Norfolk* became a celebrated study of the role of conscience and of moderation in the claims being made by the Vatican Council.

In 1877 Newman reedited the *Prophetical Office* and added to it a lengthy preface about abuses in the church. This preface was to be the last major writing of his career, and it is a marvelous example of the mental agility and keenness of the seventy-six-year-old warrior. No further battles remained, although Newman did prepare a later essay on biblical inspiration. Pius IX, the pope who began as a liberal in the 1840s and turned increasingly conservative thereafter, died in 1878 and was succeeded by Leo XIII. Leo showed his new policy by creating Newman his first cardinal, causing Newman to say that the cloud was lifted from him forever. He was allowed to remain an Oratorian, and he is buried at its rest home, Rednal, alongside Ambrose St. John.

Consideration of Newman's personal style—his manner of thinking, of sizing up complexities, of urging his convictions—will illuminate our understanding of his ecclesiology. It has been mentioned that in Newman's scheme the one who thinks and chooses is the person whole and entire, the person of ideas, feelings, memories, social constraints, ethical temper, etc. Therefore for Newman abstract argument, however sound and well based, was unlikely to be convincing; neither were direct appeals to the will likely to be compelling. Conviction and decision are a person's deepest personal features, and they are the arenas Newman's writing sought to penetrate. Consequently he was concerned with those wellsprings that define a person, that color thinking, that drive the choice for one or another path. But however central those wellsprings to decision, they exist so far below the surface of personality that most people are only dimly aware of them, if at all. The writer in Newman wanted to bring them to full light.

Newman's guide in these matters was himself. Through an introspection that revealed how he himself came to think about God and the church and how he made difficult choices as a result, Newman's own wellsprings came to light. They informed his notions of God, of moral conscience, of church and of sacraments; they influenced the way he wrote about these matters since he wrote to convince and not merely to instruct. They characterized him, and thus we need to go through them if we are to enter into his vision of the church.

What features constitute this interior side of Newman? First and foremost is the functioning of "first principles." These are convictions deeply embedded in each person, often of a hidden character, from which one reasons on any given matter. It was Newman's practice to lay bare both his own first principles and those of others, as much as they admit of disclosure. A second feature is the power that concrete experiences and the workings of imagination exercise on "assent." Newman divided assents into "notional" and "real" assents, the latter being associated with concrete experiences. Since he described religious belief in terms of "real assent," we need to examine Newman's personal orientation toward the primacy of the concrete and the imaginative. Third, Newman has portrayed the complexity of human judgment, especially when brought to bear on religious truth, in terms of a process called the "illative sense." To be followed properly the process requires "patience." Once the illative sense is appreciated, it will not be surprising to see the requisite role patience plays in Newman's ecclesiology. The final feature of Newman's style applies the other features to the purpose at hand, the nature of his theological writing. He wrote to engender "real apprehension," the source of real assents and thus of beliefs. As a writer he had no command over the real assents his readers may or may not give, but he could aim for the style of writing most calculated to evoke real apprehensions in his readers. In this regard he is a "controversialist" writer. The term means more than being argumentative or apologetical, as we shall see.

THE ROLE OF FIRST PRINCIPLES

Reasoning must begin from some judgment accepted as true. A fundamental premise for most people is, for example, "There is a world external to my senses." Most people do not subject this understanding to scrutiny; it functions as given and self-evident, and based on its truth people reason about other things. For fuller illustration of the operation of a first principle, let us take the judgment, "Roman Catholics are untrustworthy people." To the extent that this premise has rooted in the mind, it colors everything one experiences of Catholics and determines the conclusions one draws about them. It may never have been proven, and it may be obvious that many do not concur with the judgment, yet for those to whom it is true this judgment is an incontestable beginning point of thought and interpretation.

Newman understands first principles to be the propositions with which one begins reasoning on certain subject matters; they are quite numerous and vary in large measure with the person involved. In the *Present Position of Catholics,* a book of lectures examining Protestant prejudices at the time the Roman Catholic hierarchy was reestablished in England—an effort Newman called his "best written book"[3]—he describes first principles as "simple persuasions or sentiments, which come to the holder he cannot tell how, and which apparently he cannot help holding."[4] They are not innate ideas; they issue from concrete experiences now lost to view, e.g., from early family influences. To extend the example in the previous paragraph, one may have lived in a household where family conversation instilled the idea that Catholics are not trustworthy, a sentiment reinforced during early schooling by like-minded peers. It may have become so deeply entrenched that experiencing Catholics to the contrary is impossible; any good action by Catholics would be interpreted as guileful. I have drawn out this illustration of a first principle we would call a *prejudice* because the very word means *prejudgment,* a judgment not following upon controlling evidence but in fact controlling latter evidences. All first principles are something of a prejudice—not necessarily in the bad sense; they stand where reasoning begins. Newman considered himself quite deft in identifying someone's first principles, and in a rare instance of bravado he remarked, "I have a vivid perception of the consequences of certain admitted principles, have a considerable intellectual capacity of drawing them out, have the refinement to admire them, and a rhetorical or histrionic power to represent them."[5]

First principles are described differently in the *Grammar of Assent,* where they are termed "conclusions or abstractions from particular experiences."[6] They remain the initial premises of the reasoning process, but they are themselves the fruits of experiences. Newman illustrates this feature by contrasting two types of knowledge about everyday phenomena. Both animals and humans engage the particulars of the external world—what Newman terms an "instinct" for the concrete—but in humans instinct takes a higher form called "intuition." Newman likens intuition to a force spontaneously compelling people to mental acts.[7] From the ever-recurring testimony of sense experience the general notion is drawn that we are confronted by an external world having its own rules. As a lamb has an instinct about fleeing the wolf, a human has an instinct for reaching toward the generalized assertion. The judgment about the existence of an external world comes spontaneously upon the small child. The fact that some idealist philosophers deny the existence of the external world gives further support to Newman's point that the judgment is instinctual though not axiomatic; it is a sound intuition, however, since it is spontaneously accepted by nearly everyone. The *Grammar of Assent* uses for first principles the language of instinct because Newman there builds the case of the recurring testimony of conscience to the generalized moral principle behind it, the awareness of a divine being. But whether with this aim or with that of exposing prejudices, Newman describes first principles similarly in terms of their primordial quality.

First principles are, furthermore, sovereign and regulative. As

Newman explains in the *Present Position of Catholics,* "They are the means of proof, and are not themselves proved; they rule and are not ruled; they are sovereign on the one hand, irresponsible on the other: they are absolute monarchs, and if they are true, they act like the best and wisest of fathers to us: but, if they are false, they are the most cruel and baneful of tyrants."[8] The unexamined and unproven features of first principles are especially alarming in the case of prejudices because principles are so opaque to self-reflection. But when they reflect reality as it is— termed by Newman being responsible to the "nature of things"—they are hidden but wise masters of thinking.

The examination of inferential thinking in the *Grammar of Assent* leads Newman to inspect the premises from which someone reasons. Are premises not to be verified by prior premises that in turn require verification? But if so, how does Newman avoid an infinite regress? "The long retrospection lodges us at length at what are called first principles, the recondite sources of all knowledge, as to which logic provides no common measure of minds."[9] Newman wishes at this point to accent only the indemonstrable quality, hence the sovereign quality, of first principles. Although they will not allow of logical demonstration and therefore of verification in that sense, they will be open to justification. The same human instinct leading from concrete experiences to a generalized intuition searches ever for principles that universally recommend themselves, such as the principle of causation or the principle of a world existing externally to the senses. If first principles were impervious to this kind of justification, Newman would have no business in "controversial" writing.

Finally, first principles are profoundly personal. Each person operates from judgments formed from the cluster of experiences and influences making up one's individual story. Thus constituted, the principles are idiosyncratic. "By them we form our view of events, of deeds, of persons, of lines of conduct, of aims, of moral qualities, of religions. They constitute the difference between man and man; they characterize him. As determined by his First Principles, such is his religion, his creed . . . ; they are, in short, the man."[10] This statement allows us to see why Newman wrote the *Apologia* the way he did. Charles Kingsley had impugned his honesty in converting to

Roman Catholicism; with his honesty in question, Newman recognized that his denials would only be discounted as further lies. Thus trapped, Newman's sole recourse was to justify, through a meticulous account of his Anglican experiences, the personal character of the principles that led him away from the Church of England. Accordingly the book describes persons, events, and influences in vivid detail. The conversion to Roman Catholicism is depicted as a pilgrimage arising from the import of his own first principles. The reader may not agree with Newman's decision but would have to acknowledge that Newman changed churches with honesty. Laying forth his first principles was Newman's only way to rebut Kingsley.[11]

Both the hidden character of first principles, which Newman loves to uncover, and their regulative character set the framework in which he develops an ecclesiology. Throughout most of Newman's writings one meets apologetical strategies to expose prejudices about the Catholic church, such as the Protestant judgment that all revelation must be explicitly mentioned in the Bible. This first principle of Protestantism is for Newman an uncritically asserted one, and it dictates how he presents the revealed status of Roman Catholicism. Second, the nature of the Catholic church rests on more fundamental realities, as reasoning rests on regulative premises, and these first principles are actually the pillars of his ecclesiology.

Newman's own first principles are basically three in number, each interconnected: (1) A moral sovereign exists to whom conscience testifies. (2) This divine being has provided a revelation that distinguishes right from wrong. (3) God acts within our world in a sacramental way. This sacramental principle is the basis of the possibility of dogma and thus of an entity to maintain it—the church. These principles are at the root of Newman's thinking about the church, and to paraphrase his own description of the controlling power of principles, these three are, in short, Newman.

Newman begins the *Apologia* by describing his vivid experience in childhood of "the thought of two and two only absolute and luminously self-evident beings, myself and my Creator."[12] It was an experience of conscience that seared his mind, for it remained unshaken his entire life and certified an ethical awareness of God's existence. The God of truth and holiness impressed upon Newman a sense of moral duty and the need to be faithful to the voice of conscience. This inner ethical experience was as real as the impress of an external world upon his five senses. In the *Grammar of Assent* it is at the core of the argument for God's existence. "From the recurring instances in which conscience acts, forcing upon us importunately the mandate of a Superior, we have fresh and fresh evidence of the existence of a Sovereign Ruler, from whom these particular dictates which we experience proceed."[13] The experience is luminous by a kind of growing ever-insistent claim that if faithfully followed becomes even clearer and if purposely unheeded begins to haunt the person.

Newman's personalist orientation lies between the objectivist style of Thomas Aquinas and the subjectivist approach of Immanuel Kant. Kant also begins with one's ethical experiences, but his Moral Sovereign is only a *postulate* to explain normative maxims and one's striving for happiness. Aquinas begins from without, from sense experience of external phenomena, and argues to the existence of God as demanded by the nature of things. Newman, like Kant, begins from internal ethical experiences, but their direct implication is a divine reality and not simply a postulate required for the act of understanding. Like Aquinas, Newman affirms the divine reality to which experiences point, and the import Newman accords internal ethical experiences is parallel to one's sense experience of the outside world. Just as one is led as if by instinct to perceive in sense experience *things* distinct from and beyond our sensations, there is also a "religious" instinct brought to bear upon moral experiences. In the experience of concrete actions being praiseworthy or culpable, a person forms the generalized statement, "There is a right and wrong." (In Newman's terminology this generalized statement is "notional apprehension" of an abstract truth and not yet "real apprehension" of a definite reality.) As the religious instinct pushes one from concrete experiences to the generalized truth, it will push further to the moral sovereign in whom the truth is grounded, and of this being one can have real apprehension.

Newman draws a helpful distinction about what is happening. Conscience (and by implication the religious instinct driving it) has a *moral sense* by which we instinctively, i.e., without logical medium, discriminate good from bad actions. It is what most people mean when they say, "My conscience is clean on this matter," or "My conscience bothers me about it." But unlike any other interior sense, such as the sense about what is beautiful, conscience has an added yet distinct *sense of duty* that registers the unconditional command of doing good and avoiding evil. We are not allowed to rest in mere apprehension of something being praiseworthy or culpable; we feel duty bound to act. Finally, in proportion as we obey the particular dictates of this sense of duty, the religious instinct urges upon the mind an awareness of a reality beyond our sense of right and wrong. We become aware of a being who praises or blames, who promises or threatens, to whom one is accountable. As sense experience leads us to something distinct and beyond itself, i.e., an external world, our moral experiences are notices of a moral judge and sovereign. We apprehend this reality instinctively, without logical medium, and for Newman it is as concretely real as the garden flowers he looked at and smelled. He opposed that narrow British empiricism which limited "data" to the testimony of the five senses. He was quite Anglo-Saxon in giving primacy to concrete experiences, but he included inner moral sensations among them. The testimony of conscience was as real as the action of memory or of one's inner sense distinguishing the beautiful from the ugly.[14]

Another feature about conscience's testimony to a moral sovereign pertains to the moral content of its dictates. If conscience is likened to an inner voice, at times it speaks vaguely. How is it to be heard clearly, and, by consequence, how is the moral sovereign who speaks to be vividly apprehended? Newman's characteristic answer: Be faithful to conscience, however vaguely it speaks! If one follows its promptings in searching prayer and with an earnest desire to know God's will, conscience leads to true and clear apprehensions. If in good conscience one acts in error, some self-correcting insight will emerge eventually; if one acts correctly although without clear grasp of the moral truth at stake, confirmations will follow. "When men begin all their works with the thought of God, acting for His sake, and to fulfil His will, when they ask His blessing on themselves and their life, pray to Him for the objects they desire, and see Him in the event, whether it be according to their prayers or not, they will find everything that happens tend [*sic*] to confirm them in the truths about Him which live in their imagination, varied and unearthly as those truths may be."[15] In Newman's essays and in his many letters offering spiritual direction a constant theme is that the truest hold on religious issues (*theoria*) is gained by habits of personal religion (*praxis*).

Another dimension of the moral sovereign must be noted, and to it also conscience gives testimony. As our painful experiences of bad conscience bring to our imagination apprehensions of God's justice, our uplifting experiences of good conscience testify to God's benevolence. No single word seems apt to describe someone who is simultaneously demanding and benevolent. It is easier to imagine those qualities separately and exercised in turn. But the God who speaks through conscience has both qualities at once. Newman here expresses in his own style the classic and seemingly contradictory attributes of divine mercy and divine justice. For him there is an original unity of these attributes in God to which a developed conscience testifies. The language of theology may indeed have to distinguish the attributes, but they have an original unity that language should strive to recapture. The *Grammar of Assent*'s lengthy analysis of "natural religion" (i.e., those religions that in Newman's view are borne only by the voice of conscience and not by a public divine revelation) emphasizes God's demanding and awesome side. The purpose is to depict the religious instinct of accountability and appeasement, of the sense of sin and transgression. This instinct leads to ritual sacrifices and prayers of intercession. While this instinct provides impetus to the phenomena of natural religions as Newman knew of them, it is also an unbalanced view of God's true self, neglecting the self that is loving and benevolent. Newman's fuller view of conscience testifies to a moral sovereign who is also a caring moral educator. God does not leave to the unaided testimony of conscience the knowledge of his will and purposes. Conscience in and by itself is too uncertain, too prone to error, too ready to compromise itself. Conscience in the concrete conditions of life, according to Newman, has led to what is objectionable in natural religions. Therefore there is an "antecedent probability" that the God who speaks within individual consciences will also speak, and speak more clearly, through prophets. Wondering if God has spoken through prophets is a question posed from all that is laudable in natural religion's instinct of accountability, that is to say, a wonder posed from the depths of honest conscience itself. (The final argument of the *Grammar of Assent* is that either Christianity is the prophetic benevolent voice from God or a revelation has not yet been given the human race, since Christianity alone fulfills the aspirations and foreshadowings of natural religions.)

My aim is not to elaborate or defend Newman's argument at this point but merely to draw the connection between what can now be termed two first principles: the principle of a moral sovereign and the antecedent probability of a divine pedagogy, a 'revelation' as it is called in the language of theology, the latter being the implication of the moral judge's benevolence. From these two principles a third one arises, Newman's principle of sacramentality. The full effectiveness of divine teaching requires it. Newman is fond of calling the divine realm the "unseen world," or the "invisible world." People, however, are instructed and impelled by what is concrete and visible, by the things that flood the imagination with vividness. How is the imagination to apprehend the unseen world? How are people to experience the spiritual if the powers of human knowing seem so geared to the material realm? Newman's answer is the principle of sacramentality.

Newman owes his notion of sacrament to Eastern Christianity, especially to the teachings of Clement and Origen, for whom "the exterior world, physical and historical, was but the manifestation to our senses of realities greater than itself."[16] The material world does not simply point to spiritual realities. The visible, rather, realizes the invisible such that a condition of unity between both obtains. In other words, an earthly thing or event becomes God's self-expression. Newman envisions a progressively unfolding revelation being expressed sacramentally in the course of history. God's truth was first manifested through the world of nature, then through historical events such as the Exodus and the preaching of prophets, and finally in Jesus Christ in whom the divine and human realities are united in one person. The sacramental principle continues in the church, not only in its 'sacraments' but also in its fundamental structure.

To this ancient notion of sacramentality Newman adds the crucial role played by the imagination. The earthly and spiritual dimensions of a sacramental revelation existed in an original unity. The unity is lost when the event, e.g., the Exodus, is conceptually analyzed, for the mind distinguishes the two dimensions. The earthly dimension (the migration of Israelites) and the spiritual dimension (God chooses this people and becomes committed to them) are not *identical,* and thus they are conceptually distinct. But the spiritual and earthly dimensions of the Exodus exist in the imagination in *unity.* This unity mirrors the original unity of the one sacramental event, the Exodus. The language of distinction, coming from conceptual analysis, must strive for the original unity captured by the imagination. Newman's preference for the concrete to the abstract, for the real to the notional, for the totality to the piecemeal, amounts to the epistemological priority of the imagination. His religious writing aims at readers' imaginations, where sacramental images can exist undivided, where the divine is met materially, and where assent can issue from real apprehensions. For this reason Newman determined to write in an appealing style, using vivid illustration in preference to heavy, abstract reasoning.[17]

The most important application of the sacramental principle concerns revelation, i.e., dogma is the sacramental form of God's teaching. Newman understands dogma in the wide sense as any verbal expression of divine truth. Dogmas are "supernatural truths irrevocably committed to human language, imperfect because it is human, but definitive and necessary because given from above."[18] While the more restricted and customary notion of dogma as a solemn church teaching is recognized, Newman's broader notion carries more importance for ecclesiology. A number of issues requiring examination are at stake.

Whether God can truly communicate and be heard within history is the first and foremost issue. To affirm this possibility means that human language can capture God's message without distorting it. The scriptures of a religion and the words of its prophets have both a human aspect (they are, after all, produced by people) and a divine aspect (they purport to be God's message). The opposing position maintains that God's truth cannot be committed to human language; this understanding amounts to a denial that any religion could be revealed religion. Newman calls this position "liberalism," understanding it to mean "the anti-dogmatic principle and its developments."[19] He might just as well have called it the antisacramental principle.

Against this kind of liberalism he fought all his life, and at the end of his efforts, when he received the Biglietto in 1879, he described the foe in the following words: "Liberalism in religion is the doctrine that there is no positive truth in religion, but that one creed is as good as another, and this is the teaching which is gaining substance and force daily. It is inconsistent with any recognition of any religion as *true*. It teaches that all are to be tolerated, but all are matters of opinion. Revealed religion is not a truth, but a sentiment and a taste; not an objective fact; not miraculous: and it is the right of each individual to make it say what strikes his fancy."[20]

Newman believes that liberalism's logical consequence, when its subjectivism is fully played out, is atheism. In reducing a religious assertion to private judgment or personal feeling, the strength of liberalism is the strength of opinions. There is a delicate but crucial frontier marker between the testimony of conscience and liberalism's most noble sentiment. Both are interior, both are rooted in one's subjectivity, but conscience asserts a communication from God while liberalism does not. Dogma adds to conscience's inner testimony the social nature of genuine divine communication, that is to say, the message is meant for a group. Only on genuine revelation, according to Newman, can a lasting religion be grounded; on liberalism it cannot.

Newman's sacramental understanding of God's revelation, consequently, has a number of implications. First of all, dogma is a divine pedagogy. It is the communication from God of his will and purposes to conscientious listeners. If religion is to be a communion with the unseen world—a frequent motif in Newman's writings—it would soon become severed were it only to be grounded on opinions or theories about the nature of God. The devotional dimension of religion, according to Newman, flows from real assents, and such assents can only be given to what is experienced as real and true beyond doubt. One cannot be genuinely religious by halves.

Secondly, dogma is symbolic. We meet here the phenomenological dimension of Newman's sacramental principle. Symbols have an inner reality and an external manifestation. Dogma's external side is forever wedded to what is creaturely, human, and worldly. If the word of God is not merely to be a word about God or an uncertain echo, then God must communicate in human forms. Human words must somehow express divine thought and not be merely pointers toward it or veils before it. Furthermore human words must somehow be retentive of divine thought. An ephemeral connection that at any time might slip away is no connection at all, at least not for the social demands of communication, if revelation is to be a message for a community of people throughout the ages. Still, human words always remain an imperfect expression of divine thought. (Indeed, human words cannot even capture perfectly our own thoughts.)[21] The unity of the divine and the human elements in a symbol never amounts to their identity, and thus the human element contributes limitation. The symbolic nature of dogma then means that revelation is truly expressed by human words but never perfectly encompassed by them. Through human words one may truly hear God but never fully hear God.

Third, dogma is necessary. With this contention Newman joins the benevolent side of divine pedagogy to the actual human situation. Human life is crisscrossed with personal and social sin. We wish to hear God but cannot decipher the voice. Therefore God's message must enter human history in an unmistakable way and overcome the deafness caused by sin. The message is spoken by One who in love and forgiveness has claims upon the ultimate destinies of everyone. Each one remains free, though at peril, to refuse to listen.

These various features of dogma, understood in the light of Newman's sacramental principle, undergird his ecclesiology. He draws the connection succinctly: A revelation that could stifle itself is no revelation. The teachings of conscience, dimly focused in natural religions, further articulated in Judaic revelation, are most fully complemented by the teachings of Jesus. His teachings are dogma in that wider and more fluid sense described above. But is his word to endure any longer than the period of his Jewish lifetime? Newman responds that Jesus has not passed beyond our hearing but continues to communicate through the sacramental structure of the church. The church, both as "oracle of truth" and as liturgical community of sacraments, is the ongoing symbol of revelation. The church *realizes*, i.e., renders actual, and makes concrete the message of Jesus. This is the wider sense of dogma, and it underscores the need for an ecclesiology.

These most general remarks on the sacramental nature of dogma, itself rooted in the principle of a divine pedagogy that in turn is rooted in the testimony of conscience to a moral sovereign, provide the basic orientation of Newman's thinking. They are the wellspring for his vision of the church. More specific topics in ecclesiology in one way or another reflect these principles, these instinctive premises. When we sense them, we will know we have met Newman's vision.

THE PRIMACY OF CONCRETENESS

Some people, whether by temperament or training, incline toward abstract and theoretical analysis, while the bent of others is toward the concrete and the factual. Newman is among the latter, and his preference for the importance of concrete experience and for the personal implications of whatever is at stake came as naturally to him as did his own name. In theological analysis his point of departure was what people experience. Normally he began an investigation by simply wondering what happened. In his essay about the role of the laity in guarding orthodoxy, *On Consulting the Faithful in Matters of Doctrine,* he opened with a historical account of lay activity in the years between the first two ecumenical councils (A.D. 325–81). How the laity maintained the genuine faith in opposition to the Arian tendencies of most bishops was a *fact* for him, stubborn in its character against any *a priori* theory of episcopal-laity relations. The experience of fourth-century people shaped his theology of the laity.

Newman's empirical tendencies signal his preference for what he calls "real apprehension." Since he describes the task of theology in terms of "*notional* apprehension," it is necessary to be clear about the distinction. Newman calls "apprehension" the sense we give to the terms of a proposition, such sentences being the manner in which we communicate our thoughts. When the terms are abstract, e.g., "Marriage in the Christian tradition is considered a sacrament," the apprehension of the sense is "notional." One grasps the proposition conceptually, and the referents are not individual people but rather a generalized condition common to many marriages. On the other hand, the referents are concrete and particular in the proposition, "My parents love each other," My father, my mother, and the relationship between them are facts of my experience. We would brush away any claim that human love is impossible by our experience of the contrary fact. Newman calls our hold on this proposition a "real apprehension."

Notional apprehension concerns generalizations; real apprehension concerns the concrete realities of the world. Notional apprehension furthers science, and mathematics would be the clearest example. Real apprehension is a vivid knowledge of the singular, and falling in love with someone would be its best example. Both apprehensions have their necessary roles for the way knowledge grows. "To apprehend notionally is to have breadth of mind, but to be shallow; to apprehend really is to be deep, but to be narrow-minded. The latter is the conservative principle of knowledge, and the former the principle of its advancement."[22] Without notions we would neither pose questions nor range afield. Without concrete experience, captured in vivid imagination, our cognition would drift along and end in fuzzy speculations. It is quite possible that a concrete reality can be only notional for us. If I have never been to Rome, a friend's account of visiting the city can provide knowledge, but it remains generalized and sketchy. If I visit Rome and walk its ancient streets, I acquire a personal "feel" for the city. Real apprehension is a cognition providing a certain feel for the object known and is normally identical with directly experiencing the object.

Of the two apprehensions, Newman accords primacy to real apprehension, calling it the scope and test of the notional. Recognizing this emphasis is important for understanding his style of "doing theology." Theology, being a scientific inquiry, involves notional apprehension. But religious living, at whose service theology functions, involves personal belief, decision, and action—the realm of real apprehensions. Therefore theological ideas that are not supported by people's experience are airy, and theological ideas that do not in turn enrich religious experience are ideological. The real feeds the notional, and the notional in turn is gauged by the real.[23] In perceiving Newman's preference for real apprehension we are sensing his personal style.

It is with assents to propositions that concreteness of knowledge is so important. Newman understands assent to a proposition to mean the judgment one makes that a proposition in and of itself is true. Unlike the mental states of opinion or suspicion, it is the nature of assent to be total; one cannot assent by halves. Assents, however, can be weak or strong, and it is to this range of possibilities that Newman's analysis of apprehension is directed. Strength of assent varies because assent follows on what is apprehended to be true and formalizes it into a judgment of truth. Of the two types of apprehensions, real and notional, Newman remarks: "As notions come of abstractions, so images come of experiences; the more fully the mind is occupied by an experience, the keener will be its assent to it."[24] On the other hand, the more the mind is engaged with an abstraction, the duller will be the (total) assent.

How is it that assents are total and yet have varying strengths? Newman readily admits that inferences are stronger as the abstraction is of a higher level, such as the inferences based on abstract mathematical concepts (i.e., assents following notional apprehension). But as for the issues of daily life, where people must decide continually what is true and to be done, real apprehension wins out. "What is concrete exerts a force and makes an impression on the mind which nothing abstract can rival."[25] The term *mind* is used here in a broad and subtle fashion. It involves an intellectual act of insight along with the likeness of a sense experience in the imagination, a position not unlike that of Bernard Lonergan in contemporary epistemology.[26] The assent derives from insight into what the imagination presents to reflection, but the *vividness* of imagination determines the strength of the assent. While these two components are distinguishable, the activity of real apprehension within the mind moves as one, the keenness of assent varying with the vividenss or depth of the concrete experience captured in imagination. Furthermore, the imagination stirs one's affective depths (the affections of fear, love, etc.), and it is by these personal forces that assents lead to activity; thus in religion beliefs lead to witness.

To be religious is to live and act in a certain way and not merely to think in a certain way. If religion amounted to "getting one's thinking straight," notional apprehensions would suffice. But religion is an affair of doing, and for Newman religion entails real apprehensions. "Deductions have no power of persuasion. The heart is commonly reached, not through the reason, but through the imagination, by means of direct impressions, by the testimony of facts and events, by history, by description. Persons influence us, voices melt us, looks subdue us, deeds inflame us. Many a man will live and die upon a dogma; no man will be a martyr for a conclusion."[27] In a memorable definition of a human being, evoking his penchant for seeing the totality, Newman writes: "Man is *not* a reasoning animal; he is a seeing, feeling, contemplating, acting animal. He is influenced by what is direct and precise."[28] Time and again Newman opts for what is immediate, direct, and concrete, that is, for the stuff of real apprehensions, and he counsels others to do the same. The aim of religious writing—and for him this included theological writing—is to invite real assents by providing descriptions appropriate to real apprehensions. His ecclesiology follows this path, for, as he says, "Catholicism appeals to the imagination, as a great fact, wherever she comes; she strikes it."[29]

THE ROLE OF PATIENCE

Even though the word *patience* can be misleading, no quality better describes this key feature of Newman's personal style and its role in the working of the "illative sense." We fancy a patient person to be cautious and unruffled, calmly waiting out a situation. The word might even suggest stoical endurance and, from its etymology, the quality of long-suffering. Such psychological connotations have a limited application in Newman's use of the term; rather, the emphasis is on the role of patience in the genesis of insight.

As it did for the roles of first principles and concreteness, the act of making decisions illustrates the functioning of patience in Newman's style. There is no way to describe perfectly the roles of time and timing, for they relate to the incubation process of a conviction deeply lodged within someone, a process not measured by logic or subject to a time schedule but defined by a unique mental faculty Newman calls the illative sense. Newman's life illustrated this organon every bit as much as his attempts to describe it.

How do people decide about a concrete matter? The phrase "concrete matter" covers a wide range for Newman, from everyday questions such as whether to buy this or that to more life-defining issues such as how to identify the true Christian church. A concrete matter involves whatever is particular and existentially definite. It need not be a singular entity; a collectivity such as the church is concrete in Newman's sense. He contends that concrete matters do not admit of logical demonstrations, that is to say, of being proven by reasons which can be put to paper.[30] Yet everyday life involves decisions about concrete matters in which people are more than guessing; people are certain about many things they have chosen yet cannot prove. How is such certitude of assent possible?

An act of inference is quite distinct from an act of assent. To appreciate this distinction, one must be clear on two uses of the word *certain*. A proposition may be described as certain, and from two certain premises a certain and sure conclusion can logically follow. Newman prefers to say that "certainty" describes propositions. When it is lacking, a conclusion drawn from premises is only probable. Certitude, however, is a mental state; it describes a quality of people, not of propositions. A person may have certitude of something, the propositional arguments for which are, at most, probable. On this matter Newman differed from John Locke, who held that assent had degrees and varied with the degrees of inferential evidence. Newman maintained that personal certitude about nondemonstrable matters is the normal state of affairs. People are sure they will die, but they cannot prove it. People have certitude the world is round, but the overwhelming majority cannot offer convincing evidence of that fact.

To move from mental considerations to a conclusion for which one has certitude, the mind requires a special agency. In a letter to a scientist-friend, William Froude, Newman outlined his position on inference that had been at the heart of the *Grammar of Assent*. "There is a faculty in the mind which I think I have called the inductive sense, which, when properly cultivated and used, answers to Aristotle's *phronesis*, its province being, not virtue, but the [seeking of truth], which decides for us, beyond any technical rules, when, how, etc. to pass from inference to assent, and when and under what circumstances etc. etc. not."[31] This inductive organon, which Newman came to call the "illative sense," brings a person to assents far more absolute than could be reached by the legitimate action of formal logic on the results of sense experience. Abstract concepts are the normal province of formal logic, and the mental rules determine which concepts include or exclude other concepts (e.g., "Every A is B; no B is C; therefore no A is C"). Such formal reasonings about abstract matters cannot handle concrete and particular things like human activity. "They may approximate to a proof, but they only reach the probable, because they cannot reach the particular."[32]

A concrete reality is fuller and more replete than any abstract notion of it. The human being, considered abstractly, is conceptually sketchy; Aristotle defines it as "rational animal." Concrete individuals, however, abound in rich detail. "Instead of saying, as logicians say, that two men differ only in number, we ought, I repeat, rather to say that they differ from each other in all that they are, in identity, in incommunicability, in personality."[33] The power of formal logic and the range of abstract definitions do not reach far enough into the concrete. Because people do draw judgments about concrete issues, there must be a kind of informal inference or logic that reaches into the particular. The process has special characteristics: (1) It deals with a cumulation of probable reasonings, the momentum of which in their mental interplay carries the mind to the individual case. (2) The inferential process is more or less implicit, without the full and direct advertence of the mind. (3) The process is uniquely personal; what constitutes for one person sufficient evidence and the proper time to decide are not so for another person. "A cumulation of probabilities, over and above their implicit character, will vary both in their number and their separate estimated value, according to the particular intellect which is employed upon it."[34]

As is the case with first principles, so with the illative sense is individuality paramount. Each person sizes up evidences in a distinctive manner and senses *when* sufficient evidence is in hand. The person's past experiences come into play. Various likelihoods (i.e., Newman's "antecedent probabilities") provide clues to help sift through data, but the weight of these likelihoods varies from person to person. But what is to ensure accuracy if the inferential process is so idiosyncratic? The validity of a judgment about a concrete matter belongs also to the highly personal action of informal inference. The perfection or right working of informal inference is specifically what Newman wishes to call the "illative sense."[35] He likens it to common sense or the sense of beauty. We do recognize certain people as having an accurate common sense about complexities that cause other people to err; we know of others who can call upon an instinct to bring beauty to a room or garden. Analogous to this, the illative sense is an instinct to size up accurately and to conclude rightly; it is a mental agility that properly organizes intelligence and imagination. Military genius, which sizes up the particulars of a battlefield situation accurately and in timely fashion, is another instance of the illative sense.

The illative sense admits of degrees of excellence, and someone like Napoleon exemplified the promptness and soundness of its acknowledged perfection. Although saints may enjoy such ready powers of discernment, for the rest of us the working of the illative sense in matters of religion is more painstaking. From the very nature of religious issues, patience and right timing are crucial. The accumulation of probabilities and their interplay, their weight when sifting through ongoing experience, their staying power or lack of it over a long haul, all these components involve the temporal dimension of the inferential process. Patient timing, according to Newman, is a principle "as important as any other," i.e., "the gradual process by which great conclusions are forced upon the mind, and the confidence of their correctness which the mind feels from the fact of that gradualness. . . . I repeat, it is not by syllogisms or other logical process that trustworthy conclusions are drawn, such as command our assent, but by that minute, continuous, experimental reasoning, which shows badly on paper, but which drifts silently into an overwhelming cumulus of proof, and, when our start is true, brings us on to a true result."[36]

If the gradual growth of assent contributes to attaining certitude about that assent, does this not contradict what was said about real assent, i.e., that it follows on a real apprehension of experience and enjoys its instantaneity? Newman terms certitude a "complex" assent, meaning that the mind apprehends the warrants for having given assent to something; hence certitude is a reflexive and notional assent. A person may assent to the statement, "God is calling me to this task," but a further inference, more complex and taking more time, would be, "I am certain God calls me." The original act of assent could have been quite sudden, but the complex inference takes time and cannot be rushed by any type of mental calculus. An intellectual patience must reign. The complex inference (the elastic and versatile illative sense) is an incubation process not merely of ideas but also of images and memories and feelings, that is to say, it ingests and sifts through the whole range of experiences. Within this totality Newman situates the gradual and patient emergence of conclusions of which one can have certitude.

Other dimensions of informal inference signal the importance of an intellectual patience. Newman called antecedent probabilities the grand line of reasonings in coming to certitude in concrete matters. An "antecedent probability" functions as a general assumption, derived from the nature of the case and likely applicable to the concrete matter. One might think of it as an *a priori* likelihood. It is a background aiding interpretation of data. Let us take an illustration from marriage. A husband begins to return late from work. His wife interprets this as a loss of interest in the family. When challenged, he offers an explanation fully consonant with his commitment to the family but which his wife must take on faith. Is it true, and can she be certain of it? If the husband's whole character and behavior, experienced by the wife over many years, clearly affirmed the marriage, then there is an antecedent probability his recent behavior is trustworthy. The wife has a background within which his recent behavior and his explanation for it can be interpreted, behavior which in itself allows of multiple interpretations.[37]

Numerous antecedent probabilities come into play when the concrete matter is vastly more complex, as, e.g., the questions: Did Christ found a church? Where is it today? A church is likely to exist if a revelation has been given. It is likely to have features found in the New Testament. It is likely to be a community of holiness. It is likely to continue the apostolic teachings. It is likely to have abuses, yet it is also likely that none of them are countenanced by its principles. No single probability, in itself, answers the original question. But their cumulus, especially in the ways they complement each other and in some manner point in the same direction, enjoys a persuasive power when the facts of one's experience and the history one reads and the claims one hears are brought together with them.

Early in life Newman saw that antecedent probability was the guide to sound judgment. He worked to refine the idea and to protect it from the charge that it provides only probably knowledge. I have called antecedent probability a background for interpreting experience, a clue, and Newman reckons the cumulus of antecedent probabilities to be a *force* reaching to certitude. This understanding is at the heart of the *Essay on Development,* as Newman noted in the *Apologia.* "My argument is in outline as follows: that the absolute certitude which we are able to possess, whether as to the truths of a natural religion or as to the fact of a revelation, was the result of an *assemblage* of concurring and converging probabilities," and that this process was "both according to the constitution of the human mind and the will of its Maker."[38] Making use of antecedent probabilities for the affairs of daily life, the illative sense leads a person to conclude that a particular insight is the upshot of it all, that no further evidence is needed, and that now is the moment to decide.

Such a process may take years. Intimations of the final insight were likely felt earlier. Difficulties surrounding a decision begin to ease away. Significant facts have been entering our experience, many of them arising unpredictably. A particular antecedent probability becomes crisper and more telling. The group of them seems to converge on some focus. A moment arrives when one decides on deciding the question, as if the mental process itself is ruled by conscience. A personal element infuses the proof, if proof it may be called. "We are considered to feel, rather than to see, its cogency; and we decide, not that the conclusion must be, but that it cannot be otherwise."[39] This process seems to describe the most important decisions we make, especially those in religion.

The patient maturation of a religious conviction is guided, in addition, by the inquirer's moral integrity, and the connection between sound judgment and morality is a distinctively Newmanian emphasis. Just as conscience is an inner voice, it is also an inner eye enabling a religious inquirer to see through the complexities of a question. Newman draws an analogy with a secular question: Is the text of Ovid a medieval forgery? The scholar who can decide on the text's authenticity has acquired, over many years' experience, an "eye" for such matters. Scholastic philosophy calls it a *habitus mentis,* a ready facility for unraveling an intricacy; it opens an investigation and guides it to sure conclusions. For religious quesitons (e.g., Does God exist? Is there a church I should join?), the moral integrity of the inquirer guides the investigation, being a kind of *habitus* or inner eye that discerns pathways to the truth. "My book," notes Newman about the *Grammar of Assent,* "is to show that a right moral state of mind germinates or even generates good intellectual principles."[40] It is Newman's epistemological use of the biblical idea that those who seek God in sincerity will find God. He is also retrieving the Augustinian teaching that one needs to first love what one seeks to understand (*nihil cognitum nisi amatum*).[41]

The need for patience in seeking religious certitude was Newman's epistemological advice because it was first his own experience in such matters. Using the metaphor of a slow and dimly lit journey, as portended years before in his famous hymn "Lead, Kindly Light," Newman depicted the many years it took to decide to convert to Roman Catholicism. The difficulties with Anglicanism had first to be patiently sifted. "It was my business to go on as usual, to obey those convictions to which I had so long surrendered myself which still had possession of me, and on which my new thoughts had no direct bearing,"[42] But difficulties, even ten thousand of them as he says, do not constitute a doubt requiring suspension of allegiance. Doubts finally did arise and require decisions, but even then Newman moved slowly to give fair play to his heritage. Note the descriptions of his final decade of Anglicanism: 1835–38, "I honestly wished to benefit the Church of England at the expense of the Church of Rome"; 1839–42, ". . . to benefit the Church of England without prejudice to the Church of Rome"; 1843–44, "I gave up all clerical duty . . . [wishing] not to injure [the Church of England]"; 1845, "I contemplated leaving it, but I also distinctly told my friends that it was in my contemplation."[43] One can only conclude that Newman's October 1845 decision to convert illustrated everything he was to theorize later about the illative sense and its feature of patient exercise. It was stamped with his own history.

CONTROVERSIALIST WRITER

That Newman did not produce scientific or systematic theology also tells us something about his personal style. Following his own preference, I am calling him a "controversialist." He remains a theologian even though he eschewed the title. He was what Jan Walgrave has called an "intuitive visionary," yet he was possessed of systematic and reflective abilities "to analyze his intuition under different aspects and to afford us, through a meticulous elaboration of those aspects, rigorous description—though partial and abstract—of the grasped reality."[44] Newman was an "on call" writer, that is to say, he wrote when a pressing issue from the public arena energized him. "I cannot write by wishing; I can only write when power is given me to write," he explained.[45] Such internal energy came from the clash of events, ideas, and programs that to Newman's mind involved something of great stake for people's lives. He was unable to "do theology," as today's coinage has it, from sheer intellectual interest alone. In the older sense of the word Newman was an occasional writer, waiting upon those situations that primed his energies. This preference explains why he wrote essays rather than scientific treatises and why he opens up only aspects of large issues rather than presenting total treatments. His full ecclesiology, therefore, has to be put together.

Another important feature of Newman's writing derives from the style of his reflection. It is, in Walgrave's words, a "literary style."[46] The text is literary as opposed to scientific; it is pastoral as opposed to academic. We have seen that Newman favors real to notional apprehension, that is to say, the image to the concept. Consequently, a language of exposition must be used whose verve and arrangement act as a driving force for the imagination.[47] He is literary in this sense. He writes from what he has realized of the way God works "in the concrete," that is to say, in history, in the contemporary church and society, and especially in his own life. He writes so that a reader may have real apprehension. He does not write for the theological academy as such.

If one is to be accurate about Newman's views, then any synthetic arrangement of his ecclesiology must avoid paring away the salient features of his personal style—first principles, concreteness, patience, controversial writing. Style illuminates thought patterns because in Newman's case they cannot exist apart; one is at the service of the other.

CHAPTER TWO

The Foundational View of
the Church

*I*n what is Newman's ecclesiology rooted? What are
the church's most basic characteristics? Before we examine more specific features of the church, we should
understand Newman's foundational vision of it. Not
surprisingly, his vision is closely in line with his own first principles, those wellsprings of his own manner of thinking. Newman's foundation is quite simply the *dynamism* between the kind
of God to whom conscience testifies, the likelihood that God has
revealed a message, and the necessity for a church in which and
through which the message lives on. And if a church be necessary for this purpose, then in God's plan it would need to be
recognizable so that people may draw close and hear the message.

The relationship between conscience, revelation, and church
is a dynamism, that is to say, an activity taking place within
history. Newman thinks in terms of organic activity, and he likes
to call such things an "idea," as he did in describing a university.
For him the "idea" of something is not its conceptual notion but
rather the interaction going on among its various portions, as if
it were an organism. Consequently, Newman's foundational
view of the church amounts to his idea of the church, i.e., its root
principle of life and activity. And since organic activity ought not
to be aimless, one can also say that his idea of the church is its
fundamental purpose.

CONSCIENCE

Although many ecclesiologies are rooted in the analysis of
biblical data or philosophical principles,[1] Newman's is rooted in

31

a person's experience. Experience is not restricted to data from the five exterior senses. Ethical experience (conscience), with its moral sense and its sense of duty, is Newman's most important extension of the notion. He wishes to secure conscience's legitimate place among our cognitive operations, in company with seeing, hearing, and so forth, and he wants to accord conscience the same power of testimony that the others possess. But in that case, what is to secure for conscience the same blunt witness that seeing and hearing give, as in the common assertions, "I saw him do it" and "I heard her say it"? In establishing foundations for ecclesiology the question becomes: Can the existence of God, to which conscience testifies, have for us the forceful character that direct visual and auditory experiences have?

Newman distrusts most proofs for God's existence because the conditions of the world seem to undermine the cogency and appeal of the arguments. People experience so much evil that "the world seems simply to give the lie to that great truth" of God's reality.[2] Newman does not go so far as to claim that the usual theistic arguments are invalid in themselves; they are simply not persuasive for most people, nor do they influence the decisions people make about God's reality. Instead, Newman proposes the testimony of conscience. This argument uses to its very benefit the experience of evil in the world and the fact that something seems "out of joint."[3] The approach is also calculated to take heed of the things people commonly experience. In the notes Newman used in drafting the *Grammar of Assent* he jotted: "I am not to draw *out a proof* of the being of God, but the mode in which practically an individual believes in it."[4]

Just as worldly objects strike our inner sense of beauty and register themselves in a pleasing way, our human actions—and the mere prospect of certain actions—strike our consciences and register themselves as right or wrong. Through the feelings of threat or attraction, conscience urges one to do the right or to avoid the wrong. Feelings are important, being the emotional aspects of conscience, and they penetrate people more poignantly than do conceptual notions. Furthermore, inanimate objects cannot stir human feelings as profoundly as people can. A crucial point of the argument follows: "If, as is the case, we feel responsibility, are ashamed, are frightened, at transgressing the voice of conscience, this implies that there is One to whom we are responsible, before whom we are ashamed, whose claims upon us we fear."[5] If it is true in human relationships that violating another's rightful claims upon us causes disquiet, then at the most fundamental level of right and wrong, the feeling of remorse in wrongdoing suggests an object (of a personal nature) fundamental to the world itself. "Thus the phenomena of Conscience, as dictate, avail to impress the imagination with the picture of a Supreme Governor, a Judge, holy, just, powerful, all-seeing, retributive, and is the creative principle of religion."[6] Conscience testifies to a personal presence distinct from the self to whom we stand accountable. Friedrich von Schlegel called it "another me" within me, experienced as higher and distinct.[7]

Newman trusted firmly in the workings of conscience to generate the sense of God's presence. The early Anglican sermons are replete with this emphasis: We may trust our consciences without blame.[8] Self-knowledge is the root of all real religious knowledge.[9] Even when conscience speaks incorrectly, faithfulness to it has a self-correcting dimension.[10] When listened to with sincerity and a willingness to be changed, the Author of conscience will enlighten our minds.[11] All these homiletic admonitions are rooted in the powerful impress of the image of a Moral Governor who, as experienced ethically and directly, is in conversation with an individual and influences that person's path in life in the strongest practical ways.

The "royal road" of conscience has an especially recommending feature in its self-correcting function, which for Newman amounts to corrections coming from the divine Author of conscience. If reasoning is to perform right judgments, its antecedents must be true. Conscience, if followed sincerely and honestly, sharpens the mind's gaze to things as they are in their religious implications. In contrast, reason is wrongly used when its antecedents are determined not merely by "abstract false premises" but by pride, self-trust, and narrow self-interest.[12] True and unerring grasp of antecedents is of a moral order, according to Newman, and the personal (ethical) qualities surrounding thinking are sovereign. The royal road of conscience is not a proof about God's existence but a lifelong project about it, and Newman can presume what a mere logical proof cannot. "The key of the whole system is that God, since a God there is, *desires* and imposes it as a duty on men that they should seek Him and find out how to please Him, and that being the case He will bless imperfect proofs."[13]

REVELATION

With Newman's tendency to describe something in terms of its genesis and development, the depiction of conscience reaches its next stage: the likelihood that a divine revelation will aid it. Although he has used the experience of evil to augment conscience's testimony to the existence of a moral sovereign, he also recognizes that evil obscures the specific commands of personal conscience. Both individual and social sin impede the attempt of conscience to discern God's will. Each person is innerly split, being both an image of God made to hear God's voice as well as a sinner prone to deafness. Furthermore, the world itself is infected with a contagion,[14] and thus a sinful society throws up obstacles to the work of conscience and invites false priorities.

Some type of illumination or regeneration is needed to overcome the effects of both personal and social sin. The self requires an enlightenment beyond its innate powers of discernment. And lest the religious quest become a retreat into private interiority, the illumination must be socially constituted in order to engage the collective aspects of meaning by which people live and choose.[15] According to Newman, God reveals a message that conscience can follow, and the church is the historical bearer of the message, indeed its oracle. The church is the social embodiment of revelation aiding the task of conscience to do God's will, and as such it is *in the world* counteracting social sin.

The steps by which Newman arrives at this role for the church need to be retraced. The existence of a moral sovereign suggests the probability of a divine pedagogy, that is to say, the apprehension of God through conscience involves the coapprehension of God's benevolence. We have already seen this understanding to be the interconnection among Newman's first principles. Providentially God should instruct more unmistakably the moral conscience that he had created to know and hear him. But has such a Providence spoken a message? The hope that a revelation has or will be given is experienced within the midst of religious striving, almost as if it were anticipated when the experience of distance from God is keenest. "Those who know nothing of wounds of the soul, are not led to deal with the question, or consider its circumstances; but when our attention is roused, then the more steadily we dwell upon it, the more probable does it seem that revelation has or will be given to us. This presentiment is founded on our sense, on the one hand, of the infinite goodness of God, and, on the other, of our own extreme misery and need. . . . It is difficult to put a limit to the legitimate force of this antecedent probability."[16]

With this approach Newman breaks with the tradition of apologetics that sought miraculous evidences for the existence of revelation. He presents, rather, a cumulation of indicators suggesting a revelation, no one of which is probative, but, taken as a whole, together have an aggregate force. Some of these indicators or antecedent probabilities are: (1) Christianity claims a definite message, and it answers to the needs of conscience. (2) It is addressed to all humankind and seeks to become universally rooted. (3) It preaches doctrines beyond human discovery yet momentous for human destinies. (4) Its message has endured, in substance, from the first. (5) It has actually been embraced in every land, in all classes of society, among all races. (6) It has challenged destructive worldly mores. (7) Successes have been mixed with reverses, yet it remains vigorous. (8) It has produced its saints. Any one of these indicators may be found in other religions, but their convergence as "probabilities" presents itself to the illative sense as a credible basis for the truth of Christianity, leading Newman to conclude: "I do not know what can be advanced by rival religions. . . . I feel myself justified in saying either that Christianity is from God, or a revelation has not yet been given to us."[17]

Some remarks must be made about these antecedent probabilities. First, they present Christianity as the completion of conscience's instinct to be naturally God-fearing. Natural religions raised for Newman the question whether conscience could ever hope to hear the full truth of God. A revelation would answer fully the religious quest that one perceives operating in natural religions. Second, the cumulus of probabilities does not logically prove that God gave a revelation in Christ. Acceptance of Christianity, as a revelation begetting a community, remains for Newman an act of belief. Finally, the Christian revelation is nevertheless worthy of credence, and to appreciate the strength of this contention, his position on the illative sense must be recalled.

The illative sense deals with "concrete matter" where formal logic cannot reach. Christianity as a social entity claiming a revelation is a concrete reality, not an intellectual notion. Informal inference (which in its perfection is the illative sense) about concrete things is governed by a convergence of probabilities and points to their consequence. The process is highly personal and, on a time scale, unpredictable. Yet the mind has an ability to reach a judgment about concrete realities, however complex. The conclusion is not logically forced; rather, one concludes one ought not resist the upshot of the convergences. Newman uses the image of a cable to suggest the rigor of this kind of reasoning.

> The best illustration of what I hold is that of a cable which is made up of a number of separate threads, each feeble, yet together as sufficient as an iron rod. An iron rod represents mathematical or strict demonstration; a cable represents moral demonstration, which is an assemblage of probabilities, separately insufficient for certainty, but, when put together, irrefragable. A man who said, "I cannot trust a cable, I must have an iron bar," would, *in certain* given cases be irrational and unreasonable:—so too is a man who says I must have a rigid demonstration, not a moral demonstration, of religious truth.[18]

The existence of a revelation would respond to the need of conscience for a guide, and the credibility of the Christian revelation being the divinely intended guide rests on the various indicators or probabilities pointing in its direction. Newman preferred to make a case for Christianity in this apologetical manner. The revelation that former ages described in miraculous interventions "addresses us at this day in the guise . . . of coincidences, which are indications, to the illative sense of those who believe in a Moral Governor, of His immediate presence."[19]

THE CHURCH AS ORACLE OF REVELATION

Revelation that supports the task of conscience to do God's will can only be of help if it assumes for people an understandable form. A divine message that is not simultaneously a humanly shaped message is beyond human ken. Among Newman's first principles, consequently, sacramentality—including dogma as a type of sacrament—is a direct consequence of the likelihood of a divine pedagogy. We must examine more closely his notion of dogma—sometimes also called doctrine—to understand how the church is the authoritative bearer of God's revelation. Under this aspect, Newman frequently called the church an oracle.

Dogma has two roles that correspond to the two ways of mentally apprehending it. It may be a statement expressing an abstract notion, such as the traditional dogmatic definitions, e.g., "Jesus is consubstantial with God the Creator." This type of dogma invites notional apprehension and belongs properly to the work of theology. Or it may be a statement expressing a concrete image, e.g., "Jesus died to save me." However imperfect the wording, the statement invites real apprehension, or, more accurately, comes from a real apprehension, and it belongs to the realm of devotion. Religious devotion must cast into some form of wording what is experienced; otherwise devotion slips into vagueness, and what is vague is forgotten. Newman liked to call this second type of dogma the "backbone of religion."[20]

We have already seen that Newman opposed a nineteenth-century liberalism that resisted dogma because it reduced religious beliefs to the level of personal opinions. If liberalism was the antagonist on the left, then on the right Newman battled an anti-intellectualist evangelicalism. He understood the latter to maintain that "faith is *not* belief in a proposition, but is a *trust in a person* so that whatever Scripture says about its being necessary for salvation only means that a filial acceptance of Christ as our Lord and God, as saving us from future punishment and bringing us to heaven, is the only way by which we can gain these great benefits."[21] A religion admitting dogmas can indeed invite the kind of intellectualism the evangelicals feared. Newman shared that fear, and, furthermore, he agreed with the evangelicals' wish for religious commitment, what they called "vital religion." But "vital" feeling and devotion must be focused, Newman argued, because unfocused affections cannot endure. The religious imagination needs to fall back upon propositions (i.e., definite doctrines) for its stay, when direct sense experience of the divine is lacking. The focus is supplied by words, and it is the sense of words that our intellect requires in order to work. Revelation "is made to *teach* us something, which otherwise we should not know,—for our soul's good, for the education of our soul—for our preparation for heaven—It teaches us how to please God. How can we fancy we shall be saved unless we let Him guide us? and He guides us by propositions addressed to the intellect, such as . . . 'our Lord died for sinners.' "[22]

If Christ's message is the most credible source of a divine pedagogy, how is such a message to be mediated faithfully to later generations? How is a revelation, once given, not to stifle itself? "Revelation, in its very idea, is a revelation of truth—and it is a revelation not for the first century alone, but for all times. Who is its keeper and interpreter, or oracle, in centuries 2, 3, 4 as the Apostles were in the first?"[23] Newman here presupposes that those who experienced Jesus directly and enjoyed real apprehension, i.e., his disciples, were authoritative teachers to their contemporaries along the lines of I John 1:5: "This is what we have heard from him and the message that we announce to you." Newman calls that pristine situation the idea of the "Apostolic church." But this description raises the antecedent probability that something subsequent to the apostolic age will serve as a faithful teacher and guarantor of the message. Newman saw three realistic possibilities—the self, the Bible alone, or the church.

The self was not equal to the task. To Richard Holt Hutton, a magazine editor and former Unitarian who argued that God's truth was self-revealing to any thoughtful person, Newman admitted that God's message could come to someone through channels such as a Greek poem or the Koran. "But where I should differ from you is, that I should not consider such an internal acceptance or embrace of a doctrine a sine qua non condition of its being a truth. And on this ground, because, minds being very various, the subjective acquiescence in a doctrine cannot be the invariable measure and test of its objective reality or its truth."[24] More to the point, Newman notes in his first book, *The Arians of the Fourth Century,* that human intelligence, which includes the workings of conscience, enlightens people in the difficulties of their situation but not in their solutions. This function gives the mind a tendency toward skepticism, but the very sense of the self's weakness indicates that "it must be intended to rely on something" because one has trust in the benevolence of him who impresses himself on our moral nature.[25]

The Bible alone, in the sense of private interpretation of it, is another possible guarantor and teacher of revelation. Newman's response is that the Bible has never worked; it, too, is not up to the task. The fact that the Reformation accorded the Bible normative authority indicates to him the psychological need any Christian has for some enduring prophetic and decisive voice. Revelation, historically situated in the past, must carry with it as an internal feature some expression of ongoing pedagogical authority, and the reformers claimed that the biblical message bore its own warrant. The Reformation, in Newman's view, replaced a teaching church with a teaching Book.[26]

The issue is not whether this swap is justified but whether it works. Recollecting that religious devotion requires a focus supplied by definite doctrines (dogmas), Newman concludes that the Bible *alone* cannot succeed because it was never meant to adjudicate doctrinal disputes. The principle of private biblical interpretation has splintered Christianity and produced myriad churches and sects.

> "The sacred text was never intended to teach doctrine, that if we would learn doctrine, we must have recourse to the formularies of the Church, for instance to the Catechism and to the Creeds." And is not this abundantly clear? . . . Why do Wesleyan schools turn out Wesleyan pupils as their resulting process, Congregationalists Congregational youths, and the Church of England schools Episcopalians? If the Bible teaches doctrine clearly, why do some readers arise from it Trinitarians, others Unitarians, and others Calvinists? Why do not all readers of the Bible at least agree in what are fundamentals, what not? I do not know what is *meant* by saying that Scripture is adapted, is intended, to teach the very truth of revelation, if in matter of fact it does not do so.[27]

Today biblical scholars of almost all denominations conceive of the Bible as an ecclesial book. They understand it to be a reflection, in its literary forms and overall redactions, of the situation of the various mid-first–century churches. The Bible emerged from a post-Jesus church tradition and is inevitably read within a tradition. Although Newman lacked a detailed conception of the Bible's roots within church tradition, he had, however, an innate sense of this relationship, and he recognized that Protestants, though championing private biblical interpretation, cannot avoid their own traditional and confessional *dicta*. "Scripture says, 'Anoint the sick with oil in the name of the Lord'; they say, 'This was a temporary rite.' Who told them all this? they will say, 'It stands to reason'—that means, . . . 'I never heard any other interpretation—any other seems to me *strange;*' of course, every thing is strange to those who are not accustomed to it."[28] Newman would admit that he interprets the Bible within the teaching tradition of his own church, and he contends that, inevitably, so does everyone.

The only viable successor, therefore, to the authoritative teaching of the first apostles is the church. There is no other normal and ordinary channel of doctrine, none that claims to be an "authority which signs and seals a doctrine as the common property of Christians."[29] Private judgment, whether of the Bible or of edifying texts, cannot establish a community of common meaning and value or provide definite doctrines required by the devotional imagination. There is an antecedent probability that if a revelation began a community (the first Christians), it requires correct, ongoing interpretation as the community enters new eras and faces new questions. "To myself, it seems a paradox that the Almighty should give to men a revealed doctrine without giving also a standard interpreter of it. It is in that case but a half or a quarter gift, or rather a gift reversing and undoing itself."[30]

The argument in the *Essay on Development* adds to the notion of teaching office the qualification of *infallible* teaching. Infallibility is a sensitive point in current ecclesiology, especially in an ecumenical context, and Newman's position must be carefully elaborated. He contends that the notion of a developing doctrine entails some authoritative agency, external to its process, judging its aberrations or its legitimate growth. The Christian idea develops within the whole church—in its liturgy, its controversies, its pieties, its encounter with secular values and structures, in short, in the total experience of its members. The Christian idea is social, making distinct impress on different minds, issuing in manifold consequences, some true, some false. Appeal to reason cannot unite this broad mental field of the "idea" into a community of common creed. The only guide to social cohesion, for Newman, would be a teaching office divinely aided to convey the truth. "If Christianity is both social and dogmatic, and intended for all ages, it must humanly speaking have an infallible expounder."[31]

It is a matter of the church itself being maintained in the truth. Whether a pope is infallible, or a council, and under what conditions, is subsidiary to the more basic issue, the fundamental infallibility of the community. The heart of Newman's argument is simple: Unless there were provident protection from error, there would be no sense in having a teaching role in the church. "The doctrine of . . . infallibility is primarily an inference, grounded on the Church's office of *teaching*. How could the church be the organ of revelation and teach gospel truth without a security given to it that it should be preserved from *error* in its teaching?"[32] As Newman's theory on doctrinal development is the broad hypothesis to account for a difficulty (the *de facto* variations in Christian doctrines over the ages), an infallible authority is an inference that would directly follow. Indeed, he thinks of it as the "simplest, the most natural, the most persuasive" hypothesis, more winning than chance events or coincidences, to account for doctrinal developments.[33] The maturation of truths, or apparent truths, on the large mental field of Christian history varies so much, conflicts so much, that an authority is needed to decide what is genuine and what is aberrant. Theologians may draw out tests for ascertaining legitimacy, but such tests "are insufficient for the guidance of individuals in the case of so large and complicated a problem as Christianity."[34] (One notes here Newman's assessment of his own famous seven tests for development.)[35] Christian belief cannot be grounded on the probability that a doctrine is true. Belief is assent with certitude that something is true, else it is not Christian belief. And if Christian belief is also a social belief that constitutes a community of common meaning, an unerring teaching office is needed.[36]

In Newman's ecclesiology, one continually senses his appeal to the *broad issue* where the decisive judgment must be focused and within which more detailed questions and difficulties shift for themselves. Can there be any sense to a revelation without an interpreter of it, and can that interpretation, particularly about the most crucial issues,[37] be unguaranteed in its judgments? Here lies the broad issue. Conversion to Roman Catholicism never meant for Newman, or for any inquirer he counseled, a checklist of individual doctrines that had each to be gotten through and approved before one joined a doctrinal church, but rather a judgment about the church as a credible teacher. If one believed in a particular church as an oracle of revelation, its various dogmas would commend themselves. "The object of faith is *not* simply certain articles, A B C D, contained in dumb documents, but the whole word of God, explicit and implicit, as dispensed by His living Church."[38]

Our earlier portrait of Newman described him as a person of first principles, and in a certain respect his tendency to urge the broad view at the outset illustrates this mental orientation. Revelation, a teaching ministry, a community of shared vision, infallibility as a guarantor, these ideas cluster about each other in Newman's fundamental vision of revealed religion. But does an infallible authority imply for him a church of passive and docile listeners, or of theologians without any intellectual freedom, or of a process of infallible pronouncement practically automatic and somehow mysteriously inspired? Newman's ecclesiology stands against this paternalistic stereotype. He champions a highly active laity, a wide scope of intellectual freedom for theologians, and a doctrinal teaching process best described as dialogical. These specifics, however, presume his broad view.

RECOGNIZING THE CHURCH OF CHRIST

A practical question inserts itself at this juncture in Newman's foundational viewpoint. If Christ's revelation is meant to be interpreted by the church, and if many groups claim to be that church, how is the "oracle of revelation" to be identified? We know that Newman converted from the Church of England to the church of Rome at great personal cost. He left family and friends and was disowned by most of them. He gave up financial security. He lost a podium of influence in the nation. What were the main issues leading to this momentous personal decision to recognize in Roman Catholicism the church of Christ?

The Conversion of 1845

The Tractarian movement of the mid-1830s defended the Church of England's independence from the state by asserting its apostolic authority.[39] But in trying to combat Erastianism, the tracts—Newman's in particular—were thought to be too papal-ist. Newman, consequently, attempted to clarify the precise relation of the Tractarians to Roman Catholicism. The *Lectures on the Prophetical Office of the Church,* appearing in 1837, outlined a Via Media position that situated Anglicanism between Roman Catholicism and Protestantism. Using the work of the earlier Caroline divines, Newman argues that Anglicanism possesses a catholic patrimony of doctrines, such as the visibility of the church and its apostolic succession. Protestantism denies such doctrines, and Romanism abuses them. Anglicans can join Protestants in condemning Roman abuses, and they can join Catholics—indeed they claim the name Catholic, too—in accusing Protestants of heresy. However, because an Anglican principle holds that an abuse does not destroy a thing's nature, Anglicans can feel a kindredness with Rome not possible with Protestantism. The Branch Theory of churches expresses this kindredness. "The Catholic Church in all lands had been one from the first for many centuries; then, various portions had followed their own way to the injury, but not to the destruction, whether of truth or of charity. These portions or branches were mainly three: the Greek, Latin, and Anglican. Each of these inherited the early undivided Church *in solido* as its own possession. Each branch was identical with that early undivided Church, and in the unity of that Church had unity with the other branches. The three branches agreed together in *all but* their accidental errors."[40]

Certain issues emerge with this "catholic reading" of Anglicanism. A visible church is an essential feature of Christianity, a visibility Rome perverts and Protestantism denies. Second, the integrity of revelation is to be found in the church before it split into branches, hence the value given to antiquity and patristic teachings. The Protestant idea of private judgment rejects this source of authority. Rome accepts it in theory but neglects it in practice by appealing to medieval and Tridentine dogmas. Newman's empirical bent, however, senses danger in the Via Media construct. "Protestantism and Popery are real religions; no one can doubt about them; they have furnished the mould in which nations have been cast; but the Via Media, viewed as an integral system, has never had existence except on paper; it is known, not positively but negatively, in its differences from the rival creeds."[41]

Protestantism was never the threat to the Via Media that Roman Catholicism was. If Anglicans could charge Rome with introducing doctrinal novelty, Rome could say that the current Anglican church communes with no one but its British Empire self. "The Anglican disputant took his stand upon Antiquity or Apostolicity, the Roman upon Catholicity. The Anglican said to the Roman: 'There is but One Faith, The Ancient, and you have not kept to it;' the Roman retorted: 'There is but One Church, the Catholic, and you are out of it.' "[42]

The standoff in arguments was broken for Newman by two shocks. In the summer of 1839 he studied the Christological controversy of the fifth century and saw a middle-path strategy being followed by the heretical Monophysite party. "I found, as it seemed to me, Christendom of the Sixteenth and the Nineteenth centuries reflected. . . . The Church of the *Via Media* was in the position of the Oriental communion, Rome was where she now is; and the Protestants were the Eutychians."[43] Then Newman chanced upon an article on Donatism in the *Dublin Review* whose focus did not arrest him but a certain rule-of-thumb quoting St. Augustine did: *Securus judicat orbis terrarum,* i.e., the total community judges unerringly. Newman perceived that this rule was the clue to the Monophysite outcome and, more important, that these words "decide ecclesiastical questions on a simpler rule than that of Antiquity. . . . The deliberate judgment, in which the whole Church at length rests and acquiesces, is an infallible prescription and a final sentence against such portions of it as protest and secede."[44] Augustine's dictum destroyed Newman's Via Media construct because the Roman position came to be the judgment of the near-total community.[45]

The efforts of the Tractarians to ground Anglican doctrine in the ancient faith, in "catholic teaching" as they put it, quite naturally raised a practical objection. If on the basis of the Branch Theory catholic doctrine exists in the Roman church though in corrupted form, how could the Tractarians subscribe to the Thirty-nine Articles, since they are anti-Roman? Newman has to contend with two givens. The popular interpretation of the articles was Protestant, and the personal beliefs of the original framers were Protestant. Tract 90 argued that the articles do not gainsay a Catholic Anglican tradition; they were formulated to be flexible so that Christians with Catholic sentiments could sign them as readily as Protestant sympathizers. Tract 90 wanted to ascertain the limit of their elasticity in the direction of Roman doctrines so that contemporary Anglicans could claim the same flexibility. But the Anglican bishops, one after another, condemned Newman's interpretation of the Thirty-nine Articles, with the result that his last foothold in Anglicanism was pried loose. The great irony is that Tract 90 sought to keep Anglicans from Rome by proving that Catholic sentiments could coexist with subscription to the articles; the episcopal condemnations, unwittingly, caused an exodus of Anglo-Catholics by rejecting such sentiments as un-Anglican.

Four more years would pass before Newman arrived at a decision to join Roman Catholicism. Although certain signs pointed to the Roman Catholic church as the legitimate successor of the undivided early church, two serious difficulties held him back: Were more recent Roman teachings not corruptions of the ancient faith? Was not Catholic devotional life filled with pious excesses, especially regarding Mary and the saints? The *Essay on Development* was Newman's resolution of the first difficulty.[46] The 1877 preface to the third edition of the *Prophetical Office* was eventually to address the second.

Notes of the Church

Newman's conversion, showing the long and patient exercise of the illative sense, has stamped in a very existential manner his understanding of the notes of the church. A 'note,' in the context of apologetics, is a shorthand expression for a feature of Christ's church by which it can be identified and thus distinguished from false claimants. Since Newman experienced an absorbing search for this church, he tends to see a note as a beacon. Christ established a community offering gifts of grace. The gifts are meant for everyone, just as everyone's conscience is meant to hear God's voice. The signs (notes) identifying this community ought to beckon, at the level of common sense inquiry, a morally disposed inquirer. Recognizing the church, therefore, ought not to depend upon esoteric studies. The church is, and always has been, a home for the learned and unlearned alike. Its signs of recognition should possess a "simple and easy" character.[47]

From another aspect the church's notes are surface features; although they may lure someone, that person must still make a decision at the level of faith that an inner reality of the church corresponds to the external feature one sees. In the notebook Newman used to draft the *Essay on Development,* he remarked that notes are "necessarily an external view—and controversial."[48] Borrowing upon the classic treatment of the four marks of the true church, Newman developed his apologetical approach using the categories of apostolicity, visibility, oneness, and holiness.

The paramount note of the church, and the one that most influenced Newman's conversion, was *apostolicity.* The Branch Theory pictured an undivided patristic church, itself the natural growth of the New Testament church that was rooted in Jesus, which gave rise to three branch churches: the Greek, the Roman, and the Anglican. During the church's first five centuries its central doctrines were forged in the controversies over the nature of God and of Jesus. Since the controversies involved the very self-identity and viability of the community, the prevailing decisions enjoyed the infallibility required in a community meant to be God's oracle. The heretical parties became sects, which withered and all but disappeared; the orthodox party grew and its teaching took root "in the *orbis terrarum*" (everywhere).[49]

Newman used the notion of apostolicity to express the continuity between the present-day church and its patristic forebear. Anglicans considered Roman Catholicism a deformed continuation and Greek Orthodoxy a culturally constricted continuation.[50] Newman came to perceive, however, that the Roman charge against Anglicanism of lacking catholicity (i.e., being only a British Christianity) was actually a loss of apostolicity. The patristic period had shown him that those groups that lost continuity with the true biblical message (e.g., the Arians, the Gnostics, etc.) became marginal to the *orbis terrarum,* became provincial. He came to see the Anglicanism of the Via Media in the same configuration as these early groups.

Newman wished his *Essay on Development* to be read as an argument from apostolicity and not, as some maintained, from the idea of catholicity.

If that book is asked, why does its author join the Catholic Church? The answer is, because it is the church of St. Athanasius and St. Ambrose. . . . The one idea which for years was before me, was, "The Anglican Church corresponds to the Semi-arians, corresponds to the Monophysites.". . . I think I wrote to Keble, "I am far *more certain* that the Anglican Church is in loco haereseos, than that the Roman corruptions are not developments." No one can maintain the Anglican Church from *history,* (whatever they may try to do from the ground of *Doctrine,*)—and those who speak against my Essay as inconclusive, most of them, do not see its drift.[51]

In effect, Newman counters with apostolicity the Protestant accusation of having introduced doctrinal novelty: One can be *more sure* that Rome continues the patristic church than that its more recent teachings are not legitimate developments.[52] The *Essay on Development* scrutinizes Roman doctrines and sees reflected in them a teaching church more kindred to the early church than is any Reformation church. So strong is the mark of apostolicity to Newman that it overshadows any papal claims. Other Tractarians were attracted by the Petrine ministry, but not Newman. Papal prerogatives were only a doctrine of the church and not its foundation. "I think there *are* abundant reasons for holding the R.C. Church to be the true Church, quite distinct from any argument (which to some is so convincing) *through* the infallibility of Rome. A point which to some people is the *proof,* is to me a *doctrine* of the church."[53]

In addition to continuity in doctrine, Newman also applies the note of apostolicity to the external institutional features of the church. When writing as a Roman Catholic he often expresses the idea that a patristic visitor feels at home in a Roman liturgy but not at an Anglican one. "The Eucharistic service . . . would strike a stranger as the same. . . . Again, a combination of many nations into one etc. etc. Again, a one government [*sic*]."[54] Newman is overly sanguine on the similarity of a fourth-century liturgy to a nineteenth-century Roman Mass, and his reference to similar ecclesiastical polities risks oversimplification. Two features of his personal style, however, must be recalled.

Conversion is an act of real assent and the fruit of the illative sense dealing with concrete matter. This process goes forward and is spurred by images in the imagination that trigger feelings and emotions. The social features of church life, more than the interrelationships of doctrines, supply vivid images. People are lured by what they can directly experience, and the external phenomena of the church are there to be concretely experienced. Second, the appeal to continuity of institutional features lends itself to rhetorical overstatement. Still, Newman had a more nuanced sense of continuity whose careful expression was awkward in letter writing. The *Essay on Development* introduces the criteria of preservation of type and continuity of principles. The type remains preserved if the most general characteristics of a person or of an institution remain constant. The principles continue if the behavior patterns that they elicit exhibit consistency. Newman is aware that the nineteenth-century church differs in external detail from the patristic church, but at a level of type and of social principles he perceives continuity. As we form an image of a person's type (character), Newman believes we can imagine the church and produce its external type. Roman Catholicism "typified" the early church and was its contemporary heir. This institutional sense of apostolicity, as a note, is better geared to the real apprehension and hence to the real assent of some kinds of people, and that is why Newman uses it in his correspondence. The church attracts people differently.

The *visibility* of the church was another of its distinguishing notes, as important in Newman's dealings with evangelicals as apostolicity was with Anglicans. The evangelicals distinguished an invisible church from a visible one. The former was the real church of Christ, a spiritual and unseen assembly of the "saved" who were known only to God; the latter was a mere human institution containing the just and unjust alike. Newman rejected this dichotomy, not by stressing an institutional church as such, but by explaining the church's sacramental being. It was the early Newman, the Newman of the *Parochial and Plain Sermons,* who argued the case.

The visible world is an immense, attractive, and almost overpowering realm for our external senses. Its concreteness fascinates our imagination and stirs our feelings.[55] But it is a world, in and of itself, destined to crush our hearts with its burdens, its frail structures, and its unfulfilled promises. People "have tried the world, and it fails them; they have trusted it, and it deceives them; they have leant upon it, and it pierces them through."[56]

Why would people trust such a world? It is because they need to engage and seize something definite that might hold out promise. "And if there is nothing good to admire, we admire what is bad."[57] But there is a counterforce to a world of empty promises. It is an invisible world that has taken up abode here. God in his providence had given a "home in the midst of this turbulent world"[58] that merits our confidence, love, and surrender. Notice the introduction to Newman's sermon "The Visible Temple": "A Temple there has been upon earth, a spiritual Temple, made up of living stones, a Temple, as I may say, composed of souls; a Temple with God for its Light, and Christ for the High Priest, with wings of Angels for its arches, with Saints and Teachers for its pillars, and with worshippers for its pavement; such a temple has been on earth ever since the Gospel was first preached."[59] People may confidently fix their eyes and set their admiration on this temple. The church is at once a visible temple and "an outward sign of that unseen Temple in which Christ has dwelt from the first."[60] It is filled with holy symbols, spiritual ordinances, a definite revelation, ministries of grace, and the company of angels and saints.[61]

Visibility is clearly at the service of sacramentality in Newman's religious philosophy, and thus the visible church has the nature of a symbol. It is, first of all, a sign; it expresses the invisible temple by means of its activities and structures. Second, the symbol is not without imperfection, and thus the invisible temple can be veiled by this imperfect, humanly composed church.[62] Third, and most germane for the dispute with evangelicals, the visible church and the invisible church are two aspects of the one same reality; there are not two distinct churches in existence. Newman likens the visible and the invisible church to the convex and concave aspects of the same curved line.[63]

In dealing with evangelicals, Newman made no attempt to prove the sacramental nature of the church through exegetical considerations or through the philosophical analysis of symbols. His instinct is to take the patristic church as a living commentary on the *meaning* of the New Testament, i.e., that it gives social expression to the "idea" of New Testament Christianity.[64] And thus he challenged evangelicals to produce any ante-Nicene authority who maintained the idea of a spiritualized church. "As to the Post-Nicene authorities, I think they would have clapped

49

their hands to their ears and would have said, 'Bone Deus, to what times hast Thou reserved us!' "[65]

The note of *oneness* that ought to identify the church became the nemesis of the Branch Theory, and it preyed increasingly on Newman in his last Anglican years. Calling two or three churches, which were manifestly not in communion with one another, a single church of God on earth voided the normal meaning of words. "If the Church be a kingdom, a body politic, visibly, it is impossible that both the Roman and the Anglican communion can be that one body politic because they are two distinct bodies, . . . *one or the other is in schism.*"[66] To Anglican correspondents Newman pointed out their lack of institutional unity: The Church of England was barely in communion with its own branches in Scotland, Canada, and elsewhere. One had no assurance that what was taught in one diocese was taught elsewhere. Whatever cohesion the church had came from the civil government and not from within itself. Roman Catholicism, on the other hand, was *"in matter of fact* in unity" as was evident from its common ritual, legislation, moral teachings and its communion of dioceses spread throughout the world.[67]

Oneness: unity or uniformity? That is the tension within this note of the church. Within Roman Catholic circles Newman waged battle against the uniformity imposed by the ultramontanists. But his discussions with Anglicans emphasized those uniform features of Catholicism that he thought told so well against Anglican disarray. In the last resort, nonetheless, it was his insistence on oneness in doctrine more than his advocacy of oneness in ritual and discipline that mattered most. Unity of doctrine was the more substantive note by which to recognize the church that was God's present-day oracle.

The classic mark of the church, *holiness,* does not figure prominently in Newman's writings. The themes of vocation to holiness, the holiness of the sacramental ordinances, and the exemplary witness of the saints are indeed conspicuous.[68] But holiness as a note of the church and, consequently, as an argument from external features would have had a counterproductive effect on the minds of those already convinced of Roman corruptions, and Newman sensed this. The *Present Position of Catholics,* his lengthy treatment of anti-Catholic prejudice, never tries to answer charges of corruption with counterexamples of holiness;

rather, it unravels the phenomenon of prejudice. The same apologetical realism lies behind the scarcity of appeal to holiness as an identifying note of the church. Toward the end of his career as a controversial writer, Newman confided to his Anglican nephew, John Rickards Mozley, that the note of holiness does not argue well, as apologetics, since the Christian community has both good and bad members, and that the saintly life tends to be unostentatious while evil "flaunts itself and is loud."[69] It was Newman's expectation, however, that the church of Christ fosters the holy life, and he thought Roman Catholicism did this better than other churches did.

All of these notes of the church must be understood in Newman's own context. As far as being apologetical arguments put down on paper—and many post-Tridentine theologians did just that—Newman would be the first to admit the want of depth. The notes were externalized perspectives, and the "paper logic" for any one of them could be picked apart. Therefore Newman intended them as clues to one's illative sense, factors in the way someone puts together antecedent probabilities. And if to them was joined the personal element of moral conscience, he was sure that the Author of conscience would prosper one's search for the church. Accordingly, along with these "paper arguments" Newman counseled inquirers simultaneously to a life of prayer and asceticism. To miss this "moral" strategy is to miss what Newman really thought about the notes of the church and also to forget his own life's story.

The Church of England

The Church of England nurtured Newman in the Christian faith, and at midlife he left it for another church. In simplest terms these two facts underline an ambivalence in his assessment of Anglicanism.

Newman's conversion was driven by the question of apostolic identity. He left the Church of England "because I became sure that it was not a portion of that Catholic Church which Our Lord and His Apostles established, as the source of teaching and the channel of grace till the end of the world."[70] But even with this conclusion, Newman never maintained that grace was denied to individuals in his former church; the personal holiness of fellow

Tractarians such as Keble and Pusey and of so many others was undeniable. The distinction was, rather, the issue of *ecclesial* grace, that is to say, the ecclesial value of Anglicanism. Only the one church of Christ, in Newman's thinking, was the mediation of grace, and Anglicanism was in schism from it. At the English Reformation it had become a religion of the throne, grafted upon civil loyalty, almost a "new religion."[71]

The effects of the English church's schismatic state were in evidence. It did not act like a decisive and committed teacher of the Christian message. "Its disorganized state of belief, its feebleness to resist heretics, its many changes" belied that it could be God's oracle of revelation.[72] He thought the church inherited an indecisive style from its own great divines and that its current doctrinal disarray was the fruit. Bishop Joseph Butler, in his opinion, had reduced faith to a mere practical certainty, that is, to something that was safest to act upon rather than being a true conviction without reservation.[73] Furthermore, the Church of England had abandoned its apostolic heritage when it accepted royal establishment and then began to capitulate to civil interference; from that moment it became "a department of Government . . . , a function or operation of the State."[74] Newman had in mind certain doctrinal controversies that had been adjudicated by Parliament. The Church of England, finally, was more English than catholic (i.e., universal). It was in communion with no one but itself, hopelessly tied to the structures of civil government and reaching only where the civil power stretched, no farther.

Given this unflattering assessment, a problem of consistency arises. Newman had acknowledged in the *Apologia* that the Catholic sentiments which led him to Roman Catholicism had been the part and parcel of the Tractarian movement. But did not the movement of 1833 issue from the established church?

Newman first treated this quandary in the King William Street (London) lectures of 1850.[75] The experiences of grace to which the Tractarians had witnessed were indeed real and outside the boundaries of Roman Catholicism, but they were not coming from the work of the Anglican church as such; they were the graces of individuals who were responding to the direct action of God.[76] Fifteen years later Newman's appraisal of the established church is much more positive. The appendix to the *Apologia* describes the institutional value of Anglicanism as "a serviceable breakwater against doctrinal errors" of the day, "to a certain point, a witness and teacher of religious truth."[77] Is Newman not here affirming ecclesial value to the church he left?

Edward Pusey, Newman's Tractarian colleague, borrowed the idea to use in a pamphlet; he made mention of a body of Roman Catholics who rejoiced in the workings of the Holy Spirit in the Church of England and who "are saddened by what weakens her who is, in God's hands, the great bulwark against infidelity in this land."[78] Archbishop Manning attacked Pusey's statement in a pamphlet of his own, but he was obliquely glancing at Newman's favorable interpretation of the Church of England.[79] When, in 1865, Newman responded to Pusey's *Eirenicon,* he took the occasion to disown the phrase "bulwark," saying that the *Apologia* had called Anglicanism a "breakwater." A "bulwark" is an integral part of what it defends, whereas a "breakwater" implies a protection of Catholic truth without itself, as an institution, being grounded in truth.[80] Does Newman quibble over nouns?

My own interpretation is that Manning's intervention caused Newman to introduce the distinction to avoid appearing at odds with the ranking Catholic prelate of the nation. In June 1863 he had written to an old Anglican friend, Isaac Williams, describing Anglicanism as a "breakwater against skepticism," meaning that "at present it upholds far more truth in England than any other form of religion would, and than the Catholic Roman Church could."[81] One senses that "breakwater" means, practically, "bulwark." Years later, in 1875, Newman wrote of the established church being an ally in the battle against religious skepticism, a role no Roman Catholic would have wished weakened. "There is a great deal of learning, of ability, and of religious excellence in its various conflicting schools; and both directly by their controversial powers, and indirectly by the great Christian truths which they preach and on which they personally live, they are on the side of God in the great conflict of the day."[82]

When one considers some of Newman's first principles—searching conscience struggling in a corrupted world, a divine pedagogy, the sacramental nature of revelation—Anglicanism must be reckoned as an ecclesial mediation of Christian truth, as an institution possessing the grace of the church. Newman's full testimony suggests that he sensed this prerogative, but his testimony is conditioned by the diplomacy of dealing with Archbishop Manning. Newman's earlier negativity, furthermore, mellows as he moves away from his conversion experience, an experience both personally painful and—considering his stature—requiring justification. Finally, by way of anticipating my later analysis, Newman lacked the language of participation of Vatican Council II, which would have enabled him to accord ecclesial reality to many different churches without making them all on a par.

In regard to Anglican Orders and to ordination in general, Newman anticipated the contemporary ecclesiological principle that the validity of Holy Orders is judged more fruitfully as an implication of being a church rather than as resting on an episcopal geneology of apostolic succession. He thought it was backward to argue that a church is true and legitimate because its ordinations are valid. Orders are valid because a church is truly the church, with God providing to it all its requisite ministries. "Orders do not make the Church; they are but a portion of its prescribed characteristics. . . . Anglicans must prove that they are part of the Church before they can be sure that, by the promise of God, their Orders have been transmitted safely."[83]

Anglicans claimed to be a church of grace because of valid ordinations and "to prove their validity, they are bound to trace their validity through a hundred intermediate steps till at length they reach the Apostles."[84] Newman attempts to free the question of validity of Orders from the historical complexities of the past. Whether Roman Catholicism could guarantee its present-day ordinations on an unbroken succession of episcopal consecrations throughout eighteen hundred years, or whether the 1559 ordination of Archbishop Matthew Parker did or did not follow the proper ritual, would never, on historical investigation, give satisfying results. The *Apologia* calls such approaches "antiquarian arguments" unequal to the task.[85] Valid ordinations must be a theological inference. One begins with the nature of the church. Orders are valid because the church has apostolic legitimacy, and in its continuity with the New Testament church its ordained ministry continues unceasingly the ministry of Jesus.

There has been some question whether Newman himself was reordained conditionally.[86] It would appear his ordination was performed without precautionary conditions; in effect he was ordained anew. It was not required of him that he disavow the validity of his Anglican ordination as a priest. Using the "tutior principle" of Roman canon law (i.e., the safer approach in probable matters), Cardinal Wiseman had asked Newman whether it was not safer to be ordained anew since there was at least a doubt concerning Anglican ordinations, a doubt Newman himself shared.[87] "I cannot *conceive* that they are valid but I cannot swear that they are not. . . . Putting them at their best advantage, they are doubtful, and the Church ever goes by what is safe."[88] The doubt about Anglican Orders was not based upon a canon law principle, but upon Newman's experience of his former church. Anglican sacramental practice had been lax for more than two centuries, and the Wesleyan exodus reflected it. The sacramentary had been changed to the detriment of apostolic doctrines: the Eucharist was celebrated haphazardly, infrequently, and without reverence; there was no concern to determine if someone about to be ordained had formerly been baptized; many in the hierarchy did not believe in their sacramental episcopal office. Such *actual* conditions led Newman to say that one thing is claimed for ordained ministry and another is lived out.[89]

Newman's position on Anglican Orders illustrates once again the foundational character of his thinking. Instinctively he sought the broad and basic issue, the first principle as it were. Orders depend on the reality of being the church; the legitimacy of the church does not depend on Orders. The crucial question becomes: Where or what is the church? Second, Newman's empirical bent avoids "antiquarian historical investigations" of who ordained whom; he scrutinizes the quality of contemporary church life. Does its present sacramental manner indicate the possession of spiritual gifts? Are the sacraments in fact esteemed and reverenced? Theory for Newman always gives way to facts. From these two considerations he was doubtful about the validity of Anglican Orders.

Newman as Ecumenist

There are two sides of Newman the ecumenist. One is hardlined and understands church reunion as a return of erring believers to the one true Catholic church; The Roman Catholic church alone possesses the promises of salvation, and individuals outside of it can be saved only because they are invincibly ignorant of this truth. Although Newman used the official terminology of "invincible ignorance," as condescending as this may sound to Protestants, he never shared the narrowly judgmental attitude of many of his co-religionists who were skeptical of Protestant goodness. But Newman could not deny his personal experience of Anglican virtues. "I have heard of some [Catholics] who said that there were not a dozen Protestants in England in a state of invincible ignorance. They have a right to their own opinion—it is not mine."[90]

During his Roman Catholic years Newman was often asked to comment on the possibility of corporate reunion with the Church of England. His early correspondence is filled with pessimism. Since he equated reunion with the return of Anglicanism to Rome, he thought the English church would have to change too much to do so. "Its Articles are the historical offspring of Luther and Calvin. And its ecclesiastical organisation has ever been, in its fundamental principle, Erastian. To make that actual, visible, tangible body Catholic, would be simply to make a new creature."[91] Newman never raised the question: How also must Rome change? Yet, as will be seen, there were certain things about the Roman style he thought wrong and wished changed, many of them (e.g., overcentralization) being also Anglican conditions for reunion. Whatever Newman's hard-line assessment, he raised, nevertheless, the ecumenical questions that are still vexing: Can there be corporate reunion without shared common principles? What are tolerable differences? He also noted the unique difficulty of reunion discussions with the Church of England: It tolerated such a wide diversity of doctrine, from High Church to Low Church, that it was impossible to discover who speaks for the church as such.[92]

The other side to Newman's ecumenism is more positive and timely for today. His many writings attempted a careful and balanced presentation of doctrines with the aim of moderating differences by removing mistaken impressions. This impulse motivated his *Letter to Pusey* concerning Marian doctrines as well as his *Letter to the Duke of Norfolk* explaining what is and what is not meant by the Vatican dogma of papal infallibility.

Newman wished to soften theological differences by his moderate explanations of Roman doctrine. Much Catholic literature was filled with extreme interpretations, and he wanted everyone to know that more moderate interpretations were possible. He also wanted to "level up" the national ethos by inculcating a deeper spirituality. John Coulson notes quite correctly that Newman's purpose in republishing his works was to achieve these purposes.[93] A letter of 1870 articulates the groundbreaking aim. "I am quite persuaded that in this way alone religious men will ultimately arrive at unity of thought and worship. Not that it will be attained in our day, but the first step is to lay the foundation, or rather to prepare the soil. . . . To show that there is a true philosophy of religion is the first step in the development and reception on a large scale of Christian and Catholic truth."[94] By "Catholic" Newman especially meant those sentiments he had held as an Anglican and that might recommend themselves across confessional boundaries: the role of conscience, the principle of dogma, the sense of sacrament, and the legitimate role of authority. "To begin with the doctrine of the Pope is to begin to build St. Peter's from the cross and ball. We must begin from the bottom."[95] Newman sought something more fundamental. He sought to cultivate a common spiritual ethos, a sense of holiness, and a sense of responsibility to the God of conscience. He called it a leveling-up that would some day make specific doctrinal discussions easier. In this sense he was an ecumenist of fundamentals.

CHAPTER THREE

The Pastoral View of
the Church

*I*n examining Newman's pastoral view of the church, we will not be simply surveying some sort of an "applied ecclesiology." The concern will be with *processes* in the concrete life of the church, reflecting the empirical bent of Newman's interests, but such processes are not to be equated with the mere application of fundamental theories or principles to particular cases. These ecclesial processes have their own canons, as it were, and they could be considered to be the more prudent and productive ways by which the church functions best as the church. Newman has in mind processes such as theological debate in the church and the active contributions of the laity.

Newman's pastoral ecclesiology should not be identified with what contemporary theologians are describing as *practical* theology, but it does illustrate the latter's insistence on "some form of authentic personal involvement and/or commitment."[1] An analogy with individual cognition is helpful. Just as Newman insists that the whole person thinks—not only one's intellect but also one's feelings, memories, etc.—he also insists that the whole ecclesial body is involved in discerning and living out the revealed truth. The laity have their rightful role in church affairs just as the clergy do, and the process by which religious doctrines come to expression involves theologians as importantly as it involves episcopal authorities. Newman lived at a time when laity were disenfranchised and theological debate was fairly well held in check. His vision of the church in these matters is being called "pastoral" because he focused attention on the "how to" of the church's divinely given purposes. Because he was attempting to reclaim involvements that had been curtailed in the rather controlled post-Reformation Catholic church, his vision also concerned renewal and is therefore "pastoral" in that sense.

Three principal processes will be examined here: the laity, the forms of public communication (i.e., the media), and the importance of freely conducted theological debate. These were certainly not classic subject matters of ecclesiology in Newman's day. He seemed almost alone in reflecting upon them. If in the previous chapter some of Newman's views appeared rather traditional, here he will seem unconventional. In a clericalized and authoritarian church his concerns about the role of the laity, the role of the media, and the need for freedom of discussion were dangerous to pursue, and yet they belonged to his fully organic view of the church. His pastoral ecclesiology did get him into trouble.

In a certain sense Newman's fundamental view of the church is concerned with the category of *truth*. The voice of conscience, the gift of revelation, the church as oracle of revelation, and the present Roman Catholic church as heir of the apostolic church, all these topics were driven by Newman's conviction that truth is the "pillar and ground" of religion. The scriptural phrase is one of his favorites. Truth is not merely orthodox expressions, which can be written down on paper. Truth is something personal; it has a Johannine sense of walking by the light (John 12:35) and possessing the Spirit of truth (John 16:26). When shared by many people, it is the stuff or backbone of religion. Newman's pastoral view extends the same concern about truth to concrete processes of church life. What role do the laity have in articulating it? How are journals and newspapers meant to relate Christian truth to cultural and social issues? How can the implications of revealed truth be drawn out if theologians cannot debate matters freely? If Newman's fundamental view examined the "idea" of the church, his pastoral view examines the vigor of the idea.

THE THEOLOGY OF THE LAITY

Yves Congar, who has contributed so much in our times to a theology of the laity, began one of his books with the anecdote of the priest who was asked what the position of the layperson was. The layperson has two positions, the priest went on. First, he kneels before the altar; second, he sits below the pulpit. The anecdote then added that there is yet a third position; he puts his hand into his wallet.[2] Anecdotes have small grains of truth; this one, unfortunately, was too true about Roman Catholic laity in the nineteenth century. Msgr. George Talbot was a lobbyist at the Vatican on behalf of the Roman Catholic archbishop of Westminister. When a petition of support from the laity on behalf of Newman arrived in Rome in 1867, Talbot wrote to his patron, Archbishop Manning, these memorable words about the laity: "They are beginning to show the cloven hoof. . . . What is the province of the laity? To hunt, to shoot, to entertain. These matters they understand, but to meddle in ecclesiastical affairs they have no right at all."[3]

Congar's research has shown why Newman's age and even our own, at least until Vatican II, had such an unelevated view of laity. By the fourth century three categories of church members had emerged: monks, clerics, and laity. Two approaches were taken in defining the categories, both of which gave poor bases for developing a healthy theology of the laity. The monastic approach defined persons in terms of "state of life" and manner of sanctification. Monks were preeminent, and clergy began to take on the life-style of the monk; both were defined in relation to the holy and to life in a sacred milieu. Laity, on the other hand, had to live *in the world*. Their choice of worldly life was a concession to human weakness. When Pope Honorius II confirmed the Norbertine order, his bull read: "From her beginning the Church has offered two kinds of life to her children; one to help the insufficiency of the weak, another to perfect the goodness of the strong."[4] The rood screen of a cathedral was as much a real as a symbolic separation of the laity from the sacred spaces.

Beginning with the emergence of medieval canon law, the juridic approach understood persons in terms of their function. The cleric and the ordained monk were defined as those who administer sacred things. The laity, consequently, became those who receive this sacred service. St. Bonaventure described holy orders as that which separates a man from the laity in order to serve in the Temple.[5] The juridic approach fostered a clericalization of the church; laity were viewed as passive members and so treated.

From these two definitional approaches, the layperson emerges as a nonentity. "According to the monastic view, lay people only exist by favor of a concession; according to the canonical view, they are negative creatures."[6] With a canonical approach fostering clericalism and a monastic approach praising retreat from the secular world, where in the church do the laity fit? Newman left a memorandum on a meeting he once had with his own bishop, W. B. Ullathorne of Birmingham, who had become nervous about certain initiatives local laity were wishing to take. When Ullathorne asked Newman rhetorically, "Well, who are the laity anyway?" Newman simply responded that the church would look foolish without them.[7]

A fundamental shift in late medieval ecclesiology, to what Congar labels a "hierarchology," gave ideological support to the minimalistic definitions of the laity. Throughout the patristic and early medieval periods the church was understood both as a fellowship of believers and as the institution nourishing the fellowship. Theologians called the church a *congregatio*, a *coetus*, an *adunatio*, all of which describe its character of fellowship. The church was also called a *mater,* who through liturgy, sacraments, and preaching begets and nurtures her children. Beginning in the fourteenth century, the balanced perspective was upset. Spiritualist movements of an antihierarchical character advocated a totally invisible church, anticipating some of the doctrines of the Reformation's left wing. Moreover, the civil sector (e.g., the conflict between Boniface VIII and Philip the Fair) challenged Vatican authority. The papal theologians reacted by emphasizing church authority. James of Viterbo's *De Regimine Christiano* and Giles of Rome's *De Ecclesiastica Potestate* focused exclusively on the hierarchical and institutional powers of the church, themselves anticipating the later Counter-Reformation treatises of the same spirit.

The Protestant theologians of subsequent centuries emphasized the fellowship nature of the church and, to varying extents, its invisible character. "From the beginning the Reformers were in reaction against a stifling of faith by pious practices, against a prevalence of ecclesiastical machinery over inward Christianity, in favor of a direct religious contact, interior and personal."[8] Their "protest" took root because abuses were prevalent and shocking, because mechanical devotions were not fulfilling the spiritual hunger of many, and because the resistance to the old authority figures (pope and bishops) was occurring at the same time as new civic alignments and new urban classes of merchants and artisans were emerging and seeking self-expression. The old regime was under fire.

The counteroffensive was a Tridentine ecclesiology that emphasized the very thing being denied, the church as a divine authority and visible means of grace. What earlier had been a healthy balance of two dimensions became, after the Council of Trent, polemics of one over against the other. The treatise on the church "was principally, sometimes almost exclusively, a defense and affirmation of the reality of the Church as machinery of hierarchical mediation, of the powers and primacy of the Roman see, in a word, a 'hierarchology.' "[9] By Newman's time such an ecclesiology was firmly in place. The hierarchy were the church members *par excellence;* they made the decisions, dispensed the sacraments, and were the measure of the church's life and shape. The laity were passive recipients of clerical ministry, and in the words of Msgr. Talbot, they had no business meddling in church affairs.

Newman saw matters differently. The laity were to be an active force both in church and society. For this task they needed to be properly equipped, and Newman saw himself as an educator of the laity. He noted in his journal that "from first to last, education, in this large sense of the word, has been my line."[10] His Oxford experience convinced him that an educated laity could capture and form the public mind, and it was his wish in his Catholic years to provide such education. He attempted a Catholic university in Dublin; he urged the bishops to allow young Catholics to attend Oxford and Cambridge; he encouraged journals of opinion written by laypersons for laypersons. To sense how far he was at odds with the prevailing hierarchology, note this appeal he once made to a lay audience: "You [should] be able to dispense on all sides of you the royal light of Truth, and exert an august moral influence upon the world. . . . It is a moral force, not a material, which will vindicate your profession, and will secure your triumph. It is not giants who do most. . . . I want an intelligent, well-instructed laity. . . . I wish you to enlarge your knowledge, to cultivate your reason, to get an insight into the relation of truth to truth. . . . In all times the laity have been the measure of the Catholic spirit."[11]

The theoretical basis of Newman's theology of the laity is his principle of sacramentality. We met the principle in his defense of the possibility of dogmatic language; dogma is the expression of revelation committed to human words. When, however, our gaze is directed to the process by which the revealed Christian message becomes known or is propagated, then Newman's sacramental principle is expressed by the very interaction of the people who come to know and to profess the "mind" of the church. Newman's emphasis is on the totality of those who discern the mind of the church, or, in the words of Vatical Council II, on the totality of those making up the "people of God." In view of the laity's contribution, the sacramental principle asserts that the Christian message is "realized" in the fellowship of hierarchy and laity in a way that is not found in the hierarchy alone. In a sacramental reality, the human dimension (i.e., the symbol) must provide an adequate signifying role, and Newman implicitly understands adequacy in terms of totality.

Lay Experience: The Basis for a Distinctive Ministry

A theology of the laity has emerged in our own century in more or less distinct phases. After World War I there appeared in papal writings the theme of consecrating the world to Christ, by which was meant evangelizing the secular world. This emphasis was itself a major shift in tone from the anathemas flung at the modern world by Pio Nono in Newman's day. Within this context and under the influence of the early writings of Jacques Maritain and Yves Congar, the notion of Catholic Action arose. The laity were called upon to assist the clergy in evangelization. This first phase was still within a clerical ecclesiology, because Catholic Action was defined as the participation of the laity in the apostolate of the hierarchy. A second phase emerged in the decade before Vatical Council II. Congar and others came to see the ministry of the laity rooted in their baptismal character.[12] Lay ministry was not clerically defined in relation to an invitation from the hierarchy to its own ministry but rather grounded in the layperson's *baptized* identity.

The Second Vatican Council and the work of postconciliar theologians reflected the third stage. The ministry of laity was given a fully ecclesial context in light of the guiding idea, "people of God." Many see this understanding as the fundamental definition of the church endorsed by the council. God's people have a mission to the world, and the unique role of laity is their evangelization of the secular sphere. Sacramental theologians such as Edward Schillebeeckx contend that the very notion of *laicos* implies the Christian presence in the secular world.[13] All agree in connecting lay ministry with the sacraments of initiation (baptism-confirmation) as its mandate, rationale, and spiritual power.[14]

Newman had a similar vision of the laity, although the sacramental foundations were not as elaborately worked out. The laity's personal experience of Christianity, lived in the secular world and lived also in the church, is fully unique and not replicated by the clergy. Their experience is thus a source of distinctive insight, and at the same time it offers a special arena of ministry. Newman is intent on preserving this distinctive feature of the Christian "idea," i.e., the laity's insight into revelation and their profession of it in secular life. To be sure, the laity's involvement in what is being called the *concrete process* of insight and witness does not occur independent of the role of the hierarchy, since personal interests and limited vantage points can also be misleading; the process involves multiple partners, and Newman places his sacramental emphasis on the totality of church membership called to the service of the Christian idea.

Before examining the laity's role of insight into revelation, under the title of *sensus fidelium*, their proper contribution to the spread of revealed religion needs to be presented. Convinced that people are more readily persuaded by the example of someone's life than by that person's ability to argue the Christian message, Newman advocates a type of evangelization based on personal influence. He feels, for example, that Protestant prejudice will be melted away sooner by a direct experience of Catholic laity than by the strength of Catholic writings, including his own. Such is the meaning of the statement in his book on prejudice: "The great instrument of propagating moral truth is personal knowledge." The laity are to oblige people with whom they live and work to *know them*.[15]

Fully effective evangelization, however, requires a laity with clear convictions about revealed doctrines and with expertise in the affairs and intellectual disciplines of the world, and therefore the church is obliged to support superior higher education for its laity. Newman is quick to remark, nonetheless, that this education needs to be suited to the lay life as such; it cannot be a translated version of the education meant for clerics. It is to be education building upon the unique experiences of secular life, and its aim is to Christianize this milieu. These goals may not sound startling today, but the only religious education model in Newman's day was the seminary, and it would not do. Newman's proposals were unacceptable to church authorities. He proposed that young Catholic laity should attend a full-fledged university to enable their entrée into significant secular affairs. Initially he attempted to establish a Catholic university in Dublin, modeled on his own experience of Oxford and his knowledge of Louvain, but it soon failed because the bishops, in his opinion, resisted a university effort they could not control.[16] The alternatives, consequently, for superior higher education were either to establish a Catholic college at Oxford or Cambridge or to have Catholic youth enroll at one of the existing colleges. For the latter possibility Newman envisioned a cadre of highly educated chaplains to serve Catholic youth at the great universities—the model adopted at secular universities by Catholic chaplains today, whose organizations frequently bear his name, Newman clubs.

The Catholic bishops of England did not favor any form of Oxford-Cambridge education; the Catholic laity pulled behind Newman in urging the idea. The Vatican congregation, Propaganda Fidei, was to decide the issue. It was the moment for the laity to speak out, even though uninvited by the clergy, and Newman so exhorted them. "I think that the strong *will* of [Msgr.] Manning will overcome the Bishops, and that Dr. Cullen will overcome Propaganda, *unless the laity come forward*. But they must address themselves, not to Propaganda, but *to* THE BISHOPS. If you could write to particular Bishops you know, if you could get any Catholic gentleman of property and with sons to write to them, you will do good for the purpose you have at heart."[17] Newman even counseled that the laity should list titles and accomplishments after their names to make the signatures as imposing as possible. If the petition did not succeed, it would still be a precedent and assertion of lay initiative. "Our only hope," Newman advised one titled layman, Sir John Simeon, "is in the laity knowing their own strength and exerting themselves."[18]

Newman was not interested in power politics or in fomenting rebellion among the laity. The paramount issue was an educated Catholic laity having significant stature in the nation and giving witness to their Catholicism. If university life were prohibited and nothing provided in its place, Catholicism would never exert an influential voice in secular affairs. But to achieve this deeper aim, the Catholic bishops had to be convinced. "The English laity . . . could do anything, if they chose. . . . I think a (carefully weighed) pamphlet should be written by some prominent layman to state the *case* of the laity. . . . It need not commit itself to a *plan,* but to stating the grievance. It is a multiform grievance—Why is there to be a prohibition, without any positive remedial measure to meet an acknowledged want? . . . Are Catholics to be worse educated than all other gentlemen in the country?"[19]

In February 1865 the Vatican prohibited the establishment of a Catholic college at Oxford and added that parents were to be dissuaded from sending their children to the Oxford colleges. The stated reason was dangers to one's faith, but Newman thought the real reason was the clergy's fear of losing control. "The same dreadful jealousy of the laity, which has ruined things in Dublin, is now at the bottom of this unwillingness to let our youths go to Oxford. I am far from denying that there are strong reasons against that step, but these are not at the root of the dread of it. Propaganda and our leading Bishops fear the natural influence of the laity: which would be their greatest, or (humanly speaking) is rather their only, defense against the world."[20] "Defense against the world" is Newman's phrase for the need of revealed religion to combat secularism. But for the hierarchy the danger of secularism pales before the fear of an educated and articulate laity who might no longer be docile.[21]

If the hierarchy feared that an educated laity could be unmanageable, Newman feared the consequences of denying the laity education. A laity resisted at every turn, denied the possibilities of higher education, and given no sense of responsibility in the work of the church would turn anticlerical. "There will be the same miserable process set in which seems to have come to maturity in Italy, a rotting of the connection of heart between clergy and laity. This would not imply unbelief; men might be still deeply attached to their religion, frequent the sacraments, yet have no pride in their rulers and their cause."[22] Newman's own conviction is that educated laity would be the strength of the church if they were given responsibility, support, and trust. As a master of human psychology and the principles of motivation, he sees that energy and creativity are unleashed when people are given responsibility with freedom; authoritarian controls stifle the human spirit, a Newmanian motif to be met also in the matter of theological research. "On both sides of the Channel, the deep difficulty is the jealousy and fear which is entertained in high quarters of the laity. . . . Nothing great or living can be done except when men are self governed and independent: this is quite consistent with a full maintenance of ecclesiastical supremacy."[23] It was particularly painful to Newman to see the plight of Anglican converts, for the most part men and women of superior education and abilities. Their talents lay unused by the church because of the same fear of an educated and initiative-taking laity. "It has always been a real grief, and almost wound which I have carried with me, that married and especially clerically married converts, have been so tossed aside, and suffered to live or die as they may. We have lost a vast deal of power and zeal, of high talents and devotion, which might have done much for the glory of God."[24]

Newman's theology of the laity is based on the richness that their unique experience brings to what the church is about. They are not the total story, but they have a voice needed in the evangelizing work of the church. The revealed message is reflected in their experiences and discernments, and it achieves a distinctive accent that is not found in the experience of clergy. When the laity are kept marginal—such being one of the consequences of denying them the benefits of superior education—a control on the mind of the church and in fact its impoverishment is brought about. Newman attributes the fear of an educated and involved laity to the Latin mentality's need to impose order and uniformity on church life, a mentality that prior to the Reformation was held in check by the Teutonic mentality but that came to the fore as an imbalance with the German departure from the church. "All this is the consequence of Luther, and the separation off of the Teutonic races—and of the imperiousness of the Latin. But the Latin race will not always have a monopoly of the magisterium of Catholicism. We must be patient in our time; but God will take care of His Church—and, when the hour strikes, the reform will begin."[25] In this striking text one notes, once again, the value that totality (i.e., clergy/laity, Latin/Teutonic) has for Newman in the well-being of the pastoral process.

Sensus Fidelium: *The Witness to Revelation*

Newman's theology of the laity reached its most controversial level when he wrote a magazine article claiming that, during the fourth-century Arian crisis, "the Catholic people, in the length and breadth of Christendom, were the obstinate champions of Catholic truth, and the bishops were not."[26] That the article appeared in the *Rambler* was itself significant, as it was the only English-language Catholic magazine not promoting ultramontane views.

The *Rambler* was a laymen's initiative from the start. It had been begun in 1848 by John Moore Capes, an Anglican convert, and in 1857 it came into the hands of another convert, Richard Simpson, who as editor was joined by Sir John Acton, a liberal Catholic educated in Germany under Ignaz von Döllinger. Although Simpson wrote a number of pieces sufficiently critical of the church to displease the bishops, their first action against the magazine was occasioned by one of Acton's book reviews.[27] In arguing the point that no Catholic is as perfect as Catholicism itself, Acton claimed that Augustine was the father of Jansenism besides being the greatest 'doctor' of the Western church. When a storm ensued, Acton asked his former mentor, Döllinger, to provide documentation. Döllinger's letter, "The Paternity of Jansenism," appeared in the December 1858 issue. The letter was delated to Rome, and pressure to terminate was put on the magazine, both of which pained Newman.[28]

In the very next issue, Scott Nasmyth Stokes contributed an unsigned article, "The Royal Commission on Education," that criticized Catholics but particularly the bishops for refusing to cooperate with the Newcastle Commission investigating good and inexpensive education for all youths. Cardinal Wiseman had ordered his clergy not to cooperate; no Catholics were on the committee, and Smith thought these actions foolish if the church hoped to get government funding. The bishops, unused to criticism or to suggestions from the laity, threatened to censure the magazine. Both sides appealed to Newman to mediate. The bishops would not censure if Simpson were removed as editor; Acton and Simpson would step aside if an editor sympathetic to an open policy of journalism were found. Newman, the only person agreeable to both camps, assumed editorship in March 1859. He did not relish the task, but neither did he wish to see this valuable medium of progressive discussion terminated.

In the "Contemporary Events" column of his very first issue, Newman contributed some anonymous comments on the Newcastle Commission, and at this point the controversy on *consulting the laity* begins.

> This leads us to our second remark. Acknowledging, then, most fully the prerogatives of the episcopate, we do unfeignedly believe, both from the reasonableness of the matter, and especially from the prudence, gentleness, and considerateness which belong to them personally, that their Lordships really desire to know the opinion of the laity on subjects in which the laity are especially concerned. If even in the preparation of a dogmatic definition the faithful are consulted, as lately in the instance of the Immaculate Conception, it is at least as natural to anticipate such an act of kind feeling and sympathy in great practical questions.[29]

Newman supported Stokes's contention that the laity's opinion should be heard on the education question. If the hierarchy consulted the laity before the Dogma of 1854 was promulgated, then on the nondogmatic and practical issue of primary education, which involved the laity's children, one would expect consultation all the more. Dr. John Gillow, professor of dogmatic theology at Ushaw College, immediately objected. He contended that the hierarchy had never consulted the laity in the preparation of a dogmatic definition and that to espouse such consultation as a principle would imply that the infallibility of the church resided in the laity rather than exclusively in the hierarchy. For the episcopacy to consult the faithful "with a view to guiding itself to an infallible decision . . . would be characterized as at least *haeresi proxima* [nearly heresy]."[30]

An exchange of letters with Gillow sharpened Newman's own thinking on consultation of the laity and prepared the groundwork for his famous article in the magazine's July issue. The word *consult* can mean to seek an opinion, but it can also mean to ascertain a fact, as when one consults a barometer. Newman told Gillow that consulting the "sense of the faithful" meant ascertaining what in fact the laity believed, and it was what the bishops, under papal direction, did six years prior to the promulgation of the Immaculate Conception in 1854.[31] Second, Newman located infallibility in the totality, that is, neither in the laity nor in the hierarchy exclusively, but in the whole church as such. He quoted the "approved Roman author," Fr. Giovanni Perrone, that infallibility resides in the laity and magisterium in a unitary way, as a figure is contained both on the seal (magisterium) and on the wax (laity).[32]

The metaphor of a signet and wax might suggest that the laity were mere reflectors of what the bishops believed, but a passive and mechanical understanding of the laity "being stamped" is not Newman's meaning.[33] Newman holds for the possibility that there could be a suspense of clear and orthodox doctrine from the bishops but nevertheless a maintenance and steadfast reflection of it from the laity. His perspective asserts a kind of resiliency and durability in the laity's faith and hence ascribes a robust quality to its *sensus fidelium*.

Had the only disapproval with the May issue come from Prof. Gillow, the *Rambler* might have continued under Newman. But Bishop Ullathorne informed Newman of widespread discontent with the magazine. Newman offered to resign, and Ullathorne immediately advised him to make the next issue his last.[34] Newman decided to use the July issue to present an extended discussion on the *sensus fidelium*. The article, "On Consulting the Faithful in Matters of Doctrine," left a legacy for later ecclesiology, but Newman paid a price: Bishop Thomas Brown of Newport delated it to Rome, an accusation of which Newman was never officially informed, and he remained under a cloud of Vatican suspicion for years.[35] The article, currently out of print,[36] posed two key questions.

First, is it correct to say that the faithful can be consulted? The Latin sense of *consult* implies taking counsel and requesting a judgment, and the laity in this sense are not meant to be judges of orthodoxy. The English sense of *consult* may mean both asking an opinion and inquiring into a factual matter, as when one consults a barometer; in this sense the laity's beliefs can be sought as a "testimony to that apostolic tradition, on which alone any doctrine whatsoever can be defined."[37]

Second, can a consultation of the laity's faith be a preliminary to a dogmatic definition? Yes, Newman argues, because the laity as a group is one of the witnesses to what are revealed doctrines in the tradition, and its "*consensus* through Christendom is the voice of the Infallible Church."[38] (Newman often uses *consensus fidelium* for *sensus fidelium* to carry the flexibility of *consult* in English, but he clearly has the latter phrase in mind because of his references to Perrone's work.)[39] Revelation, the single soul of the church, manifests itself variously; at times it is expressed in the teachings of bishops, in the positions of theologians, in the liturgy, and in the laity. Accordingly, no witnessing source may be disregarded in ascertaining the tradition, even though the gift of discerning and defining the tradition rests with the teaching authority (magisterium) alone.

Some will stress one or another of these channels, but Newman chooses to stress the "sense of the faithful" because doctrines, in their earliest stages of development, had a clearer basis in it than in the testimony from theologians or the magisterium. He suggests five ways to understand the testimony that the laity's faith offers: (1) as a witness to the existence of an apostolic doctrine, (2) as a sort of instinct, or *phronema,* deep in the heart of the church itself, (3) as an impulse of the Holy Spirit, (4) as an answer to the laity's own prayer, (5) as a jealousy of error, an error the laity at once feels as a scandal. In illustrating the fifth manifestation of the laity's witnessing process, the unsigned July article refers to Newman's *Arians:* Although the fourth century was an age of learned clerics—Athanasius, Ambrose, Jerome— nevertheless, "in that very day the divine tradition committed to the infallible Church was proclaimed and maintained far more by the faithful than by the episcopate," and that "the body of the episcopate was unfaithful to its commission, while the body of the laity was faithful to its baptism."[40]

Newman's unsigned article drew two further conclusions from the fourth-century Arian crisis that were to alarm his more conservative co-religionists. During the half century following the council of Nicea, bishops taught inconsistently and argued with each other, leading Newman to conclude that "there was a temporary suspense of the functions of the 'Ecclesia docens' [magisterium of the church]."[41] Furthermore, the episcopal synods meeting during this period were divided and pitted against one another, such that "general councils said what they should not have said, and did what obscured and compromised revealed truth."[42]

Newman justifies his appeal for the use of the *sensus fidelium* with a principle he takes from his work on the development of Christian doctrines. A Christian truth undergoing development is usually grasped only vaguely or implicitly at first, and it comes to clearer light under the catalyst of some issue or challenge. In somewhat the same way, the truth contained in consulting the laity on a doctrinal matter had fallen into the background because the magisterium had been exercised so vigorously in recent centuries. However, the possibility of defining the dogma of the Immaculate Conception illuminated once again the importance of the laity's testimony to the revealed faith, since their belief in this doctrine provided crucial testimony, especially when support for it from the church's teaching tradition was weak.

In addition to Bishop Brown's denunciation of Newman's article to Vatican authorities, J. B. Franzelin, professor of dogmatic theology at Rome's Gregorian Univerisity and soon to be a leading figure at the Vatican Council, objected to Newman's contentions that there had ever been a suspense to the *Ecclesia docens*, that the *body* of bishops failed to witness to orthodoxy, and that general councils had erred. Newman waited until he reedited the *Arians* in 1871 to answer Franzelin and to offer further precision to his startling statements. By suspense of the church's teaching office, he meant that the period between the Council of Nicea (A.D. 325) and the First Council of Constantinople (A.D. 381) was marked by intense doctrinal confusion and that a clear and consistent teaching from the bishops was lacking; he did not mean to imply that there was simply a lull in the teaching office. As to the body of bishops' failing, Newman thought Franzelin understood him to say that the bishops, in a conscious collegial act of teaching (e.g., an ecumenical council), erred; Newman meant that the "great preponderance" of bishops, considered as individuals but nevertheless amounting to a sizable number, did not witness to orthodoxy while the body of the laity did. Finally, "general councils" did not refer to those gatherings now recognized as ecumenical but rather to those large synods that indeed can err and have erred.[43]

In defending the *Rambler* article, Newman was pushed into issues about the hierarchy and about the legitimacy of institutional authority. It was never his purpose to undermine the teaching office of the church, a fact evident from his defense of it in the *Essay on Development*. But Newman's vision of the laity as an actively contributing, personally involved, and even doctrinally testifying force in the social life of the community simply touched raw nerves among those accustomed to view the church from the top down. If the primary vision of the church is institutional, then emphasis is placed on hierarchical office and on the authority of those ordained to office. If the focus is more organic and communal, then account is taken of the church's nonclerical features and of other ways the institution works. Newman's article arose from the latter orientation, the response of critics from the former. More than just a question of phraseology and nuanced theological description, the conflict was a clash of mentalities at a deeper level.

Newman's advocacy of the *sensus fidelium* was also intended to stem the loss of the church's laypeople. If the laity were to have no involvement in the process by which revelation is discerned, they would be reduced to having an "implicit faith" in the church's teachings, "which in the educated classes will terminate in indifference, and in the poorer in superstition."[44] Implicit faith, in this sense, refers to the psychological feeling of alienation resulting from exclusion in those matters in which one ought to be involved. If doctrines are imposed on people from sources extrinsic to their experience or if they deal with subjects removed from what people apprehend of their own faith, then the laity are likely to become alienated from the very revealed message intended by God to clarify and to support their lives of faith. Among reflective people such doctrines will encounter indifference if not outright rejection; among other, less educated laity such doctrines are likely to be appropriated as superstitions, that is, as unconnected with the basic and fundamental affirmations of their simple faith.

Finally, the stakes were too high to keep the laity at arm's length from the processes of discerning the church's faith. As Newman looked ahead, he perceived that the challenge to ministry would lie outside the church's institutional boundaries. When the issues are intramural, and to a large extent the concerns of the post-Tridentine church were, then a clerically preponderant ministry can succeed. But the challenge to revealed religion, in Newman's forecast, was to come from secular life. The philosophy of the day, its literature, and especially the growing techno-scientific ethos had abandoned Christian roots and were destined to clash with religion. Educated, committed laity were the proper witnesses to a living faith and were the best evangelizers of the secularist society that was surely coming.

THE ROLE OF THE MEDIA

Newman never conceives of revelation as a deposit of divinely given propositional statements that can be readily promulgated by the magisterium, nor does he think of it as a full body of knowledge given to the apostles, of which the Scriptures were the definitive written answers and detailed blueprints for Christian living. God's revelation is more like the inner life of the Christian community, the knowledge of which needs to be articulated from the community's memory and experiences; in other words, God's truth is not prepackaged but rather needs to be lived out. The processes by which the church expresses itself as a church, in its interactions within its own walls and also in the wider world, are the agents by which revelation undergoes development and is clarified in the church's consciousness. Thus, quite naturally, Newman is led to assert the laity's rightful role in these processes, as has been described above. An immediate practical consequence of this viewpoint is the use of the means of communication—journals and newspapers—to further the processes of discernment.

A revealed religion like Catholicism does not possess a ready-made bundle of statements that a Catholic journal communicates to its readers as if it were sending out dogmatic news. Religious truth awaits exploration and grasp. Every insight prompts further questions, every truth has unfathomed aspects, and every doctrine has the need for reinterpretation within a new situation. Given this sense of process, Newman is more inclined to speak of journals of religious *opinion,* by which he means the engagement of those questions of Christian faith and contemporary life whose solutions are yet to be worked out. The church is impelled to understand its revealed patrimony in ever-fresh situations. To take a contemporary example, Christian revelation is fully concerned with the dignity and quality of human life. How is this concern to be understood in reference to the proliferation of nuclear armaments? Does the older doctrine of a just war apply any longer, or is the contemporary situation posing a brand new question? Such an important question is "at the edge" of revelation, as it were, not indeed implying that such a crucial issue is peripheral to God's revealing word but rather that the mind of the community is currently in a process of discernment. In just this sense Newman sees religious journals as pushing at the edges of Christian faith, and thus they constitute an important ingredient in his ecclesiology.

Monopolized and Suppressed Opinion

Newman assumes that questions under discernment are too complex for any single author or school of religious thought to exhaust. Such matters need to be sifted and examined under their various aspects by the reflections of many religious minds. Views will conflict, positions will be overstated, and select aspects will be chosen as paramount. These activities lead to healthy debate, out of which a truer discernment comes. Such is the dialectical process Newman wished to see in the Catholic community. What he actually experienced was a monopoly on Catholic opinion exercised by ultramontane journals advancing a particular agenda.

Rather than fearing public criticism and differences of opinion on matters of faith and religion, Newman urged their importance for the way revealed truth comes to be known. When in the 1870s he asked his friend, W. J. Copeland, to re-edit his Anglican sermons, he was at first tempted to suppress some things he had written as an Anglican that he no longer held, but he resisted. "My view has ever been to answer, not to suppress, what is erroneous. . . . It seems to me a bad policy to suppress. Truth has a power of its own, which makes it way—it is stronger than error."[45] When Prof. Döllinger published historical material critical of papal infallibility just prior to the First Vatican Council, for example, Newman did not see Döllinger's actions as disloyal or spiteful, as did others who wished Döllinger silenced. Rather, Newman preferred that the troublesome historical incidents be debated publicly by scholars, and he himself contested Döllinger's interpretations of the data.[46] Newman encouraged Pusey to bring forward in print the strongest arguments against Catholic positions because "there are objections, and grave objections, to the simplest truths, and the cause of Truth gains by their being stated clearly and considered carefully."[47]

These incidents portray Newman's healthy respect for dialectical discourse and for the confidence he had in the strength of truth to assert itself. It is as if truth has a life of its own, and it makes its way by the very clash of religious minds. But where thinking is controlled or monopolized, the life of truth withers. For such reasons, Newman supported journals that would counterbalance the prevailing ultraconservative viewpoint, such as that of the *Dublin Review*. He did not begrudge that magazine its outlook, but he wished to see that outlook debated.

The *Home and Foreign Review,* successor to the *Rambler* and continuing its progressive orientation, met the same kind of hostility its predecessor did. Sir John Acton was on the verge of retiring it when Newman wrote to dissuade him. "I think you cannot prudently stop the Review. . . . Such a course would be a smothering of feelings and opinions which exist, which are allowable in a Catholic, which it is healthy to out with, dangerous or injurious to bottle up. If these opinions imply uncatholic instincts, let this be shown; else, we cannot be sure that what happens to be called an instinct, is any thing more than the sentiment of a particular school in the Church."[48] The "instinct" to which Newman refers was the *Dublin Review*'s method of labeling its ultramontane views as the sole Catholic instinct and calling any divergent viewpoint a heresy. Newman fears the power of a monolithic and unchallenged viewpoint to tyrannize opponents and eventually to drive thoughtful people from the church. Reminiscent of his argument in the preface to the *Via Media* that the kingly office (governance), unchecked by the prophetic and priestly offices in the church, drifts toward tyranny, his point here is that the same danger of organic imbalance applies to control of the media.

Curiously, Newman blames the imbalance on the more progressive members of the clergy and laity who do not seize the ministerial possibility of using journals and who allow extreme Catholic views to go unchallenged. What is needed, he advises, is a "periodical organ of moderate views, yet unassailable in point of theology. But we have left the field open to extreme opinions and their fanatical preachers—or what is worse, we have suffered what is sober Catholic truth to become unpopular by mistakes in the opposite direction."[49]

A healthy pluralism of views and open debate among journals of various persuasions run the risk, in matters of religion, of false statement and of promoting confusion within the church. This risk has always been the argument of those who, in the name of church order and protection of tender consciences, have suppressed debate. But such risk cannot be avoided. "I have felt it as a most anxious task to have to write on the subjects which have engaged me lately—no one can write without making mistakes—I don't doubt have made some, though I hope not great ones. If a man waited till he could write without any mistakes, he would not write at all. There is in every man's work matter which may be taken up for hostile criticism, if readers are so minded."[50] Newman's hope for journalistic writing, and for that particular genre of religious writing aptly done by laity, clearly envisions those matters[51] where the implications of Christian faith for daily life are probed. These are uncharted waters, and mistakes are inevitable. If essayists retreat to prosaic topics within safely defined perimeters, Christian reflection will stagnate, and that is too high a price to pay.

Furthermore, Newman trusts the resiliency of people's faith. Debate within the Catholic community can indeed be unsettling to simple believers, but, where others sought to close off legitimate dissension in the name of protective concern, Newman thought that the faith of Catholics could bear challenge, self-reflection, and public debate. "Faith ought to be tried and tested, if it *be* faith. I don't like that faith, which, (as I have seen written to a new convert) is a 'precious tender plant,' to be sedulously guarded under a glass cover, or in a hothouse—an exotic—if so, our religion is a mere 'alien religion,' and 'Oriental faith and worship'—but it is a tough principle within us, bearing heavy weights and hard work, or it is worth very little."[52] Such thoughts come from Newman's vision of revelation as an inner light of truth, itself grasping a believer rather than merely being *grasped by* someone. Newman emphasizes God's hold on us rather than our hold on God. The ultramontanists treated the laity as if Christian fatih were precariously rooted and ever to be shielded. But Newman perceives that the suppression of debate and a monopoly over public opinion lead to stagnation in the church and to isolation from the outer world.

Notes on a Media Ministry

When Newman became editor of the *Rambler* in 1859, albeit for two issues only, he sketched in the initial advertisement the main aim of a journalistic philosophy. The magazine was to achieve a refinement and enlargement of the Catholic mind by what Newman termed a "manly investigation of the subjects of public interest."[53] The low state of Catholic intellectual life, itself a result of a patriarchical attitude of the clergy toward the laity, was a scandal to the church's mission. For Newman, the church's impact on the wider society varied with the measure of the laity's influence. It was necessary to galvanize this vast potential of the church, through it shaping the public sector; therefore, the use of publications to educate and cultivate the Catholic mind made obvious pastoral sense.

One must recall the two sides to Newman's concept of religion. One side is intensely private, the domain of personal conscience that seeks to obey God. The other side is the social reality of religion. Religion shapes a culture's *ethos;* it influences a society's basic instincts, because societies as well as individuals operate from sovereign principles. England and Anglicanism were prime examples; the church was, in large part, one with the culture, and it imprinted on that culture certain values and instincts. The Roman Catholic church was also meant to shape the public sector. This purpose necessitated a lay membership educated to the germane social issues and well grounded in the implications of the Christian faith. Four years after the *Rambler* had been taken from him, Newman confided to his lifelong friend, Emily Bowles, his aborted purposes. "I not only made the best of it, but I really determined to make it *my work.* All those questions of the day which make so much noise now, Faith and Reason, Inspiration, etc. etc., would have been, according to my ability, worked out or fairly opened. Of course I required elbow room—but this was *impossible*."[54] Catholics had first to see the real questions and understand the new situation. This emphasis may be called Newman's primary purpose for a media ministry, stemming from the public nature and responsibilities of religion.

Journals, for Newman, are also meant to retrieve the pluralism and flexibility of Catholic theology that had characterized its vigor and appeal in former centuries. "There should be in the English Catholic body a witness of a freer and larger theology than appears in the Dublin [magazine]. . . . Whether it should be exclusively theological I cannot quite decide—but it should be prominently and especially so. It might embrace among its subjects the Curiosities of (theological) literature—criticism, chronology, metaphysics—as well as theology proper—controversy, history. But it must not be written ad captandam."[55] The concluding caveat refers to the magazine's overall style. It should avoid a party spirit, as if it were merely the antagonist to the *Dublin Review*. A weapon, Newman advises, cannot be all edge lest it become tiresome. "Power, to be powerful, and strength, to be strong, must be exerted only now and then."[56] It should range beyond parochial disputes to matters of letters, history, political commentary, etc., and give evidence to a catholicity of perceptions.

Newman's clearest advice on the pastoral purposes of journalism was sent to a Jesuit who was contemplating beginning a new magazine. Since Catholics were despised for having anti-intellectual attitudes—a view Protestants took of an authoritarian church—a magazine of high caliber was the best apologetic. "As secular power, rank and wealth are great human means of promoting Catholicism, so especially in this democratic age is intellect. Without dreaming of denying the influence of the three first named instruments of success, still I think the influence arising from repute for ability and cultivation of mind, in this age, is greater than any one of them." Second, a magazine should address topical questions, since English Protestants viewed Catholics as pawns of a foreign power and uninterested in British matters. Third, the magazine should avoid polemics, which tend more to alienate than elicit sympathy. "It seems to me that what is to be aimed at, is to lay a Catholic *foundation* of thought—and *no* foundation is above ground. And next, to lay it with Protestant bricks: I mean to use as far as possible, Protestant parties and schools in doing so."[57] The most persuasive writer enters into opposing positions, exposing their first principles and ramifications. Journals offer a way of doing theology "in undress," as Newman noted to the Jesuit editor of the *Month*. Theology "should address itself to common sense, reason, received maxims, etc. etc., not to authority or technical dicta."[58]

Newman had launched the *Rambler* with the aim of courageously investigating all subjects. It was to involve the strategies of persuasion listed above, but above all it should challenge the domination of Catholic thought by the ultramontane party, which reproached its opponents as disloyal Catholics, if not heretical ones. So strong was the ultramontane hold on the Catholic establishment that freedom of debate was largely curtailed. Intellectuals outside this dominant party were suspect, Newman most of all. He know that every word he published would be "malevolently scrutinized and every expression which can possibly be perverted sent straight to Rome—then I shall be fighting *under the lash*, which does not tend to produce vigorous efforts."[59] But he would not capitulate to this tyranny. The principle of legitimate Catholic freedom was at stake.

FREEDOM OF THOUGHT IN THE CHURCH

Newman's pastoral ecclesiology, concerned as it is with the concrete processes of ecclesial life and with a method of theological reflection based on personal involvement in the issues, comes to a head on the matter of theological freedom. The issues surrounding the print media, just examined, are symptomatic of Newman's broader concern for intellectual freedom. When he refers to his journalistic efforts as "fighting *under the lash*," he is bemoaning not only his own experience of censorship from an overly cautious exercise of authority in the church but also the undue influence on Catholic thinking exercised by a particular theological school.

To appreciate his advocacy of theological freedom, Newman must be measured against two backdrops. One, not surprisingly, is the ultramontane mentality,[60] and with it we may also associate the "hierarchology" spirit of a large portion of the church's leadership in the nineteenth century. Newman opposed the ultramontane tendency to stifle legitimate freedoms. The second context is Newman himself, as classically understood, that is to say, the Newman reflected in the thirty-seven volumes of the Uniform Edition and fairly well known. In these books he is the great defender and apologete of Roman Catholicism. It was not the purpose of these "classics" to offer institutional critique.[61] But neither was the church perfect, and Newman's, experience as a Roman Catholic gave him definite views on how it should renew itself. His private letters offer ample expression of these views, and they modify the classic picture many people have of him.

The modification is most apparent in the matter of theological freedom. The Uniform Edition provides only moderate awareness and appreciation of Newman as an advocate of freedom in the church. For example, the *Idea of a University* considers the necessity for academic freedom to conduct proper inquiry, but its fuller ramifications and concrete applications to church structures are found in the letters. There is no implication that the Newman of private letters is inconsistent or contradictory; the principles are detectable in the books, but the letters make them crystal clear and apply them. The same can be said for the topic of authority. In sundry books Newman treated the role of authority as a distinguishing feature of the true church. In the *Essay on Development* an infallible teaching office is argued as the most winning hypothesis to account for true developments of doctrine that then serve as the basis of social unity and action.[62] In the *Difficulties of Anglicans* the "unitive and integrating virtue" of the Petrine ministry [papacy] is advanced as the practical source of church cohesion that overcomes the divisive tendencies of nationalisms and ideological parties.[63] Other instances could be listed, and their cumulative effect on later generations has been to promote a view of Newman as a strenuous advocate of the magisterial office of the church. This he was, but there is another side, concerned with the practical operations of authority, with the need for self-imposed restraints, and with the misuses of power. The letters exhibit this kind of person.

Legitimate Latitude in Theological Thinking

Newman's argument for the legitimate place of theology in a university curriculum, presented in the *Idea of a University*, is based on the same principle by which he would defend greater latitude in theological reflection itself. Everything that exists forms one large complex "fact" that no human mind or particular science can embrace in its unity. The complex fact has an indefinite number of aspects or portions, each with many relationships toward the others. Even though the intellect strives toward a vision of the whole, the whole cannot be taken in at one glance. The mind grasps aspects and moves by steps toward a fuller vision. Each aspect is an abstraction from the concrete whole, and where the whole refers to all of reality, then each aspect corresponds to one of the sciences. The sciences are "the results of mental processes about one and the same subject-matter, viewed under its various aspects."[64] If all of the sciences were taken together, they would in principle approximate to a representation of the whole. Whenever a legitimate science is excluded, to that extent is an aspect of the whole being neglected. Consequently, if a university seeks to investigate reality under all of its knowable aspects, and if theology offers knowledge of a particular aspect, theological science has a rightful place in the curriculum.

Embedded in this argument is the principle of disproportion. The mind grasps only aspects of reality; it can never master the whole. The whole is webbed by aspects, each one in relation to the others, each one needing the others to complement itself. Every mental view is partial and can, in principle, be indefinitely complemented by other views. As further aspects are integrated, a step closer to the grasp of the whole is made. Yet the whole, for which the mind is made, is always beyond one's ken; there is disproportion. This principle of disproportion is Newman's explanation for the mind's drive to investigate and to pursue continually the whole of truth.

Theological reflection is no exception to these laws of mental operation. In fact, the drive within religious thinking is heightened by the whole it seeks to grasp and never can achieve. The whole is the mystery of God and God's sundry relationships to the world, e.g., creator, redeemer, voice of conscience, and (for Christians) Incarnate One. The doctrine describing each of these relationships is but an aspect of the full reality; each doctrine relates to the others, and each has aspects under which it may be viewed and further explicated. There is never a final human word that may be said of a religious truth, for whatever is said is only a partial articulation. The religious mystery outstrips our reflection on it and continually invites further scrutiny.

Two conclusions follow from this sense of disproportion between the sacred and our human apprehension of it. A religious doctrine, which is a conception of the mystery expressed in human language, is still truthful even though it is partial. Partiality is not falsification provided it does not claim to articulate more than it in fact grasps. Second, and more germane to the matter of theological freedom, every doctrine has aspects and relations yet to be investigated but necessary to complement what is now known. These aspects and relationships are to the doctrine as questions naturally generated by prior insights. If a doctrine is itself the truthful culmination of a mental process—and the mental process must be seen *socially* as an ecclesial process—the doctrine is, in a sense, a fresh question posed to the restlessness within religious reflection. A doctrine such as papal infallibility is not a closed issue, a settled matter from which one moves on to other matters. It invites theological reflection on its aspects, on its relations to other doctrines, and on what is not being addressed by its present formulation.

Newman's epistemological principle of disproportion is the justification for the need for theological freedom of inquiry. Theological reflection is given certain restraints by defined doctrine (dogma), that is to say, the dogma commands assent to some partial aspect of the full truth. It is normally a minimal hold on intellectual freedom because many aspects of the issue remain open to debate, and in these areas there is legitimate freedom for speculation. Newman experienced the ultramontane party attempting to close off these areas from debate by claiming as defined what was only their opinions on the nondefined aspects of the dogma.

As editor of the *Dublin Review*, W. G. Ward was in a singularly influential position to advance ultramontane views. His main interest was the authority of the magisterium, especially for those teachings never defined as dogma.[65] He claimed for them an infallible force consistent with the ultramontane tendency to aggrandize the papal position. Those who thought this emphasis to be excessive found their loyalty to the church questioned; *real* Catholics, Ward argued, would never minimize papal authority. Newman detected in Ward's attitude an echo of the ancient Novation heresy that advocated a true church of strict observance and that anathematized backsliders.

> Pardon me if I say that you are making a Church within a Church, as the Novations of old did within the Catholic pale, and as, outside the Catholic pale, the Evangelicals of the Establishment. As they talk of "vital religion" and "vital doctrines," and will not allow that their brethren "know the Gospel" or are "Gospel preachers" unless they profess the small shibboleths of their own sect, so are you doing your best to make a party in the Catholic Church, and in St. Paul's words are *"dividing Christ"* by exalting your opinions into dogmas, and shocking to say, by declaring to me, as you do, that those Catholics who do not accept them are of a different religion from yours.[66]

Formal dogmas are carefully circumscribed teachings that only addressed a specific aspect of a complex issue. Regarding papal prerogatives, there were aspects allowing diversity of opinion and legitimate debate in the church. As Ward continued to equate ultramontane opinions with official dogma, one of Newman's younger Oratorians, Ignatius Ryder, countered with *Idealism in Theology: A Review of Dr. Ward's Scheme of Dogmatic Authority.*[67] Newman sent Ryder's work to Ward and reiterated his own anxiety about confusing opinion with dogma; the covering letter ends with the famous phrase associated with Newman: unity in essentials, freedom in doubtful matters, in all things charity. "I think he is but a specimen of a number of young Catholics, who have a right to an opinion on the momentous subject in question, and who feel keenly that you are desirous to rule views of doctrine to be vital, which the Church does not call or consider vital. . . . I rejoice in believing, that, now that my own time is drawing to an end, the new generation will not forget the spirit of the old maxim, in which I have ever wished to speak and act myself. 'In necessariis unitas, in dubiis libertas, in omnibus charitas.' "[68]

After Vatican I's formal definitions of papal primacy and infallibility, definitions Newman thought restrictive in their word-ing, the ultaramontanists pressed even further their maximizing interpretations. Newman had a keen sense how preconditioning influences the task of interpretation. With his penchant for psy-chological analysis, he thought that the recent loss of the Papal States was such an emotional blow to the ultramontane party that ultramontanists exaggerated the import of the council's dogmas in a compensatory way.

> All enunciations of doctrine, as all legal documents, admit of a wider or of a narrower interpretation. Take, for instance, the "Extra Eccle-siam Nulla Salus—" Now there are those who will take it in the one sense, and those who will take it in the other, and thus schools of opinion will be formed. And so again of the dogma concerning the Pope's prerogatives; and his party, as it may be called, will use it in that sense which best subserves his aggrandisement. But these parti-zans, when brought to book, are obliged to confess that an interpre-tation of it less favorable to him is allowable—though they will try to discredit it. In like manner, the Pope of the day himself may make himself one of his own partizans, and defend that view which is most favorable to himself—but since such comments are not ex cathedra, but the words of a private doctor, they do not impose an acceptance of the sense, which they advocate, on the consciences of the faith-ful.[69]

Genuine theological insight needs an environment of freedom within which to operate. The mind must have range if the crea-tivity involved in insight is to be activated. Newman thinks of freedom in regard to both the subject matter and an attitude church authorities adopt toward theologians. The subject mat-ter, as just seen, refers to that legitimate region of opinion that does not fall under dogmatic definition. More crucial, perhaps, is the feeling of support and trust a theologian should sense from church authorities. It is freedom's psychological side. New-man is concerned with this dimension, and he likens its require-ments to those of a healthy plant. A plant must be allowed vigor-ous unchecked growth before it is pruned; if pruned or checked too early, it will not flower. If prematurely restricted, it will wither. It needs room to expand, to overstate itself as it were, before excesses and misdirections are cut off. The life of the mind is a great instance of this law of growth. A remarkable statement in Newman's *Letter to Pusey* expresses the idea eloquently. "Life has the same right to decay, as it has to wax strong. This is specially the case with great ideas. You may stifle them; or you may refuse them elbow-room; or again, you may torment them with your continual meddling; or you may let them have free course and range, and be content, instead of anticipating their excesses, to expose and restrain those excesses after they have occurred. But you have only this alternative; and for myself, I prefer much whenever it is possible, to be first generous and then just; to grant full liberty of thought, and to call it to account when abused."[70] One cannot, as Newman said in other context, think under the lash.

For any living and complex reality, such as the church, Newman likes to envision a dialectical interplay of forces, each with its proper aims, each with momentums somewhat at variance with the others. The activity of an organism is again his paradigm. Viewed separately, each part of the organism contributes to the overall good, but any part may assume for a time a dominant role over the other organs, as when in traumatic injuries the brain has greater claim on the body's blood than the other organs; this period is followed by a return to balance (homeostasis). Theologians and magisterium are two such forces in the organic life of the church. The momentum of theology is toward discovery, the molding of new formulations, the expression of the ancient faith in new situations; theology is a constructive enterprise. The magisterium's momentum is toward conservation and protection, holding faithfully to the revealed inheritance, effecting and ensuring the ordering of common faith and action. There are times when the health of the organism demands the dominance of the conserving element, as when Nicea rejected Arius.[71] Other times need the free play of theological inquiry being conducted without premature incursions of authority.

Newman's great instance of the free play of theological inquiry was the university theology of Aquinas and the scholastics. The rediscovery of Aristotle challenged the hold of Neo-Platonism on Catholic thought, especially as the latter philosophy was embedded and consequently sanctioned in the theologies of Saints Augustine and Anselm. Church authority could have stepped in and "exterminated the spirit of inquiry with fire and sword," but it took instead the wiser course of letting the university theologians debate. "It is the splendid and palmary instance of the wise policy and large liberality of the Church. . . . If there ever was a time when the intellect went wild and had a licentious revel, it was at the date I speak of."[72] For centuries, Aristotle was reckoned a foe of Christianity, and Augustinian Neo-Platonism was its congenial ally. Yet Aquinas was given the opportunity to relate Aristotle to the faith and made of him, in Newman's words, "a hewer of wood and drawer of water to the Church."[73]

Great ideas, be they true or false, cannot be suppressed. They may only be engaged, sifted, tried for awhile, and accorded their proper place in a community's mental soil. New ideas of this sort will unsettle the community for awhile; they come as foreign bodies into an organism at mental balance. And indeed it is practically a law that they are never fully domesticated with what was there. This truth, for Newman, explains why religious ideas are not homogeneous and why the church must be a home for the different ways people understand themselves, their church, and their world. "Differences always have been, always will be, in the Church, and Christians would have ceased to have spiritual and intellectual life, if such differences did not exist. It is part of their militant state. No human power can hinder it; nor, if it attempted it, could [it] do more than make a solitude and call it peace. . . . Man cannot, and God will not."[74]

Does not such championing of freedom for theological inquiry undermine the value of oneness in doctrine, a note of the church to which, as we saw in the previous chapter, Newman made strong apologetic appeal? His tenth lecture in the *Anglican Difficulties* argued the compatibility between unity in faith and diversity of opinions on the basis of Catholicism's ability to hold together without "thought control." Private judgment begins at the point where a dogmatic teaching ends, and in Newman's view a dogma is narrowly worded and limited in what it teaches. The intellect's natural tendency is to assert its personal view, to be independent of the pronouncements of any external authority. In the *Idea of a University* Newman uses the term "imperial intellect" not as a criticism but in recognition of the intellect's sovereign sway. There is only one external voice before which the human mind rightly humbles itself—the voice of God—and that voice might be heard through a variety of channels. Still, the mind is naturally self-willed, self-dependent, self-satisfied. For these reasons, "There ever has been, and ever will be, a vast exercise and a realized product, partly praiseworthy, partly barely lawful, of private judgment within the Catholic Church. The freedom of the human mind is 'in possession' (as it is called), and it meddles with every question and it wanders over heaven and earth."[75] Considering the varieties of private judgment (Catholicism's schools of spirituality, its theological parties, etc.), Newman found it remarkable that the ecclesial character of Catholicism has remained so coherent and unified; it has held together almost in spite of differences. The differences in Catholic thinking, in fact, have delineated more clearly the common faith of the community when that faith has encountered new situations. Theological differences have been at the service of church unity rather than being its nemesis.

These insights have been Newman's justifications for the need to preserve freedom of inquiry in the church. Furthermore, as if it were God's providential guidance of the process of discernment, Newman was convinced of the self-destructive quality of error. When insight is wrong, it will wither; when it is true, it will secure itself. Error is "like other delinquents; give it rope enough, and it will be found to have a strong suicidal propensity."[76] Therefore error should not be feared unduly. Error can even promote truth and at times is its necessry mental soil. "Theories, speculation, hypotheses, are started; perhaps they are to die, still not before they have suggested ideas better than themselves. These better ideas are taken up in turn by other men, and, if they do not yet lead to truth, nevertheless they lead to what is still nearer to truth than themselves; and thus knowledge on the whole makes progress."[77] Given this general orientation to the legitimacy of freedom in religious inquiry, the actual *processes* advocated by Newman require more detailed examination.

Theology within a Dialectics of Discourse

Because the model of an organism served Newman in understanding the processes of church life, he tended to view the healthiest state of affairs as a balancing of forces. For example, a "hierarchology" and a passive laity depicted a church off balance. When forces are in balance they are not, respective to each other, inactive or at rest. Each force has a characteristic dynamism that seeks to fulfill its natural propensity. But each needs also to be *balanced off* by the rightful assertion of the other forces. The state of healthy equilibrium, then, is dynamic rather than static. When the image of a dynamic organism is used disclosively of the church, Newman is suggesting that every component of the church is a gift from God and has a necessary role to play in the totality. As an idea has many aspects, each with its own power to stretch the totality toward itself, so does the church have aspects (e.g., clergy/laity, Franciscan/Dominican spiritualities) each with its distinctive aim, its own teleology. Similarly, theologians and magisterium are teleological forces in the organic functioning of the church.

The organic model also suggests what the church is not and must never become. It is not a mere amalgam of heterogeneous forces, each in devisive struggle against one another. The church itself has a teleology in which its diverse forces share. The common objective is expressed variously: one Lord, one Faith, one Baptism; the one confession of Jesus as Lord. A Roman Catholic Christian adds further ecclesial specifications, such as "being in communion with the Apostolic See," when reference is made to the unifying role of the papacy. Organism, then, does not suggest an internally chaotic situation. On the contrary, there is an interplay of internal forces that in their very interplay maintain a unity while avoiding a uniformity. Newman was attracted to the need for dynamic equilibrium because he feared the hegemony of an ideological party or cadre. In a draft of a letter to a Jesuit friend about the sheer size and influence of the Society of Jesus, Newman elaborated on the operation of equilibrium. "I dread their [the Jesuits'] unmitigated action on the Church. Every religious body is good in its place; every religious body is dangerous, if it aims to engross the whole Church. The Jesuits, the Dominicans, the Franciscans, the secular Priesthood, the Colleges of a University, the Theological Faculties, are so many distinct and independent influences modifying each other, subserving the whole Church."[78]

The notion of equilibrium applies especially to the topic of theological discourse. New theological ideas are like particular forces in the church. They have a right to a hearing. Their proper forum is the theological academy, at least initially. Newman refers to courts of appeal to describe the various stages at which theological debate occurs as the idea makes its way forward. Under scrutiny by other viewpoints, a theological idea may be modified, augmented, or placed in context with other doctrines; it may even be rejected. Such should be the history of its path to achieving its balanced place.

Balancing is achieved in at least two ways. Within the theological arena (e.g., in a journal), a theological insight seeks to hold its own in relationship to the views of other theologians. Each theologian, or each school of theology, brings a particular point of view to bear on it. In Newman's language, each operates out of certain first principles of thought that even extend to the cumulus of feelings, memories, and present experiences shaping *how* one thinks. From such first principles, viewed concretely, inevitable differences emerge. I am calling the theological arena a "dialectics of discourse" to express this personalized multiplicity of viewpoints; no two persons look on the world in exactly the same way.

Second, the theological academy itself must seek balance with the ecclesiastical authority, that is to say, each has accountability to the other. Theological insight eventually comes under the scrutiny of the magisterium, and for Newman theologians must accept its judgments. But church authority also has a responsibility to let the theological process assess the place and worth of new ideas, that is to say, the teaching office has a judgmental role subsequent to a dialectics of discourse. But this layered strategy was being usurped too often by a premature exercise of authority. An instance in which Newman's letters provide an application for ideas expressed more guardedly in his books occurs in his candid assessment of a Vatican office.

> I will tell you what seems to me the real grievance; viz. that in this generation, the Bishops should pass such grave matters (to use the Oxford term) by *cumulation*. The wisdom of the Church has provided many courts for theological questions, one higher than another, and with an appeal from the lower to the higher. I suppose, in the middle ages, which has a manliness and boldness of which there is now so great a lack, a question was first debated in a University; then in one University against another; or by one order of friars against another; then perhaps it came before a theological faculty; then it went to the metropolitan; and so by various stages and after

many examinations and judgments, it came before the Holy See. But now what do the Bishops do? All courts are superseded, because the whole English-speaking Catholic population all over the world is under Propaganda, an arbitrary, military power. Propaganda is our only court of appeal; but to it the Bishops go, and secure it and commit it, before they move one step in the matter which calls for interference. And how is Propaganda to know anything about an English controversy, since it talks Italian? by extempore translation, (I do not speak at random) or by exparte assertion of some narrow-minded Bishop,—narrowminded, though he may be saintly too. And who *is* Propaganda? one sharp man of business, who works day and night, and dispatches his work quick off, to the East and the West, a high dignitary, perhaps an Archbishop, but after all little more than a clerk.[79]

The *Apologia* also mentions the medieval courts of appeal, only to draw the less combative conclusion that such a process "tends not only to the liberty, but to the courage, of the individual theologian or controversialist."[80]

The assimilation of new ideas into the church's self-understanding involves a further feature of the theological process having both pastoral and dogmatic implications. Newman speaks of the purposes of the *schola* (literally, the school) of theologians. Thus far, Newman has described the theological process as an arena of many viewpoints assessing a proposed insight. But a dialectics of discourse, when successful, moves beyond a diversity of insights to the truth of insight. Newman calls this latter phase of the process the *schola*.

The process is supple and normally quite lengthy, as is the case in the following example. It has been a Christian doctrine that salvation comes through Christ. About this doctrine one may wonder whether non-Christians are saved, and the phrase "Outside the Church, no salvation" has certainly been understood by some to preclude salvation for non-Christians. Through a process of theological debate on this question, refining the concepts of 'church', 'salvation', 'personal conscience', and 'mediation of grace', theologians came to a consensus that salvation in Christ involves the possibility of salvation for everyone. The consensus predated the clear teaching of Vatican Council II on the same question and in fact was a basis for the conciliar teaching. The *schola* of theologians also functions as a milieu for interpreting a church teaching concerning further questions that arise about it. The *schola* is thus an important agent in Newman's vision of the pastoral process and has many purposes.

> It defends the dogma, and articulates it. Further than this, since its teaching is far wider and fuller than the Apostolic dogma which is de fide, it protects it, as forming a large body of doctrine which must be got through before an attack can be made on the dogma. And it studies the opinion of the Church, embodying tradition and hindering frequent changes. And it is the arena on which questions of development and change are argued out. And again, if changes of opinion are to come, and false interpretations of Scripture, or false views of dogma to be set right, it prepares the way, accustoming the mind of Catholics to the idea of the change, and preventing surprise and scandal. It is a *recognized* institution with privileges. Without it, the dogma of the Church would be the raw flesh without skin—nay or a tree without leaves—for, as devotional feelings clothe the dogma on the one hand, so does the teaching of the Schola on the other. Moreover, it is the immediate authority for the practical working and course of the Church—e.g., what are mortal sins? what venial? what is the effect of the mass? what about indulgences? etc. etc.[81]

The pastoral purposes of the *schola* are obvious. Convictions mature slowly within the *schola,* and by consequence, within the church. There may have been *understandings* among Catholics in their pieties, about Purgatory for instance, which were never dogmatically taught. As theologians examine such understandings and the history of the question, they shift the emphasis to aspects more central to the Gospel. The shift occurs gradually, gaining clarification within the *schola,* and it then filters into pastoral preaching and catechetical materials. This process conditions the Catholic imagination for change because the change has been gaining an imperceptible momentum.

The dogmatic purposes of the *schola,* furthermore, concretize a doctrine, and given Newman's preference for what is concrete and for what vivifies the imagination, this contribution is crucial. To take another example, the Catholic doctrine on the Mass understands it as meal and sacrifice, preceded by proclaimed Word (Scriptures and homily). Even when all the official teachings on these aspects are gathered together, they are as threads trying to cover the concrete richness of the experience of the Mass. The fuller cloth is woven from the history of interpreting these doctrines, and this interpretation is the work of the *schola*. (The image is in harmony with Newman's philosophy, since the experienced reality is always larger than any explanation of it.)

The *schola*'s dogmatic purposes serve mainly the development of doctrine. It is true that not every dogmatic development initially happened within the theological schools; some have occurred within the devotional life of the community. But most dogmatic developments underwent gestation in the *schola*, often in the context of intense debate and possible heresy. In the *Development of Doctrine*, Newman points to the debate between Arius and Athanasius as a clear instance. Arius objected to the Son's divinity, arguing that the exaltation texts of the New Testament describe Jesus as *becoming* divine (e.g., at the Resurrection). Athanasius was led to apply these texts to Jesus' humanity, being convinced by the weight of tradition that they could not be describing the divinity. From this debate, which lasted a very long time and with many nuances, the doctrines of the exaltation of Jesus' human nature as well as the 'deification' of all humanity in baptismal regeneration came to maturation. Controversy helped doctrines develop that initially were not clearly realized.[82]

Newman finds theological controversy to be very healthy. It is an instance of his principle that religion is so engrossing a matter, and minds are so varied, that controversy ought to be expected and is, in fact, a sign of vitality. Every error, as we have seen, suggests, in the dialectics of debate, insights more fruitful than itself. The dynamics of the *schola* lead to aspects of the idea not previously sensed to be present; precision is achieved on what formerly was vague. Normally, the dynamism of the process results from new questions being posed to the Scriptures and tradition, questions that the original authors never had in mind. As a result, mere repetition of the past cannot meet new questions. The Christian idea must expand toward fresh aspects of itself to engage the new questions being posed, as if they are pulling the idea. Thus does development occur within Newman's *schola*, prompting Jan Walgrave to describe it as the "intellectual work house in which development of doctrine is ultimately achieved."[83]

Tactics against Doctrinal Extremism

It was one thing for Newman to describe the freer exercise of theological reflection in the fourth or thirteenth centuries; it was quite another matter to achieve it in the latter half of the nineteenth century. Yet that is what he attempted in a hostile ecclesiastical climate. He compared the mentality of the ultramontane party—and one must recall its influential hold on Vatican theology—to those nurses of old who shut off infants from fresh air as if the infants "were not healthy enough to bear wind and water in due measures."[84] Against such paternalism he became, as it were, the loyal opposition.

Of open criticism and the clash of ideas Newman had little apprehension. His great fear was that he sensed a growing climate of inquisition.

> I have a clear conscience that, in the works of mine they profess to criticize, I have said nothing which a Catholic might not say, though I am not of their way of thinking. If then they are strong enough to put down me, simply on the ground of my not succumbing to the clique, no one else has a chance of not being put down, and a reign of terror has begun, a reign of denunciation, secret tribunals and moral assassination. . . . As to the actual attack upon me, I shall outlive it, as I have outlived other attacks—but it is not at all easy to break that formidable conspiracy, which is in action against the theological liberty of Catholics.[85]

The intimidation is not limited to theologians alone. Newman is pastorally alert to the adverse climate for the laity and to the particularly cruel way the ultramontane party forced its interpretations of papal infallibility on everyone. Letter after letter in the early 1870s captures his indignaiton, of which the following is typical.

> The definition, if we are to suppose it legitimately passed, is producing most untoward effects, as far as I have experience of it—and, when poor people ask me categorically "Is it binding?" I don't know what to say. That "securus judicat orbis terrarum," I am sure—but time has not been given yet to ascertain this, and the very cruelty of certain people, of which I complain is, that *they will not let people have time.* They would come round quietly if you gave them time—but, when you hold a pistol to their heads and say, "Believe this doctrine, however new to you, as you believe the Holy Trinity, under pain of

damnation," THEY CAN'T. Their breath is taken away—they seem to say "Give me time, give me time—" And their confessors all about the country, say "No, not an hour—believe or be damned—we want to sift the Catholic body of all half Catholics."[86]

To help the many laity who appealed to him, Newman was unable to attack directly the ultramontane theology, since one of its strongest advocates was Edward Manning, archbishop of Westminster. Newman was aware of the recent schism of the Old Catholics in Germany and in the Netherlands;[87] he did not wish to be a catalyst to an English schism. Neither, however, could he remain silent about this infringement on legitimate liberties. His strategy of response came from two features of what has been called his personal style.

Newman's commitment to God's providence convinced him that if his cause were just and if his interpretations were truer than those of the ultramontane party, God would provide some ripe situation in which he could act without fear of an English schism. "The Almighty Lord of the Church will heal over the great offense as He has obliterated other offenses."[88] Second, truth comes to the patient person. As someone's illative sense cannot be forced to a conclusion, so also the discerning process in the church cannot be calibrated by time. "Beware of desperate steps . . . live till tommorrow," he advised harassed inquirers with these lines of the poet, William Cowper, during the bleak days of ultramontane extremism. His strategy, consequently, was to wait for a propitious moment when the most effective blow to extremism could be made. He wrote to Matthew Arnold: "It often happens that those who will not bide their time, fail, not because they are not substantially right, but because they are thus impatient. I used to say that Montanus, Tertullian, Novatian, etc., were instances in point, their ideas were eventually carried out."[89]

The propitious moment came in 1875. In the previous year Archbishop Manning had written a defense of the dogma, *Caesarism and Ultramontanism*.[90] Disgruntled by a parliamentary defeat that he attributed to the Catholic bishops, the former prime minister William E. Gladstone published an expostulation which assumed Manning's interpretations to be official and binding; Gladstone questioned, in view of the dogma, whether Catholics could be loyal British citizens and loyal to Rome at the same time.[91] Newman seized the opportunity to write his celebrated *Letter to the Duke of Norfolk*. While Newman's moderate explanation of the dogma ostensibly replies to Gladstone's attack, it is actually a rebuttal to the ultramontane position. In it Newman does make a veiled reference to those who have "done their best to set the house on fire [and] leave to others the task of putting out the flame."[92] His private correspondence, however, indicates how thankful he was to Gladstone to have allowed him to trim ultramontane excesses without ever having mentioned Manning and Ward by name. "We can speak against Gladstone while it would not be decent to speak against Manning."[93]

Newman's patience was richly rewarded. His thorough response to Gladstone's indictment was so able a defense of the dogma and became so universally applauded that the ultramontane party could not afford to attack Newman's moderate interpretation of it. To attack Newman would be to undo his successful defense of Catholic loyalty to both faith and country. Newman's pastoral tactics were not lost on Bishop David Moriarty of Kerry, a moderate, who wrote: "Many thanks for the coup de grace you have given to the faction who would allow none to be Catholics but Dublin Reviewers and Tablet Editors. . . . You . . . have *shut them up*."[94]

Through patience and with a confidence in divine providence, Newman was able to make his voice heard in the arena of debate. The dogma of papal infallibility especially invited a dialectics of discourse so that its implication, restrictions, and relationship to other doctrines might be further clarified. Newman's *Letter to Norfolk* will remain an important contribution to those dialectics, but whatever its final value as insight, his pastoral tactics to gain for dialectics a hearing will remain admirable, given the restrictive climate on theological freedom in which he lived.

The climate would only change substantially when fresh air got into the Roman establishment. By this Newman meant the same thing Pope John XXIII meant when that reforming pope spoke of opening the Vatican windows to fresh ideas. Experience was Newman's great teacher, and Rome needed to open itself to the experience of worldwide Catholics. "When Rome goes out of Town, it may gain experience which it never would gain at home—and admit views, which at present it does not tolerate—and then it will return home in God's time with re-newed wisdom and energy."[95] Newman predicted that the loss of the Papal States would be one catalyst to force Rome out of its isolation. When this loss indeed occurred, he shed no tears. It is difficult to gauge to what degree Newman's pastoral vision of the church pushed it on the road toward Vatican II, but clearly he stands on the side of those who advocate open windows, an active laity, pluralistic journalism, and theological freedom.[96]

CHAPTER FOUR

The Theological View of the Church

*M*aking distinctions runs the danger of creating permanent separations. If the scholastics are taken as the masters of distinctions, one should also follow their advice that whatever has been distinguished must finally be conceptually reunited. Notions ought not to be left in compartments. Distinguishing Newman's ecclesiology into foundational, pastoral, and theological components does not mean that aspects of the church considered under any one of these categories have no applicability elsewhere. The notion of apostolicity in Newman's foundational view, for example, has obvious pastoral consequences and is deeply theological. In distinguishing a theological dimension of Newman's ecclesiology, the caveat about separation and exclusion is especially germane. A chapter on Newman's theological view of the church might seem to imply that here is where his *real* ecclesiology emerges, that the aspects treated in the following pages are at the heart of what the church means to him. Yet distinguishing these aspects as *theological* is not meant to bear that weight; it is meant primarily to suggest the graced dimensions of features of the church. The aspects that follow (i.e., authority, theology of abuses, the church as sacrament) seem to me to have greater affinity to the inner workings of grace than to a foundational argument (from conscience, through revelation, to church as teacher) or concrete church processes.

The relationship to grace is suggested by the etymology of the word; something *theological* is an expression (*logos*) of God or godly grace (*theos*). Notionally, *theology* describes a word or study about God; really, in Newman's sense of real apprehension, it refers to a concrete manifestation of God's being and activity. When Newman thinks of sacraments as actions of the invisible world, or when he considers conciliar authority, his emphasis is on the gifted nature of the church, which is appreciated only in faith. Although Newman may be describing something quite concrete and thus empirically observable, his own vision penetrates to the event as *graced*. The example of infallible conciliar authority may be helpful. It was one thing for Newman to argue the hypothesis of an infallible teaching office, as he does in the *Essay on Development*. The argument does not appeal to faith; Newman addresses it to any reader of church history who wishes to make sense of differing doctrinal formulations, and he simply calls it the most winning and most natural hypothesis. It is quite another thing to describe an ecumenical council as infallible; here he has to assume in the reader a shared belief that such an ecclesial event is a *graced* expression of divine pedagogy, that is to say, Newman is making a theological statement about it.

Under a theological viewpoint three aspects of the church will be considered: (1) We return to Newman's views on authority and give particular attention to the two modes of infallible authority, conciliar and papal. (2) We examine his notion of the prophetic, priestly, and kingly offices of the church in their dialectical affinities. This aspect could be called Newman's "theology of abuses," and it addresses why he loved the church, stayed in it, and sought to reform it even though he was acutely aware of its faults. (3) The church is itself a sacrament. Newman's thought constantly moves back and forth between the visible and the invisible worlds. These are not bifurcated worlds in his mind but rather two sides to the one graced reality.

AUTHORITY IN THE CHURCH

Newman's strenuous championing of theological freedom as a necessary condition for a dialectics of discourse is misconstrued if one does not take account of his *attitude* toward church authority. Just as ecclesiastical authorities have a responsibility to support free inquiry, members of the church are accountable to hierarchical authority. Accountability runs in both directions, and since its lines are not always clear, one may think of the interplay of authority and freedom as itself dialectical.

The fact that Newman stressed the freedom-of-inquiry side of the dialectic followed from the climate of his time. Ultramontane theology was ever trying to shift matters toward unquestioned obedience to authority. Newman threw his weight to the other side, yet he had no wish for free inquiry to become itself an excess. Respect for authority is ingredient to his ecclesiology, and, more important, positive *attitudes* toward church authority are essential to the proper religious disposition of someone who lives by conscience. Though he wrote in the *Letter to Norfolk* that he preferred drinking toasts to personal conscience first, and to the pope second, he never meant to imply thereby an antiauthoritarian attitude whose only masters were personal insight and personal conscience.[1]

Freedom of thought and accountability to authority always exist in tension. In certain situations their spheres were clearly marked for Newman; in others, the demarcations were foggy. Whenever he was sure ecclesiastical authority spoke with the voice of God, he aligned his thinking with it. When he was sure it did not, as when the pope as a private theologian advanced interpretations of some doctrine favorable to his own position, Newman felt free to decide the matter himself. When he was unsure, he gave the benefit of the doubt to ecclesiastical authority, and Newman's readiness to trust church authorities illustrates an important *attitude* at the heart of his views on authority.

Attitudes and General Considerations

According to Newman, authority in the church functions in two contexts, to which two types of submission correspond.[2] When the church is viewed as the oracle of revelation, authority expresses itself as a teacher of the faith. In this instance, a doctrine is proposed *de fide,* to which is owed an internal submission of the mind to what the doctrine states. Such an act of belief (i.e., Newman's real assent, with certitude) is owed only to what is proposed *de fide* as dogma. When the church is viewed as a social polity, authority determines communal activity; the unity of the church, as a sociological entity characterized by harmonious behavior, is achieved by the specification of disciplinary law. (*Disciplinary law* is a technical term for Newman and for traditional ecclesiology; it does not have the modern connotation of sanction but rather connotes regulation, around which group behavior unites.) To disciplinary law is owed a submission of will; individuals agree to *act* in harmony on a matter that someone may or may not *think* is true or prudently best. It allows the possibility of dissent because of the supremacy of personal conscience, given the proper circumstances.

This broad distinction between dogmatic teaching and disciplinary law invites may further precisions, the most important being the difference between infallible *de fide* teaching and the church's authoritative, noninfallible teaching role. Newman never elaborated all the aspects of church authority in any systematic fashion, but the basic distinction between dogma and discipline operates in his thinking. I wish to map a terrain of materials and within that mapping capture his attitude toward both kinds of authority.

That which constitutes a doctrine as *de fide,* in consequence asking one's internal assent, is based on the principle that the church teaches it as God's revelation. Newman advised people to focus on the church *as oracle.* The decision to be a Catholic Christian, he often told inquirers, arises when one's illative sense has concluded that revelation demands an ongoing interpreter of it and that the Catholic church is this interpreter. Although the church may have taught many things throughout the centuries, a prospective convert need not sift through and assimilate each one. Rather, at some point of inquiry, the illative sense turns from a material consideration (What is this or that doctrine taught by Catholocism?) to the formal consideration (Is or is not the Catholic church a *credible* teacher of revelation?). At that point a convert makes the decision—because the illative sense leads one to decide—that he or she believes in the church. Since the object of religious belief must always relate to God, believing in the church expresses one's conviction that the church is a divinely assisted teacher. The church is apprehended as *graced,* which for Newman is a "real apprehension."

Such a formal consideration of the church entails certain attitudes. Openness to faith's future is one of them. Just as belief in God is not only an acceptance of what God has done (i.e., Scripture's *mirabilia Dei*) but also involves a trust in what God will do, belief in the church-as-teacher entails an implicit acceptance of whatever might be taught as dogma. Newman urges prospective converts to decide on this future orientation of faith, and he describes such faith in terms of piety. One might call it the attitude within which faith is lived. "While it would be illogical not to give an inward assent to what [the church] has already declared to be revealed, so it is pious and religious to believe, or at least not to doubt, what, though in fact not defined, still it [sic] is *probable* she might define as revealed, or that she *will* define, or seems to *consider* to be revealed."[3]

In keeping with his penchant for holistic viewpoints, Newman's conception of Christian faith involves not only the content of one's belief but also the attitude of trust one should have in the church's teaching office. This perspective becomes clearer when Newman describes the opposite attitude, which he termed "minimism." Minimists believe only what is formally defined, holding everything else in abeyance, as if one could cut cleanly between doctrine revealed and doctrine not revealed. Such a distinction is impossible, according to Newman, and the church itself cannot codify revelation with such precision. "It has always been trusted," Newman wrote to Pusey, "that the received belief of the faithful and the obligations of piety would cover a larger circuit of doctrinal matters than was formally claimed, and secure a more generous faith than was imperative on the conscience."[4] Minimism changes faith's focus from an organic community maintained in truth to a written code of dogmas. In Newman's philosophy, this change would involve notional assent" replacing "real assent." Real assent engages what is concrete, actual, living, and opening into the future, viz., a community whose convictions about revelation are broader and richer than any checklist would involve.

This kind of piety made Newman ready to sacrifice his own opinions to those of church authorities, if asked, because he viewed the bishops as the legitimate guardians of doctrine; if they censured his writings, he was prepared to withdraw them. Many letters mention that he submitted his writings to ecclesiastical review, that he spoke "under correction" in his proposals, and that he promised retraction should he be condemned.[5] While one may wonder to what degree this attitude was dictated by Newman's prudence in dealing with the ultramontane climate, it does capture his own sense of accountability to church authority and his hesitancy to insist on his own views no matter what.

One must not mistake the attitude of trust in the magisterium with any abandonment of critical reflection that questions whether a particular church doctrine is part of revelation. Newman's whole struggle with ultramontane theology provides proof of his belief in the importance of critical reflection, and the instances are too many to recount. Let his own illustration of the Galileo case, however, suffice to situate the fuller context for his attitude to the magisterium. If Galileo had thought that geocentrism was implied by revelation, his heliocentric theory would have involved "bad faith." If he thought that it was part of the nonrevealed doctrinal heritage, and if he lacked compelling reasons to doubt it, he would have been deficient in "piety" to urge heliocentrism. But if he had good reasons to doubt geocentrism, it would be in keeping with piety to question if it were part of revelation, and if convinced it were not, he would have been free in conscience to advocate heliocentrism.[6]

Disciplinary law is a term of vast scope, embracing a spectrum of ecclesiastical decisions governing external behavior within the church, from the liturgical laws on ritual to the regulations an individual bishop sets for his diocese. For Newman, the proper attitude to such decisions is ready obedience. When the *Home and Foreign Review* was censured, Newman wrote Sir John Acton, its editor, that a continued open defiance of legitimate authority placed one "in a false position."[7] It was not a matter of submitting one's inner convictions to the bishop. Newman even told Bishop Ullathorne that his own sympathies lay with Acton's general intentions for the magazine. He felt, however, that open rebellion would undermine the unity of the church and subvert whatever claim to authority the church rightly enjoys.[8]

In this matter, Newman's holistic vision again guides his thinking. Authority in the church is a graced feature of a community called to maintain unity within itself and continuity with its heritage. Authority expresses itself in sundry ways and legislates matters of varying importance. Although theology must draw careful distinctions among the various modes and levels of authority, people overall cannot relate to church leadership in such atomistic fashion that its every decision is subjected to intense scrutiny. Newman is always thinking of the practical order; the daily life of a diocese, or of the universal church, would become chaotic if every authoritative decision is met by suspended judgment, carefully drawn distinctions, or a rebellious spirit. He thinks that pastoral authority should, on one level, be taken as a whole. It is the "office of nurturing the fold of Christ,"[9] to which the religious conscience owes trust and obedience. This trust and obedience should be one's fundamental inclination. On another level, however, distinctions about disciplinary law are necessary, and Newman readily draws them: One may internally dissent from disciplinary laws, e.g., thinking them imprudent, unwise, or in error; a bishop's laws are confined to his diocese; papal injunctions affect behavior, not faith, etc.[10] These distinctions have their proper place within the context of the fundamental attitude, described above.[11]

This sketch of Newman's attitude toward authority does not resolve the tensions between the claims of personal freedom and those of ecclesiastical obedience. Because both exist in a dialectical tension, there will never be a clear formula dictating concrete solutions. Newman, however, provides an orientation, a sound first step, with his insistence on attitudes. Everyone should begin with trust in the *office* of authority and seek to be its loyal supporter. Then, and only then, might someone claim the right to dissent. In a moment of autobiographical testimony, Newman confided to Archbishop Georges Darboy of Paris, "If by some fiction those who love me will have it that I am a teacher of the faithful, I am above all a disciple of the Church, *doctor fidelium discipulus ecclesiae.*"[12] This loyalty is not a sacrifice of intelligence or conscience to blind obedience; it is a stance of personal humility before that more august reality of grace, the church as a trustworthy guide to conscience.

Conciliar Infallibility

The only authority having absolute claim on our minds and hearts is God. This is Newman's first principle of conscience, and on it the principle of divine pedagogy follows: God has entered into personal dialogue with searching consciences through revelation that has culminated in Jesus Christ. The word of Jesus continues in the community established by his risen Spirit. It is a word of light for a searching conscience, a word of forgiveness for a sinful conscience, a word of authority for a submissive conscience. Human conscience has been constituted by its Creator as if it were one's inner ear waiting for God's voice. To emphasize its sovereign authority, Newman calls it "the aboriginal Vicar of Christ."[13]

It becomes critical to establish how one's conscience engages a definite and unmistakable word from God and not its own projection or rationalization. This engagement, according to Newman, is provided by God as a historically situated grace. It must be historically situated, for we are only made to listen from within history; it must be of the nature of grace if it is to be God's self-expression. History and grace come together as the Christ and continue as a community begotten by his message. But what is to guarantee that a word about God is a word of God in a community that speaks about God, teaches about God, argues about God, and at times has been wrong about God (e.g., Newman's own account of pervasive Arianism in the fourth century)? The only guarantor is God's Spirit itself, ensuring that what is taught by the community is true to Jesus' message. Newman calls this guarantee the infallibility of the church that, under special circumstances, comes to expression as a definite and unerring teaching. It is a graced event of a particular kind of authority. Its foundation is not a collective wisdom or the majority vote or the imposed views of ecclesiastics but only the act of God in the act of teaching.

The notion of infallibility has various aspects, and its general features in Newman's ecclesiology have already been noted: Infallibility primarily describes the church as a whole. The laity's *sensus fidelium* is a witness of God's truth. Infallibility is best understood in the unity between hierarchy and laity. There are two concrete modes of infallibility as an act of teaching authority, conciliar and papal, that require separate examination.

Newman thought that an ecumenical council is the strongest and clearest expression of the church's teaching office. It is the highest expression of its authority addressed to personal conscience. Moreover, it is the normal way the Holy Spirit guarantees infallible utterance. So, when it became known in 1867 that a council was to be convened, Newman thought it would confirm the dogma taught by Pius IX in 1854. "The *normal* mode of deciding a point of faith is a Council, not the Pope speaking ex cathedra, and . . . the first thing which a Council would do, if called, would be to recognise and reaffirm the Immaculate Conception, not as throwing doubt on the previous definition, but as normalizing the ecclesiastical proceeding."[14] When, in 1870, the council defined papal infallibility itself, Newman ceased using the language of "normal mode" for ecumencial councils, but there are reasons to think he maintained his views. First of all, the image, or *type,* of the church he used to illustrate a definitive teaching authority was its succession of councils. These synods of the early church were such a commanding paradigm of vitality and authenticity that it is unlikely Newman's preference for conciliar authority would have been altered by the dogma of 1870 about the pope. Second, councils by their very nature were events of theological debate, dialectics, and the accumulated experiences of their participants. They were a microcosm of the very interaction Newman wished for the church at large.

The actual process that a council exemplified had numerous benefits, the strongest being the breadth of vision it could provide. The present council, he wrote to a former Anglican colleague, is "bringing into personal acquaintance men from the most distant parts. . . . Each part will know the state of things in the other parts of Christendom, and the minds of all the Prelates will be enlarged, as well as their hearts. . . . Further, the authorities at Rome will learn a great deal which they did not know of, and . . . this will be a wonderful gain."[15] (Newman's concern about the Vatican's isolation from the world of ideas has already been noted.) Furthermore, the dialogical processes of a council should have a marked influence on its participants; an ecumenical council would be like a pentecostal renewal which so changes the gathered bishops that they return to their local diocese with a wider vision of church.[16] Such benefits are simply applications of Newman's preference for a dialectics of discourse in the discernment of religious truth.

It is well known that Newman opposed a defining of papal infallibility. He himself believed in the pope's infallibility, but he felt that a dogmatic definition of it was *inexpedient.*[17] A dogma would force Catholics, who had difficulties with the doctrine for any number of reasons, to accept it immediately or be forced out of the church. Time and the work of the *schola* were needed to educate the entire church about the papal teaching office. Second, conciliar dogmas were not doctrinal luxuries. Dogmas were meant to redress a heresy threatening the very fabric of the church. "Where is the Arius or Nestorius," Newman asked, "whose heresy makes it imperative for the Holy Church to speak?"[18] Conciliar definitions, the most intense act of teaching authority, were to be used only at times of gravest necessity.

Newman's strongest words against defining papal infallibility were in a confidential letter he sent his bishop, William Ullathorne, during the council. In this letter, which caused him great embarrassment when it became public, one sees poignant application of Newman's principles about the work of councils.

> Rome ought to be a name to lighten the heart at all times, and a Council's proper office is, when some great heresy or other evil impends, to inspire the faithful with hope and confidence; but now we have the greatest meeting which ever has been, and that at Rome, infusing into us by the accredited organs of Rome and its partizans (such as the Civilta, the Armonia, the Univers, and the Tablet) little else than fear and dismay.
>
> When we are all at rest, and have no doubts, and at least practically, not to say doctrinally, hold the Holy Father to be infallible, suddenly there is thunder in the clear sky, and we are told to prepare for something we know not what, to try our faith we know not how. No impending danger is to be averted, but a great difficulty is to be created. Is this the proper work for an Ecumenical Council? As to myself personally, please God, I do not expect any trial at all; but I cannot help suffering with the various souls which are suffering, and I look with anxiety at the prospect of having to defend decisions, which may not be difficult to my private judgment, but may be most difficult to maintain logically in the face of historical facts. What have we done to be treated, as the faithful never were treated before? When has the definition of doctrine de fide been a luxury of devotion, and not a stern painful necessity? Why should an aggressive insolent faction be allowed to "make the heart of the just to mourn, whom the Lord hath not made sorrowful?" Why can't we be let alone, when we have pursued peace, and thought no evil? I assure you, my dear Lord, some of the truest minds are driven one way and another, and do not know where to rest their feet; one day determining to give up all theology as a bad job, and recklessly to believe henceforth almost that the Pope is impeccable; at another [time] tempted to believe all the worst which a book like Janus says; others doubting about the capacity possessed by Bishops, drawn from all corners of the earth, to judge what is fitting for European society, and then again angry with the Holy See for listening to the flattery of a clique of Jesuits, Redemptorists, and converts. . . .

With these thoughts before me, I am continually asking myself whether I ought not make my feelings public; but all I do is to pray those great early Doctors of the Church, whose intercession would decide the matter, Augustine and the rest, to avert so great a calamity. If it is God's will that the Pope's infallibility should be defined, then it is His Blessed Will to throw back "the times and the moments" of that triumph which He has destined for His Kingdom; and I shall feel I have but to bow my head to His adorable, inscrutable Providence.[19]

Leaving papal infallibility for later analysis, one may ask why Newman would restrict the purposes of conciliar definitions to the stern necessity of responding to major heresies. Abstractly considered, a dogma is a truth of revelation answering to a conscience's quest to know the God in dialogue with it; the submission of mind and heart (Newman's "real assent") is connatural to a being made for communion with God. In the concrete, however, an individual conscience acts from its own perceptions of truth, governed by those first principles of thought, highly personal and sovereign, that distinguish one person from another. Defined doctrine, if experienced as merely imposed by ecclesiastical authority, is not connatural to conscience's quest for truth but experienced as arbitrary; conversely, conscience accepts as congenial to itself a dogma articulating that which is implicitly known in the depth of faith. Given this background, dogmas are pastoral emergencies. They assert a truth concerning a matter threatening the church's self-identity. They immediately divide proponents and opponents of a controversy, as Nicea divided the parties of Athanasius and Arius, and Chalcedon divided the parties of Cyril and Eutyches. However necessary to the well-being of the church a definitive teaching may be, it forces allegiances. Applying this principle to Vatican I, Newman thought a definition would force allegiances around understandings of the papal teaching office. No heresy threatening the church called for it; schisms would likely result.[20]

Recalling that patience is a component of Newman's personal style, one recognizes that his preference for the gradual maturation of convictions, even within the rather short period of a council, is typical. His criticism of Vatican I, as a *process*, was the "railroad pace" at which it was speeding toward dogmatic definitions. Conciliar decisions, above all, should show the fruits of patience, both for the sake of truth and for the sake of charity.[21]

In terms of discerning the truth, the preparation of an infallible teaching should evidence the work of years. Newman illustrates this belief with the example of the Immaculate Conception, an infallible teaching prepared for by centuries of debate that eliminated extreme interpretations and secured a unanimity of conviction within the Catholic world. Of papal infallibility Newman wrote: "What we require, first of all, . . . is a careful consideration of the acts of Councils, the deeds of Popes, the Bullarium. We need to try the doctrine by facts, to see what it may mean, what it cannot mean, what it must mean. We must try its future working by the past. And we need that this should be done in the face of day, in course, in quiet, in various schools and centres of thought, in controversy. . . . This is the way in which those who differ sift out the truth."[22]

Patience, for the sake of charity, enables dogma to find a congenial reception in the consciences of the entire church. "The Church moves as a whole; it is not a mere philosophy, it is a communion. . . . You must prepare men's minds for the doctrine, and you must not flout and insult the existing tradition of centuries."[23] Newman has in mind the traditions of Ireland and England, which had been silent on papal infallibility and into which ultramontane views only recently had come; the doctrine germinated in the Mediterranean parts of the Catholic world, and the soil of northern countries was as yet unprepared for it. "Charity" is Newman's expression for the unity of the universal church. Conciliar authority, responsive to the demands of charity, should not jeopardize the existing communion of churches by the imposition of a doctrine felt as novel. As he bluntly puts it, "We are not ripe yet for the Pope's Infallibility."[24]

Papal Infallibility

Many books in ecclesiology, when describing the church's teaching office, used to begin with the topic of papal infallibility. Had Newman ever written a systematic text, he would have moved from the notion of conscience to that of revelation and then to the church as *oracle*, or to use his frequent phrase, to the church as "ground and pillar of the truth" (1 Tim. 3:15). Infallibility would be a consequence of the church's being an oracle of revelation. Newman calls it "a doctrine *derived from*" the apostolic doctrine that the church is an authoritative teacher; it cannot succeed without infallibility.[25] The ways of being infallible came to light only gradually, under the impulse Newman calls development of doctrine. First was seen the role of ecumenical councils, then in time the role of the papacy in formal teaching.[26] In moving from the basic doctrine that the church is a teacher of revelation to its consequences within historical developments, Newman places papal infallibility within the more fundamental notion of *ecclesial* infallibility. Papal infallibility is not a starting point for him but a consequence.

Besides thinking that a definition of papal infallibility by the Vatican Council would be inexpedient, Newman also thought it unlikely to transpire. Though the definition was, in fact, proclaimed, his original reasons for thinking it would not be remain instructive.[27] A dogma has twin supports: the divinely assisted act of infallible teaching—what I have labeled its "theological dimension"—and the human actions of discernment. Newman's empirical tendencies attracted him to the human processes that employ historical investigation, theological reasoning, and attention to the *sensus fidelium* in order to discern if a doctrine is rooted in revelation. Consequently, it becomes an act of pedagogical prudence for the magisterium to refrain from formulating a dogma until there is a moral certainty about its rootedness in the apostolic revelation. Concerning papal infallibility, although Newman had believed in it since 1845,[28] he thought that the historical problems attending it were still unresolved in the collective mind of the church and that a moral certainty about it was unlikely to emerge. If the council were to define it, however, then faith in the guidance of the Holy Spirit should overcome one's misgivings about the doctrine's historical supports.

But does not Newman's readiness to believe a conciliar definition collapse the twin supports for a dogma and make everything depend on the chance that a conciliar teaching is simply inspired? To prepare for a dogma, historical evidence and theological reasoning need to be perused, but their benefits are limited. Evidence "reaches a certain way, more or less, toward a proof of the Catholic doctrine," but "in all cases there is a margin left for the exercise of faith in the word of the Church."[29] There is an ecclesial illative sense by means of which the church reaches a perception of truth beyond the supports of scholarship alone, and in this conviction it teaches that a particular doctrine is to be believed. One does not believe a dogma because a commanding reasoning process or a historical proof can be adduced. Ultimately, one believes in the word of God and in whatever shares in the reliability of God's word, such as a council's infallible teaching.

On July 18, 1870, the Vatican Council solemnly defined the doctrine of papal infallibility. The restrictive language of the definition actually pleased Newman. It said far less than the ultramontane party had wished. The pope's infallibility was limited to the deposit of revelation; it did not apply to the political arena, such as the pope's temporal powers. Furthermore, the dogma was to be understood negatively; it was a protection from error in the statement alone that was explicitly being taught. Thus, whatever might be said as prefatory to a papal *ex cathedra* statement did not enjoy infallibility as such. Finally, Newman sensed that the wording looked to future modifications—he called it "trimming"—from another council or pope.

Newman's strategy of interpretation is governed by a principle of "wise and gentle minimism"[30] that is brought to bear on three aspects of papal infallibility.

1. NATURE OF THE DOGMA. Infallibility is not a personally enduring quality of the pope but is a transitory graced assistance in his action of *ex cathedra* teaching only. "What Providence has guaranteed is only this, that there should be no error in the final step, in the resulting definition or dogma."[31] The pope, and the whole church for that matter, must make the necessary human effort to learn the truth. The process is not inspired, and there may well be stages that were false steps. Even when a doctrine is taught *ex cathedra,* it is possible that "the grounds suggested for it in the definition, the texts, the patristic authorities, the historical passages, are all mistakes."[32] Infallibility is simply the protection from error in the statement of the definition itself.

The protection from error, furthermore, secures only *ex cathedra* papal teaching. Popes may teach many things, at various times, using the firmest language, but only those instances of teaching that are *intended* to be solemn definitions are infallible.[33] Newman lists four signs by which to recognize them: (1) The pope must speak as a teacher for the universal church. (2) He must claim to speak in the name of apostolic authority. (3) He must teach on a point of 'faith and morals' only (i.e., on a matter of revelation, or intimately connected with it. (4) He must expressly intend that the teaching is to be believed.[34] Newman calls these signs contracting conditions; they limit what may be defined, they stipulate when a definition is had, and they place a sense of caution on a pope who would wish to teach so solemnly.

2. OBJECTIONS TO THE DOGMA. Infallibility has often been confused with personal virtue, as if the claim to infallibility involved a claim to impeccability. If that were the meaning of the dogma, history's testimony to the moral wrongdoings of certain popes would render impossible any reasonable belief in it. Infallibility and impeccability are entirely distinct, however. In 1872 the London *Times* had editorialized that the recent dogma would make it impossible for popes ever to accept responsibility for moral faults. Newman responded to the newspaper: "No Pope can make evil good. No Pope has any power over those eternal moral principles which God has imprinted on our hearts and consciences. If any Pope has, with his eyes open, approved of treachery or cruelty, let those defend that Pope, who can."[35]

Objections to the dogma, on the charge of past papal heresies, are analyzed by Newman on a case-by-case basis. Although too varied and complex to be recounted,[36] two principles guide his analysis. First of all, one must be certain one is dealing with a papal teaching of the highest authority. It must be shown to have been a teaching *intending* to solve a controversy in the name of the apostolic office, because the teachings of popes, as private theologians, are fallible. Second, the authoritative tone of papal teachings is no automatic indication of an instance of infallible authority. "Every one, who teaches, must by the fact that he is teacher, 'lay down the law,' as it is called. . . . Every Bishop in his Pastoral speaks as if he were infallible, for he is the teacher of his flock; he speaks, from the nature of the case, as if no one could answer him."[37] Firm language is to be expected from any pope and, in itself, is no sure clue of an infallibly intended statement.

3. EXTENT OF DEFINABLE MATTERS. As much as Newman thought a definition would be inexpedient, its restriction to faith and morals aided him in his struggle against ultramontane extremism. It limited the range of papal infallible teaching to mat-

ters "referable to the Apostolic *depositum*."[38] Newman perceived here a rejection of ultramontane wishes to extend papal powers to the widest arena, such as political teachings and disciplinary decisions. In fact, the definition actually protected the liberty of Catholics in matters not dealing with revelation, securing their freedom to be guided by scholarship and prudence in these wider arenas.

The restriction of papal infallibility to faith and morals was fully consonant with Newman's fundamental vision of the church as the oracle of revelation. As God guides the church to teach unerringly the revelation of Christ, papal dogmas enjoy the same protection from error that the church has, and not more than it. Papal infallibility is a concrete mode of the church's infallibility and is not an alternative to it or an expansion of it. Newman's holistic tendencies prohibited his perceiving dual sources of infallibility; for him, conciliar and papal infallibility are grounded in the single grace of the church to be maintained in the truth.

Definable matters must be *referable* to the apostolic revelation. Newman's use of "referable" preserves the historical nature of knowing revelation. The postapostolic church grasped dimensions of revelation that were not clearly articulated or fully appreciated in New Testament times, e.g., the distinct personhood of the Holy Spirit. The teaching of dogma, consequently, must go beyond a verbal repetition of the biblical texts to those aspects of the original revelation that have subsequently come to light. The limitation of papal infallibility, then, to a teaching about faith and morals is not to be measured by its verbal repetition of Scripture but by its *relatedness* to that original witness, thus allowing a historical growth in understanding the teaching.

Generally speaking, Newman perceives dogmas to be "more or less abstract" utterances, since they admit of exceptions or different interpretations in their concrete applications.[39] This impression is especially the case with moral dogmas. There are, however, dogmatic *facts* that describe concrete matters. They refer to the apostolic revelation in a necessary way; thus they, too, can be defined. "The Church (or Pope) can determine the sense of the depositum—she can declare its implicit meanings—she can declare what contradicts it—she can declare what in its nature subserves it . . . or is prejudicial to it. . . . She can

declare its concrete manifestations, as that the inspiration originally given at Pentecost is carried out in the *particular* Epistle to
the Hebrews. . . . But all these enunciations are to be received
by Catholics BECAUSE they *directly* relate to the depositum."[40]

Those who wished to extend the reach of papal infallibility
beyond revelation realized that the motive for assent had to lie
elsewhere. To claim that the church could infallibly teach nonrevealed matters meant that its credibility had to reside somehow in itself, protected by God in all that it does. One believed,
not on God's word, but on an ecclesiastical word. Newman neither shared such a sanguine view of an unerring church nor
understood what this hybrid faith meant.

> These writers, when urged to reconcile their teaching with the old
> and received view that the Church is infallible only *in ordine ad* the
> original depositum of faith, make these verbal and unintelligible
> distinctions, which to me sound like shuffles. Oh, they say, we don't
> absolutely say that the Church is infallible in such matters, but she is
> certain, errare non potest. Next we don't say that the faith that
> receives them is divine faith (that is, I suppose, from *grace*)—we only
> say it is not human—that is, it neither is from grace—nor is it not
> from grace, and therefore we will call it "ecclesiastical.". . . to my
> mind it is utterly *un*intelligible.[41]

Newman's "wise and gentle minimism" is also a pastoral strategy in the aftermath of a dogmatic definition. He maintained
that the burden to faith ought not to be increased by the church.
Faith assents to what reason cannot prove, and as the object of
faith is further removed from the reach of reason and the direct
testimony of experience, the difficulty of relying on an authoritative *word* increases. Newman was speaking psychologically
about "real assent" (i.e., without reservation in mind and heart).
Although grace does make possible what the unseen nature of
faith makes difficult, the church "has ever shown the utmost
care to contract, as far as possible, the range of truths and sense
of propositions, of which she demands this absolute reception."[42] As minimism, therefore, urges the nonproliferation of
dogmas, it also prompts theologians to trim broad readings of a
dogma to a narrower frame. In this case the *schola* contracts the
range of the dogma's claim on the church's faith by indicating
what is minimally necessary for the unity of faith. (The work of
the late Karl Rahner was illustrative of this strategy; he was

famous for paring away an inherited and nonbinding penumbra of issues from the core of a dogma.) "Minimizing theology," as Newman would term it, aids the pastoral responsibility to restrict, as far as possible, the binding claims of authoritative teaching on personal consciences.

Ecclesial Reception: Securus Judicat Orbis Terrarum

The two vehicles of infallible authority, councils and popes, are *theological* views of the church because they are *graced* protections from error in the teaching of revelation. Newman's view of infallibility, however, takes in the whole church. Because he tends to see things in their wholeness, or *per modum unius,* the conciliar decree or the papal *ex cathedra* teaching is a partial picture of the full truth. To understand the two teaching vehicles properly, they must be related to the infallibility of the entire church.

The aftermath of the First Vatican council underlined the problem. When the council adjourned,[43] Newman was unsure if its decrees had the authority of infallible conciliar teachings. Was there the moral unanimity necessary for a conciliar teaching? A number of bishops absented themselves from the final vote. What did their "walkout" mean? Were the decrees being 'received' by the various episcopates throughout the Catholic world? Second, what was to be the judgment of the general Catholic membership about the meaning of the decrees? Newman wondered about the so-called *passive* infallibility of the universal church. These questions are aspects of what is called *ecclesial reception.* An authoritative teaching enters the mental soil of the church. What does the teaching contribute? What do the people contribute? Newman viewed the relationship dialectically; each influences the other, and from that mutual interaction the church comes to a secure understanding of a dogma. *Securus judicat orbis terrarum,* the phrase of St. Augustine that struck Newman so powerfully in 1839, became his expression of the dialectical relationship and its resolution: "The judgment of the whole Church has no chance of being wrong."[44]

In the bishops' final vote of July 18 on papal infallibility, 533 were in favor and 2 were against the definition; more significant, about 60 bishops avoided voting by leaving Rome the day before.[45] As recently as June 6, Newman had written Bishop

Ullathorne that a moral unanimity among the bishops was indispensable, "for how could we take as the voice of the council, which is infallible, a definition which a body of Bishops, of high character in themselves, and representing large masses of the faithful, protested against?"[46] Thus, when news of the minority walkout reached him, Newman was not sure the Vatican decree was infallible. He raised three suppositions that related to the ecclesial reception of a doctrine. (1) If the nonvoting bishops maintained their protest as a *body*, there would be serious reasons to think the definition invalid. (2) If their protest were not corporate, then their individual dissent would not undermine the needed moral unanimity. (3) Finally, if the definition were eventually received by the whole body of the faithful, "it will claim our assent by the force of the great dictum, 'Securus judicat orbis terrarum.' "[47]

The Augustinian formula was a barometer of a teaching's orthodoxy. If a teaching were indeed true, it would find a receptive soil in the collective belief of the church. The community would recognize, as if instinctively, that a particular teaching captures in its human wording the faith that animates the church, just as the early church recognized itself in some writings (i.e., the canonical Scriptures) and not in others (i.e., the Gospel of Thomas). The process of recognition is gradual and implicit, and a teaching more or less settles in and is absorbed. On the other hand, the church may not recognize itself in a teaching, in which case the teaching never takes root universally.

Since the bishops of the minority party represented a significant portion of the universal church (i.e., practically the entire episcopate of Hungary, and large portions of the French, American, Austrian, and German episcopacies), their continued and collective protest against the definition would constitute a strong countersign to morally unanimous agreement. How could the authority of the July 18 decree be gauged? Reception was not equated with majority vote, and although moral unanimity was difficult to measure, it was for Newman the only way to judge the harmony of a teaching with the universal church's instinct for the true faith, its *sensus fidei*. "Till better advised, nothing shall make me say that a mere majority in a Council, as opposed to a moral unanimity, in itself creates an obligation to receive its dogmatic decrees. This is a point of history and precedent."[48]

A judgment about corporate dissent is not easy. Newman recognized that *groups* had gone into schism as a result of those early councils that he recognized as ecumenical. Were the corporate protests of Donatists, Nestorians, and Monophysites not countersigns invalidating the respective councils? He called such groups "local disturbances" within the one distinct body of the church, "branches" that separate from it and claim to be heard in matters of doctrine and discipline.[49] Because he could not be sure that a dissenting group at the council invalidated the proceedings—the group might merely be the early form of a schismatic sect—Newman was therefore forced to another criterion that followed instinctively from his organic philosophy. That which is true, he concluded, lives and grows; what is false, decays. Error has the seeds of self-destruction within it. "In every age bodies have fallen off from [the church], and have shown in the event that the falling off was death—that they tended to lose all definite faith, as *bodies*. . . . The Arians came to nought, and the Donatists—and the Greeks show no signs of life, but remain shut up as if in the sepulchre of the past."[50] With this theory of corporate decay one has, perhaps, the most empirical verification Newman gave on dissent, and it offers a way to discriminate between group protest that undermines moral unanimity and protest that does not.

The issue of corporate dissent, following Vatican I, never fully materialized. The bishops of the minority, either individually or in regional synods, came to accept the decree and to promulgate it in their dioceses.[51] As this opposition was melting away, the decree was gaining conciliar authority in Newman's mind. The doctrine of papal infallibility, in which he had long believed, was receiving *de fide* corroboration.

The second phase of *securus judicat* then began. If the first phase could be called its judgmental moment (i.e., its reception ensuring its validity), its second phase was an interpretive moment. Newman phrased it as follows: "The securus judicat orbis terrarum is the real rule and interpretation of the words of the Church, i.e. the sensus theologorum primarily, then the consensus fidelium next."[52]

The secure judgment of the whole church is not only an acceptance of a doctrinal decree but is, in the very same process, an interpretation of it. In 'receiving' a teaching by recognizing itself in that teaching, the church assimilates it by *understanding* it. An analogy with individual knowing is helpful. Knowledge is not simply a mental photograph of what is "out there." The knower personally contributes to what is known. The external world impresses itself on a knower whose knowledge is already filled with a wealth of experiences; the knower is not a *tabula rasa*. What modern philosophy describes as the turn-to-the-subject, what Newman describes as first principles already lodged in an experiencing subject, and what Lonergan calls insight as opposed to a "taking-a-look" theory of knowledge, are all describing the intellect's interpretive role in assimilating information. The collective mind of the church does the same thing.

Wanting to maintian that a teaching ends up being correctly understood, Newman attributes an active power to the mind of the universal church by which a teaching, which is undergoing assimilation by the church, is also undergoing the process of being understood correctly. He calls the process "passive infallibility." I wish to emphasize the more active sense his notion involves. The word *passive* is misleading because it suggests total determination from without. Then why does he employ it? He does not want ecclesial reception to be confused with the teaching office. The magisterium alone remains the *active* teacher, and the general faithful are not infallible teachers of doctrine. Newman follows the classical distinction that attributes active infallibility to the teaching office and passive infallibility to the phenomenon of reception. But reception is quite *active* in its own way, being a discriminating power and instinct for the truth. "There are no words, ever so clear, but require an interpretation, at least as to their extent. For instance, an inspired writer says that 'God is love'—but supposing a set of men so extend this as to conclude '*Therefore* there is no future punishment for bad men?' Some power then is needed to determine the general sense of authoritative words—to determine their direction, drift, limits, and comprehension, to hinder gross perversions. This power is virtually the *passive infallibility* of the whole body of the Catholic people. . . . Hence the maxim 'Securus judicat orbis terrarum.' "[53]

The two aspects representing active and passive infallibility express the dialectical movement between the *Ecclesia docens* (magisterium) and the *Ecclesia discens* (the faithful). That which the magisterium teaches comes from the church's faith, hence Newman's retrieval of the *sensus fidelium* as one instrument in ascertaining this faith. Formulation into language, however, never expresses perfectly the *content* of belief, as language carries inherent ambiguities. The teaching is then addressed back to the church, which, in assimilating it, interprets it. The church is guided by a gift of infallibility to understand that, and only that, which the dogma's words attempt to convey as revealed truth. The dialectical movement between the magisterium and the baptized faithful occurs, of course, at the level of grace, and the process can be described in terms of the original unity that is the Holy Spirit. All dialectical movement attempts to recapture the original unity from which it arose. The faith is externalized into words (i.e., Newman's principle of dogma), and the words are assimilated, under the action of the Holy Spirit, so that there is proper understanding (internalization) of what had been externalized. The faith of the church returns to itself in more articulated form but not as a stranger.

The *schola* makes a special contribtution to the interpretive aspect of ecclesial reception. As the dialectics of debate move forward, within a milieu of freedom of discussion, Newman perceived that agreement would emerge about what is central to a dogma. While there will always be differences aobut details, common first principles of the discussion will emerge. Through its disputes, which are its very life, the *schola* "keeps the distinction clear between theological truth and theological opinion, and is the antagonist of dogmatism. And while the differences of the School maintain the liberty of thought, the unanimity of its members is the safeguard of the infallible decisions of the church."[54]

The *consensus fidelium* is the other interpretive agency that operates in ecclesial reception. In one respect, the consent of the faithful is the culmination of the entire process, for the theologians themselves are part of this wider consensus, being members of the baptized. The *consensus fidelium,* of which Newman speaks at this point, is to be distinguished from his *Rambler* essay's use of the phrase "sense of the faithful," even though he employed *sensus* and *consensus* interchangeably in the 1859 essay. In the steps toward a dogma, the faith of the laity is consulted "for a fact," that is, the state of their belief is ascertained but they do not act as judges. In the ecclesial reception of a dogma, in the final step of the full dialectical process in other words, the *consensus* of the entire body of the faithful (bishops, theologians, laity) is judgmental. By this Newman does not mean the Gallican notion of a separate act of ratification by the church subsequent to a magisterial decision. That would rupture the unity within the dialectical process. In my opinion, Newman means the assimilative process that is simultaneously a process of understanding. The phrase best capturing Newman's non-Gallican insight is "the teaching ends up being understood correctly." One may call the infallibility *passive* to indicate it is not the infallibility of the teacher, as such. Still, it is an active instinct for the truth. At the deepest level passive infallibility is the work of the Holy Spirit keeping the church on course. *Securus judicat* is Newman's *theological* vision of the church in terms of the Holy Spirit.

THE THEOLOGY OF ABUSES

Honest ecclesiology cannot avoid reflecting on the sinful features of the church. They are there and must be taken into account. This honest acknowledgment was especially incumbent on Newman, whose empirical bent and preference for the concrete had to take things as they were. But everyone who belongs to a church has to come to terms with its faults; no one can skirt having some kind of "theology of abuses," however rudimentary. The phrase refers to a view of the church that can affirm the presence of grace coexisting with sin in the same reality. Grace and sin are indeed distinguishable, but they are not separable in the concrete reality of the church. By way of contrast, take the classic axiom, "holy Church, sinful members." It purports to be a theology of abuses but is not. It distinguishes *and separates* by claiming that the church itself is "without spot or wrinkle," even though individual members are sinners. But this rationale makes an abstraction of the church, as if it is something apart from its members; the rationale is also blind to abuses in the church's very structures and processes.

A realistic theology of abuses must acknowledge institutional sinfulness and offer a rationale why, in spite of its presence, it does not discredit one's conviction that the church is a community of grace. Someone might go so far as to claim that abuses are inevitable, and Newman did precisely that in the context of a sacramental analysis of conflict in the church's fabric. Realistically, also, a theology of abuses concerns itself about affections. Christians do not simply believe in the church as it if were the right or best idea; such belief would be a cold *notional* assent.

Christians are expected to love their community. But can one love what is not perfect? If it is to happen, a person needs some vision of a sinful church that does not suffocate the possibilities of loving it. Newman's vision may not appeal to everyone, but it was his, and it enabled him to join the Roman Catholic church, to love it, and to want to stay in it to improve it.

Newman's fullest reflection on abuses appeared in 1877, when he republished his 1837 lectures, the *Prophetical Office*, adding to it a lengthy preface[55] that examined institutional faults from a sacramental perspective. Long before then, however, Newman needed to account for abuses, particularly in his 1845 decision to become a Roman Catholic. His *Essay on Development* responded to the indictment of doctrinal innovations, but he also needed to address whether *actual* Roman Catholicism was a corruption, even if its offical doctrines were orthodox. Was it simply an orthodoxy-on-paper?

Prior to the sacramental analysis in 1877, Newman had used the categories of worldliness, expedience, and dialectics to reflect on the church's sinfulness. Worldliness carried the notion that even good things get distorted in the kind of world in which we live. He liked to describe it with the Latin phrase translating 1 John 5:19, *mundum in maligno positum* (the world is in the grip of evil). Take, for example, Newman's description of natural religion. It is the system of religion borne by the voice of human conscience, behind which is none other than God. But God's voice is heard in a sinful world, which muffles or distorts the communication. Consequently the structures and ideology of natural religion become laced with distortions and abuses.

With worldliness connoting evil's influence on all things, Newman gauges that the church is not only in the world but of the world. "I begin by assuming that the Church is in the world, and the world in the Church, and that the world, whether in the Church or not, *totus in maligno positus est.*"[56] His notion is developmental rather than dualistic. Jesus has overcome the powers of evil, and the church lives this victory *in principle*. Grace did not overcome evil at once, but it is in the process of overcoming it on the strength of a victorious change in direction; thus Jesus' death and resurrection have begun the victory of the church.[57] Until the process is completed "at the consummation of all things," the church itself is undergoing redemption. Sin disfigures its features, and any religion of the multitides, what Newman calls "popular religion," has inevitable deformations. He never tries to whitewash this fact, and of the post-Reformation Catholic church he acknowledges that "three centuries have taught us that a case may be made against us."[58] In taking things as they are (i.e., the church's worldliness), he accepts the validity of the Reformation dictum, *ecclesia semper reformanda* (the church must always be undergoing reform).

The category of expedience gave Newman another angle on abuses. Expedience is a response to a complex situation in which one refrains from pursuing what abstractly is best, since it would entail greater difficulties in the concrete. Newman thought the exercise of ecclesiastical authority often had to use expedience—what he termed "temporizing"—such that it had to tolerate certain evils to avoid greater ones. Expedience has varied applications to institutional abuses. In some cases it involves a toleration of an evil that it appears to be countenancing. In other cases "temporizing" is the choice of political aims over the claims of truth, and this choice may perpetuate harmful structures in the church. In whatever case, the complexity of actual church life presents a number of conflicting values, and the choice of certain ones entails the rejection of others. (More matured reflections on expedience appear in the 1877 preface.)

The category of dialectics refers to the interaction of forces within a large and complex system. Newman views the church in its vast complexity, permeated with the energies of individuals, groups, special interests, and ideologies. In 1845 he was calling these forces "great apparent anomalies" that were connected with institutional pathologies. Any large system, he noted, has inherent tensions; pope is against earlier pope and one council overturns another. Scripture itself is complex and filled with anomalies. *"You must begin* by *expecting* this, and making allowance for it—that some things perhaps must ever be difficulties, (as there are insoluble difficulties in Scripture)."[59] Newman's early notice of anomalies in the church becomes more clearly articulated years later as three conflicting instincts: the church's devotional life, its political life, and its reflective theological life. Being at once all of them, the church will illustrate their conflictual nature, and one should not be unduly surprised or scandalized by such conflict.

Newman's theology of abuses received fullest treatment in the 1877 preface. The three conflicting instincts are perceived to be the ramifications of a sacramental energy whose multiple expressions (polity, devotion, theology) never perfectly capture the originating unity of which they are the signs (Jesus as priest, prophet, king). Newman locates abuses in the dialectical interaction of the three instincts, and with a certain inevitability of happening.

The preface, drafted in six days when Newman was seventy-six years old, is a model of subtlety and clarity.[60] It responds to two major indictments against Roman Catholicism: that there is disparity between the primitive church and the present Roman church "in teaching, conduct, worship, and polity," and that a disparity exists between Rome's formal teaching and Catholicism's "popular and political manifestations," i.e., between what is preached and what is lived.[61] Since the 1845 *Essay on Development* responded to the first charge, the preface is concerned chiefly with the second.

Two examples of disparity are offered: The tone of various devotional manuals deviates markedly from the official prayer book, the Breviary; the statements of various ecclesiastics deviate from the Official Catechism. Newman summarizes the thesis he will argue. "From the nature of the case, such an apparent contrariety between word and deed, the abstract and the concrete, could not but take place, supposing the Church to be gifted with those various prerogatives, and charged with those independent and conflicting duties, which Anglicans, as well as ourselves, recognize as belonging to her. Her organization cannot be otherwise than complex, considering the many functions which she has to fulfill, the many aims to keep in view, the many interests to secure."[62] As it is difficult for one person to fulfill several roles, such as being a parent and a minister of religion, conflicting goals are more likely to be found in the church's several roles.

Newman resists the apologetic temptation to ground these conflicts in the personal sinfulness of individuals. While personal sinfulness is always a contributing factor, he perceives an inevitable friction in the very functioning of sacramental symbolism. The church discharges, in a sacramental manner, those ministries that are primarily and supremely its Founder's. Christ is the prophet, priest, and king; the prophetic, priestly, and kingly works continue sacramentally in the church's current life, but not without conflicts among them.[63]

In its prophetic role, Christianity is a *philosophy,* meaning that it has a doctrinal life. A doctrinal religion requires theological reflection and the various processes of discernment that lead to dogmatic teachings. In its priestly role, Christianity is a *worshiping* body. It is a community striving for holiness and meeting the holiness of its Lord in the various religious rites and practices that express its devotional instinct. Christianity is a *polity* in its kingly role. It is a governance with legitimate authority. Pope, bishops, and pastors express the kingly rule of Christ; they are "symbols" of the Lord who continues to lead the church.

In cryptic prose Newman describes the three roles of the church in terms of ends, means, and propensities for abuses. "Truth is the guiding principle of theology and theological inquiries; devotion and edification, of worship; and of government, expedience. The instrument of theology is reasoning; of worship, our emotional nature; of rule, command and coercion. Further, in man as he is, reasoning tends to rationalism; devotion to superstition and enthusiasm; and power to ambition and tyranny."[64]

This analysis is a crucial move in Newman's argument, and it sets the later agenda. Theology, worship, and authority are legitimate expressions, at the level of sacramentality, of Christ's threefold ministry, but their aims and means are distinct among themselves. The roles existed in Christ in an original unity, each expressed in harmony with the others; they exist in the church in dialectical tensions. The three ministries, realized by a multitude of persons, seek a harmonious coexistence, but they never recapture the unity they had in Christ himself. The dialectical interaction of the three offices reaches for the original unity in the manner in which multivalent symbolism seeks to recapture its originating and unified ground. Each office, seen in itself, seeks its own aims, for only in this manner is the necessary dialectical movement assured. "Each of the three has its separate scope and direction, each has its own interests to promote and further; each has to find room for the claims of the other two."[65] But if inevitable opposition arises from the very nature of these separate dynamisms, it is exacerbated by the principle of worldliness: human reasoning tends toward rationalism, devotion toward superstition, and, most important, power gravitates toward tyranny.

If the root difficulty lies in fulfilling the three sacramental roles of Christ simultaneously, is there any correcting feature given in the dynamics of the dialectical (sacramental) process itself? Is the process simply destined to perpetuate conflicts that in some instances are genuine abuses? Newman responds that *theology* (the prophetical office) is the reforming norm. He uses the word broadly; it is the community's reflection on its originating truth, and it uses not only the work of theologians but also the instinct of faith possessed by the laity. Theology is called the "fundamental and regulating principle" of the whole dialectic because its subject matter is revelation, which is the "essential idea of Christinaity . . . and, as being such, has created both the Regal Office and the Sacerdotal."[66] Simply put, revelation determines the styles of worship and the reaches of authority, and therefore the prophetical office should regulate the other two offices, even though these "are ever struggling to liberate themselves from those restraints which are in truth necessary for their well-being."[67]

The remainder of Newman's argument illustrates the conflicts between the three offices. Theology's conflict with the devotional instinct, and the compromises it must tolerate, will lead Newman to conclude that "there will ever be a marked contrariety between the professions of her theology and the ways and doings of a Catholic country."[68] This point was one of the two disparities he had set out to answer. Other conflicts can be noted. Theology insists on the *merit* of good works; a theologian such as St. Robert Bellarmine, nevertheless, who "lets his devout nature betray itself between the joints of his theological harness," will write of placing one's whole trust in the sole mercy of God.[69] Thus devotional language might exceed the strictness of orthodoxy, and theology will consent to a truce lest its more precise language suffocate devotion. St. Paul's admonition against scandalizing the weak is another example of the prophetical office's responsibility to back down from the priestly office. Similarly, a dubious relic devotion might be tolerated because of the "overflowing popular devotion towards Our Lord or the Blessed Virgin, of which the legend is the occasion";[70] superstition, in Newman's view, is an infirmity of human nature, but it is also the companion of a faith that is vivid and earnest, and it is sometimes faith's price.

The prophetical office collides with the kingly office as well. At times authority takes the part of an erring devotional practice against a theological truth. Under pressure from Judaic Christians, Peter approved kosher dietary practices until Paul confronted him. In his effort to spread Christianity, Gregory Thaumaturgus allowed converts to retain certain pagan games. In these cases, theology's advice was overridden by a political decision. The only example given of the clash between the priestly and kingly offices involves the misuse of a devotional symbol. Constantine, with the approval of church authorities, used the Cross as his banner in warfare. For reasons from which the polity of the church benefited, the sacred symbol of unresisting suffering was used to rally troops to inflict suffering.

In all these illustrations, one senses that partial values are being realized at the expense of other values. It is not the case that something good gives way to something fully evil; rather, abuses come from an imbalance between the legitimate aims of the three sacramental offices of the church. One suspects, however, that Newman's real worry is the unchecked activity of the political (kingly) office. Abuses are most glaring in the misuse of institutional power. Newman opts to make theology the reforming principle, not because theologians have more or better thoughts than ecclesiastical authorities, or because they are better people, but because revelation is the supreme norm of Christian life and has authority over church authorities. Deformations are measured by and corrected by it.

In addition to its role of checking and balancing, each office also supports the others. Theological reason is at the service of piety and policy; devotional feelings condition reason and temper the use of power; authority supplies political prudence to the claims of theology and to the energies of worship. In the abstract all these relationships are true; the dialectical interaction has these ideal goals. Concretely, the goals never avoid institutional imbalances and the imperfections of the people involved. For apologetic purposes Newman uses the softer language of "inconsistencies" and "anomalies," but he has in mind abuses and instances of institutional sin in precisely the church's efforts to be at once prophetic, priestly, and kingly.

"Whatever is great," he concludes the preface,

> refuses to be reduced to human rule, and to be made consistent in its
> many aspects with itself. Who shall reconcile with each other the
> various attributes of the Infinite God? and, as He is, such in their
> several degrees are His works. This living world to which we belong,
> how self-contradictory. . . . We need not feel surprise then, if Holy
> Church too, the supernatural creation of God, is an instance of the
> same law, presenting to us an admirable consistency and unity in
> word and deed, as her general characteristic, but crossed and dis-
> credited now and then by apparent anomalies which need, and
> which claim, at our hands an exercise of faith.[71]

In a five-letter exchange with his nephew, John Rickards Mozley, the son of his sister Jemima, Newman dealt with abuses in
the church from yet another angle.[72] Mozley argued that the
moral faults of Catholicism's highest ecclesiastics have disproved
any of Rome's claims to apostolic authority. Baron von Hügel, a
little later, sought Newman's advice on essentially the same
charge. For both correspondents Newman pushed the issue to
the deeper question: If evil in the world does not tell against
theism, then why must ecclesiastical evils tell against the church?
"I can quite understand, shocking as it is, a man's saying, 'The
existence of evil by itself proves there is no God,'—*there* is the
field of battle—but to argue, 'the existence of evil in the *Church* is
a proof that the Church is not from God,' is not going to the root
of the matter."[73]

For his Anglican nephew Newman drew out the analogy. Of
the great difficulties involved with belief in God, the greatest is
the presence of evil in life. One can form hypotheses to assuage
the difficulty, but they are always fragile rationales. Difficulties,
however, do not constitute doubts, as one sees from the experience of many people in the world who believe in a God; the evils
all around them do not destroy their belief. Newman then introduces into the difficulty the fact that God experiences evil too.
"Our Lord's death to destroy evil is as tremendous and appalling
a confession of [evil's] existence and of its power, as can be
conceived." The Crucifixion, in which Jesus died under the
forces of evil, suggests two contrary expectations: Either evil was
to be annihilated at once or it will be destroyed only gradually.
The natural expectation is the former, but "unless we unravel
our convictions and run back to belief in nothing, I must give
this thought up. . . . I allow then . . . the existence of that flood

of evil which shocks you in the visible Church; but for me, if it touched my faith mortally in the divinity of Catholicism, it would by parity of reason, touch my faith in the Being of a Personal God and Moral Governor."[74]

What underlies this method of arguing? By introducing God's involvement in the problem of evil (i.e., the Crucifixion), Newman provides support for his contention that difficulties do not add up to doubts, and doubting alone is incompatible with real assent (faith). God's personal experience of suffering on the Cross at least makes one pause and wonder how God and evil coexist. Ultimately and in any rationally satisfying way, the coexistence of goodness and evil cannot be fathomed, but the *ability* to believe in goodness does not depend on having rational solutions to the problem of evil. Belief in God is based on experiencing God, even though there are concomitant difficulties in getting one's experience fully clear and straightened out. In fact, Newman would have the experience of God-Creator be the parent mystery that is never comprehended in its implications, and all other things beyond our comprehension have their roots here.

> What has been most congenial to my own mind, is, to consider the beginnings of evil involved in the very idea of creation—though this of course is only throwing the difficulty a step back. The creature *must* be imperfect in itself—the question is whether *imperfection* is not a *kind* of evil—and then we go on to the different kinds of evils, and the certainty or chance of their resulting. Thus, for instance, it is often said that, for what we can see, the creation of a free agent is inseparable from the risk of sin. If the principle I am supposing can be maintained, it has this advantage—that it throws back the difficulty upon an act of the Divine Will which approves itself to our reason—for creation as such seems worthy of the Benevolence of God. Again, it throws it back upon what is at least, to *my* mind, as great. I mean how it was that the Almighty, after an eternity of quiescence and solitariness, began to create. People feel things very differently, but, though I acknowledge that creation is suitable to God's goodness, it is to me incomprehensible that He should *begin* to create, yet quite as incomprehensible that He should have created *from eternity*.[75]

With this synthesis we are brought to the heart of Newman's religious philosophy in which theology (notional assent) is not belief (real assent), and *theological failure* does not mean that someone's theism is dubious. Notional assent is never up to the demands of real assent. Real assent affirms a reality in its concrete wholeness. Notional assent comprehends aspects of the concrete whole, but the cumulus of those aspects never adds up to the richness of the concrete whole, a richness that is at once an incomprehensibility. The ability to believe in God does not depend on a comprehensive grasp of the multiple aspects of the world or on a need to have a *solution* to the problem of evil. The second part of the *Grammar of Assent* contends that one *can* believe what one cannot understand, and this ability is more common than not.

I began my examination of this aspect of Newman's ecclesiology by stating that belief in the church requires a theology of abuses if belief is to be possible in the face of evils. His position is that ecclesiastical abuses present a serious difficulty to belief, but that they do not constitute a sufficient ground for doubt. He argues reductionally. The preface pushes back the fact of abuses to the inevitable conflicts in the dialectical workings of the church's sacramental roles. Elsewhere Newman reduces the question of evil to its parent mystery of creation, or to the mystery of the Cross. In both of these reductions, the ability to believe that the church is divinely founded and guided is not overcome by the presence of evil, but by the same token it is not rendered impossible. With Newman's theology of abuses, one meets the most enigmatic aspect of grace—it coexistence with evil in the church—which, ultimately, theology fails to solve. One simply loves that which one cannot fully understand.

THE CHURCH AS SACRAMENT

The examination of Newman's first principles presented the notion of sacramentality as an implication of divine pedagogy. It described how human language could capture adequately, even if imperfectly, the truth of God's revelation. The examination of sacramentality now needs to be broadened, with a more direct application to the church as such. Recent Roman Catholic ecclesiology has moved decisively toward a sacramental philosophy.[76] It has represented a corrective balance to the institutional description of the church in prominence since the Council of

Trent. In the Tridentine model, primary stress was placed on precisely those aspects of the church that the Protestant reformers attacked: its visible structures and its claim to authority. Contemporary Roman Catholic ecclesiologists, somewhat in reaction to a tired polemics, have sought to synthesize the church's external institutional features and its interior dimension of grace. The sacramental model of the church, in the words of Avery Dulles, "harmoniously combines both aspects."[77]

Newman came to a sacramental vision of the church from another direction. His vision sprang from Anglican roots, and in particular from that part of Anglicanism that maintained a continuity with the sacramental emphases of the early doctors of the Church, both Latin and Greek. The Greek patristic influence was especially important, just as it had been for Thomas Aquinas, because of its more mystical elements. Newman's sacramental orientation was already fixed in his mind when he became a Roman Catholic. One of the more remarkable features of his conversion was the maintenance of his fundamental principles; he did not have to reject any of them in becoming a Roman Catholic. His theology was built on patristic sources, and even if aspects of this tradition were less noticeable in the Tridentine theology of his day, his roots were legitimately *catholic*.

John Coulson has recently argued that Newman's sacramental vision of the church stands in a common Anglican tradition with S. T. Coleridge and F. D. Maurice. For all three writers, the church manifests sacramentally the presence of Christ to the world. They differ, nevertheless, in the ramifications of the idea. For Coleridge, the idea of the church is an "experiment proposed"; one enters into the truth and understanding of it by trying it.[78] This understanding leads Coleridge to distinguish the *Enclesia* from the *Ecclesia;* the former is the church realized in the cultural life of the nation (the established church), while the latter is the church universal, that is to say, the transcendent principle which can become incarnated in this or that culture. Maurice is more directly in line with Coleridge, distinguishing the church in itself (God's power in all the structures of the world, transforming them) from the "churches" (those particular organizations that act for God). Newman does not distinguish different levels of the reality of the church. The church that one directly experiences is the visible expression of the in-

131

visible Spirit of Jesus. It is not as closely identified with secular society as Maurice would have it, but on the other hand it is a single historical reality *in* the world, as opposed to Coleridge's affinity for an ideal principle that can be realized here or there. John Coulson is correct to perceive the family resemblance among Coleridge, Newman, and Maurice, but Newman is more like the middle child, positioned between Coleridge's transcendent emphasis (*Ecclesia*) and Maurice's immanent emphasis (the power of social transformation in the world.)

Newman's divergence from Coleridge and Maurice is indicative of a sacramental theory more uniquely his own. According to Dean Church, the Oriel Fellows thought Coleridge to be a "misty thinker,"[79] and if one could hear the common room walls speak, Newman was probably referring to Coleridge's distinction between church as universal (*Ecclesia*) and church as established in culture (*Enclesia*). For Newman, the church is one and undivided, its visible and invisible dimensions being separate impressions that the one concrete reality makes on the mind.[80] Consequently, his sacramental theory begins with the original unity of spirit-as-matter, of grace-as-incarnate, which is, of course, prior to someone's conscious reflection upon it on behalf of a theory. Reflection can never capture the original unity, but it approaches it from different conceptualized aspects. These aspects are reflected in the multiple propositions theological reflection produces. Thus the church is truly an invisible reality, *but* it is simultaneously visible in history; it is truly hierarchical, *but* at the same time laical; it is a power of social reform within history (Maurice), *but* also a power of sanctification whose goal is beyond history.

The *Apologia* has acknowledged the influence of Bishop Joseph Butler and John Keble in the area of sacramental theory.[81] Both represented those Anglican sensitivities whose roots lay in the pre-Reformation tradition of Sarum-rite England and that subsequently resisted Calvinist inroads. From them Newman took the notion that material things are the expression and genuine offer of spiritual realities. But this influence contributed to a foundation he already had. His conversion experience, in the autumn of 1816, implanted in him the vivid realization of God. It was so strong that it confirmed his boyish mistrust in the reality of the material world around him; his Creator and his own self, these alone, were self-evidently true. This conversion experience seems antithetical to sacramental thinking, and in the Calvinist theology Newman then followed, it was. In truth, however, his conversion experience became the first foundation for his sacramentalism. From that time forward the reality of God was immediately and intimately at hand, as close as God ever comes in a sacramental encounter. The unreality of the world was the distortion in Newman's interpretation of the conversion experience, but the true part was the immediate and undeniable reality of God.

Butler and Keble supplied the dialectical key, what might be thought of as the "yes, but." God is met in experience, *but* we also experience a world of real matter. Butler helped Newman overcome his distrust for material things by enabling him to maintain the truth of his first conversion (the immediacy of God) and to accept the importance of material phenomena as symbols of God.[82] On these two legs Newman's sacramentalism came to stand. One is immediately present to God in being present to material phenomena; therefore Newman might well find Coleridge's distinction "misty." The church is not above or beyond its historical expression; it is one with it and found only there. Keble's strong insistence on the real presence of Jesus in the Eucharistic element is a merger of the same themes: materiality and divine immediacy. Newman called Keble's *Christian Year*, music to his ears, the music of a teaching long forgotten in England.[83]

Any discussion of Newman's sacramental philosophy must consider his famous imagery of the visible and invisible worlds. A cursory reading of his sermons might suggest a platonic separation between spirit and matter that, if true, would destroy a genuine sacramentality. To understand his emphasis on the unseen world (of God, the angels, and the communion of saints in glory), before which this world of matter is like a veil, we must keep in mind the purpose of his sermons and his method of presentation.

In a university sermon of 1832, Newman made the case that Christianity is more readily spread by the personal influence of committed people than by display of miracles or the inherent excellence of its teaching.[84] Holy people are Christianity's best argument. In a real sense, the heart of the Oxford movement was a call to a renewal of holiness. But if one is to have the holiness that radiates into the hearts of others, one must know the Lord in a deeply personal way. This instruction sounds like good evangelical theology, and indeed it is. It also sounds like the beginning of Newman's own spiritual pilgrimage, the conversion experience at fifteen years of age. The key to understanding Newman's unseen world begins here. Through his sermons, he leads people on the spiritual path he experienced himself. Egotism is true modesty, Newman used to claim, meaning that he could only recommend to others what he had experienced himself. The linchpin, of course, will be *conscience.*

The sacramental foundation to conscience requires deeper explanation. The world in which we grow up floods our minds with its manifold impressions. Its vast natural beauties, its human attainments, can literally overwhelm the imagination. Satisfaction in them seems its own justification. On the other hand, the world disappoints us. It is a mercurial and fragile world, and whatever we place our hopes on can slip away. As we grow into personal autonomy, we experience the anxiety of misused freedom, of what theology calls our 'fundamental sinfulness.' In this great mixture of experiences a glimmer of something beyond the immediate phenomena can catch our eye. In Newman's novel, *Callista,* the pagan heroine travels this very journey. She comes to perceive "a higher beauty than that which the order and harmony of the natural world revealed," beside which "everything looked dull and dim."[85] The beauty is neither an ethical principle nor a noble ideal but a person in whose presence Callista feels herself to be. "He says to me, 'Do this: don't do that.' You may tell me that this dictate is a mere law of my nature, as is to joy or to grieve. I cannot understand this. No, it is the echo of a person speaking to me."[86]

Newman's Callista travels the road he did and the road he wants the listeners of his sermons to follow. Absorption into the world around us is broken by a power beyond it. In the sermon, "Dispositions for Faith," Newman calls the power an inner authoritative voice. "It praises, it blames, it promises, it threatens, it implies a future, and it witnesses the unseen. It is more than a man's own self."[87] Conscience is our inner ear for God, and when it hears that voice forcing itself through the din of the world around us, another world unfolds, more real and more important than the one we have called "real" until now.[88]

The language about visible and invisible worlds strikes a chord with those who have had dramatic conversion experiences. St. Paul translated the experience into a language of dichotomies: the old man/the new man; fix your eyes in heaven where Christ is/not upon the earth. The vocabulary of conversion cannot claim theological exactness, because the dichotomous images can easily suggest a dualism. Newman's visible/invisible syntax, however, is the language of vivid imagination, of someone in the grip of the ultimate, of someone redefined by his or her transformation.

Beneath the language of the seen and unseen worlds is the one reality that maintains these worlds, against any possible dualism, in sacramental juncture—the Incarnation. If the Christian experience was the teleological outcome of the drive of conscience in natural religions, the Incarnation is the true finality of the way one experiences the visible and invisible worlds. "The doctrine of the Incarnation is the announcement of a divine gift conveyed in a material and visible medium, it being thus that heaven and earth are in the Incarnation united. That is, it establishes in the very idea of Christianity the *sacramental* principle as its characteristic."[89] Newman's sacramental view of Jesus displays the strong influence of Athanasius and Cyril of Alexandria, who insisted on the unity of the human and the divine. So cardinal is this Christological point that Newman defends the usage of "the one nature in the Incarnate One" by these Alexandrian theologians to express the oneness of the person we experience, even though the description skirts Monophysitism.[90] Jesus is fully of spirit, fully of matter, inseparable into parts or levels. "In truth, until we contemplate our Lord and Saviour, God and man, as a really existing being, external to our minds, as complete and entire in his personality as we show ourselves to be to each other, as one and the same in all his various and contrary attributes . . . , we are using words which profit not."[91] Since it begins with the oneness of experience, Newman's Christology avoids a divine Jesus whose humanity is little more than a livery, and it avoids a human Jesus whose divinity is problematic.

This Christological point of departure comes naturally to Newman's empiricist orientation: Take things as they are, and this means in their concrete wholeness. The wholeness of experience is prior to the partial aspects given in reflective thought. Through conscience, the Moral Governor is experienced as a *person*. Through faith, Jesus is encountered as the divine and human *One*. And it is through baptism that the *one* church, both visible and invisible, is met and entered. In having the Incarnation establish and ground the principle of sacramentality in Christianity, Newman directs our attention to an original unity that exists between the spiritual and the material realms. Thus the humanity of Jesus is not a pale reflection of the divinity but rather its very manifestation. By the same token, the visible church is not a distant echo or a partial realization of the invisible church, as if the latter were the truly real; rather, it is the selfsame reality undergoing an earthly history. When Newman asks himself the question, "Where is the Church of Christ to be found?" he spontaneously looks into the world of his experience to find it.

It was customary in the early nineteenth century to distinguish the visible and the invisible churches in order to explain the sinfulness of baptized Christians. Sinful Christians were members of a sociological entity called the church, but they were not predestined to glory; only the predestined belonged to the true church, invisible to our eyes but known to God. This belief reflected a Calvinist influence in Anglican theology that Newman first absorbed from his mother and later rejected. "The word Church, applied to the body of Christians in this world, means but one thing in Scripture, a visible body invested with invisible privileges. Scripture does not speak of two bodies, one visible, the other invisible, each with its own complement of members. But this is a common notion at present; and it is an erroneous, and . . . dangerous notion."[92] The danger lies in ascribing impotence to God. God's Spirit is being quenched if God has no possibility of forgiving the sinner. To account for sinful Christians, Newman preferred to say that sinners are not true or full members of the church rather than saying that they are not members of the true church.

Another description of sacramentality is provided by the teleological density of the church. One may think of a sacrament as having a twofold movement within itself. At the point of experiencing it, there is a movement *from below* by which those on earth express themselves with a divine language; in the Eucharist, for example, the prayer of Jesus is appropriated by the worshiping community as its own language of prayer. There is also a movement *from above* in which God's own life is offered to the recipient of the sacrament. This double movement has been analyzed by Edward Schillebeeckx to describe for each of the sacraments the twofold activity of Jesus, corresponding to his humanity and divinity.[93]

Newman's idea of the earthly church being in communion with the heavenly church, and tending toward it as a goal, contains both kinds of movement. The visible church reaches toward the church of glory through the language of prayer. "Prayers and praises are the mode of [one's] intercourse with the next world. . . . He who does not pray, does not claim his citizenship with heaven, but lives, though an heir of the kingdom as if he were a child of earth."[94] The world of heaven does not exist only after death, but now. We can commune with this world as much as with the world of our senses, being present to it, taking part in its heavenly liturgy, and being joined to those who have passed from this life into everlasting life.[95] Through baptism, one enters into the church and learns the language that reaches into heaven itself. All of this represents movement from below.

Conversely, heaven stretches itself to us, in and through the church. In his sermon, "The Visible Temple," Newman describes an abode set upon the earth, having God for its lamps, Christ for its High Priest, and the apostles for its pillars. Christ has furnished this house with all manner of "holy symbols and spiritual ordinances," through which the Spirit is bestowed on those who enter this abode to take their rest.[96] Each of the church's sacraments is a point of contact by which the power of the invisible world is manifested and offered to Christians on earth. The sacraments render actual and perceptible the realities of the heavenly world in the visible temple, the church. People need to fix their eyes on something, Newman observes, and if it is not something salutary, it will be something harmful to their spiritual lives. As an aid to us, God makes certain earthly realities (e.g., water, bread, oil) to be expressions of the Spirit. "Our hands, or our head, or our brow, or our lips become, as it were, sensible of the contact of something more than earthly."[97]

The symbols of God's movement toward us are not restricted to the classic sacraments, however. The teachings of Christ live on in the church today, in its Scriptures, its creeds, and its apostolical office. Just as the apostles continued the teachings of Christ in the New Testament era, their successors in the apostolic office continue this pedagogy in the contemporary church. Thoughts such as these found their way into the tracts of the Oxford movement, reminding the bishops of their divine gifts and awesome responsibilities.

This brief look at the dynamics of sacramentality in the church, the upward movement of worshiping prayer and the downward movement of Christ's activity in the symbols, is part of that larger view of sacramentality that does not hesitate to call the church itself a sacrament. Because Newman refuses to separate its visible aspect from its heavenly and invisible aspect, then the church he experiences in its historical and tangible forms is none other than the heavenly community of grace.

This view of the church finds support in the contemporary discussion about sacramentality. Every human life is characterized by two polarities: a movement toward transcendence in which the human spirit seeks freedom in the ultimate, and a movement toward structure in which the affairs of daily life are ordered to enhance our goals. These poles reflect the constitution of a human life, which is both spirit and matter: the unlimited openness of the spirit; the accountability of matter to a historical existence. Since we are not spirit *and* matter compartmentalized, but rather incarnate spirits, a perfectly integrated life would experience the movements harmoniously. But imperfect human lives, our human lives, experience them as competing polarities. We must necessarily structure our lives, even though we feel the structure to quench the spirit; on the other hand, the drive toward spirit, in a structureless life, evaporates.

Christianity confesses that in the Resurrection Jesus achieves a perfect integration of spirit and matter.[98] Of his life the church is a symbol (sacrament), in the sense that a symbol *realizes* and partakes in the reality it signifies. But a sacrament retains the limitations that its material side carries with it. Eucharistic elements, for example, are indeed the symbol of Jesus' incorruptible life, but if uneaten for a long enough time, they undergo decay. The church, symbol of Jesus' resurrected life, is also a community of limitations on this side of the Parousia. Thus the two movements of Jesus' life, transcendence answering to spirit and structure answering to matter, are experienced in the church as polarities. From a sociological viewpoint, Peter Berger calls these the charismatic and structural aspects of Christianity;[99] the community is always in danger of losing the charismatic style of its Founder to the demands of structure and, at the same time, also in danger of drifting into directionless *enthusiasm* if it neglects structure. What existed in Jesus as an original unity of charisma and structure is experienced in the church as dialectical forces in opposition. I would term this situation the *dialectics of sacrament* in regard to the church.

Jan Walgrave has pursued a similar line of thought from a basis in the symbolic philosophy of Coleridge.[100] From the one spiritual power of Christ that constitutes the church, two forces emerge, distinct but inseparable. One force tends to infinite expansion, beginning in the seed of faith and moving toward the infinite inner life of God. This force is mysticism. The second force leads to structures in which the mystical element expresses itself. Walgrave takes Coleridge's polarity one stage further. Corresponding to the two features of human existence, thought and action, the structuralizing force takes two forms in the church. Ecclesial life is structured by reflective thought (theology) and by sociological organization (church government). These three forces (mysticism, theology, and authority) course through the body of the church at a sacramental depth. For all of them to remain vital and expressive of their original unity (the Spirit of Christ), they should seek a mutually contributive coexistence. Mysticism, theology, and polity should intrude into each other's concerns, otherwise they will draft apart and set up their own priorities and rules.

If, as I have said, a sacrament retains the limitations of its material aspect, the consequences for the sacramentality of the church amount to an experience of polarity between competing forces. Structure and charisma contend; within structure, theology and magisterium contend. One may bemoan this contention as unfortunate, thinking that conflict ought never to characterize the church Jesus founded. Newman thinks otherwise. In his famous dictum, "In a higher world it is otherwise, but here below to live is to change, and to be perfect is to have changed often,"[101] he is aware that organisms struggle in order to advance. Although he was applying the dictum to developments of doctrine, it is equally applicable to the way a sacramental sign seeks to achieve in itself, at the phenomenal level, the original unity at its heart. In having somewhat autonomous lives, charisma (the quest for holiness), theology (the quest for insight), and polity (the quest for order) each wish the entire church to adopt its aims. Church authorities will urge the order Christ gave the church; theology will seek the wisdom Christ represents; the mystics seek a church of the holy, as Jesus was holy. In the abstract, none denies the values of the other two; in the concrete, their aims clash. Newman's theology concerns the concrete, and he perceives in the clash of aims the church reaching for that original unity of values found in Jesus. Precisely in the dialectical interaction of competing forces does the real and complete Christ come to expression. The sacrament of the church becomes more perfectly what it symbolizes at the level of interacting persons and their counterbalancing aims.

For a moment recall Newman's earlier concerns. Conscience hears a voice beyond and sets out on the quest for holiness. Dogma, already a structuring of religious thought, is a needed guide for a searching conscience. Dogma is impossible without an infallible voice. But an infallible teaching can only articulate a faith existing in the bosom of the community, and the faith of the laity is germane in order to discern it. But even then every dogma needs to be interpreted, and ancient ones need to be reinterpreted, hence the work of theology and the phenomenon of ecclesial reception. Magisterium preserves the tradition, theologians explore its edges, and the laity are there to instruct on its relevance to the world in which we live. Behind all these energies is the primal quest coming from conscience. Such a complexus of interacting forces! Such an array of different concerns and aims!

Newman would have thought that such a situation is a healthy dialectics of interaction in a church fully alive, not because historical studies told him it had previously been so, but because life ought to be this way all the time when one is on pilgrimage.

Dialectics is the way the church discovers its original ground. It is the way a sacrament achieves the primordial unity of the Christ out of whom it arose. In a higher world it will be otherwise; polarities give way to integration, and of course sacraments just give way. But here below, dialectical interaction is the story of the church as a sacrament.

Epilogue

*I*n offering a systematic framework for Newman's idea of the church, I have let him speak for himself as much as possible. Simple reasons dictated the choice. He is the master of the turn of phrase; his prose is delightful to read, and readers ought not to be denied it. Next, his vast inventory of observations on the church, scattered throughout half a hundred volumes of essays and letters, is here brought into some manageable order, and readers can use the sources given in the endnotes to pursue selected "aspects of the [church's] idea," as Newman would have termed specialized topics. Last and most important, I wish others to have the sense that my tripartite framework—foundational, pastoral, theological— is not a procrustean bed into which Newman is being squeezed. I trust his own words convey the impression that he genuinely viewed the church from these three perspectives.

In earlier chapters various aspects of Newman's ecclesiology— especially his theology of the laity—were placed in wider contexts. It is now time to take soundings, as it were, of his *idea* overall, and I offer five of them.

1. THE ASSESSMENT OF OTHER CHRISTIAN CHURCHES. Newman was too negative about other Christian churches. For him, Roman Catholicism alone was the church of Christ, and though the other communities—Greek Orthodoxy, Anglicanism, and Protestantism—have certain values, they were not *churches* as such. This exclusivism is not the teaching of Roman Catholicism today, as enunciated by the Second Vatican Council. Although Newman was a precursor to a number of the more liberalizing

teachings of the recent council, he differed from it on the "churchness" (ecclesiality) of the other churches.

In evaluating other Christian communities, the Second Vatican Council replaced an *essentialist* manner of thinking with a *participational* one. In the former, either the essence of the church was present or it was not. Just as one cannot be half a person, so a group cannot be half a church. The essence of the church, in the classic descriptions up to the recent council, meant having what I call the three Cs: creed, code, and cult. The church needs to preserve all of revelation in its creed; its polity requires having all the authority Christ willed to the church; and all the sacraments are to be available to Jesus' followers. As ingredients essential to the church of Christ, creed excludes nonbelievers and heretics, code excludes schismatics, and cult excludes excommunicated persons. One conclusion could be drawn from what might be called the essentialist syllogism: Certain qualities constitute the essence of the church. Roman Catholicism alone possesses all these qualities. Therefore, Roman Catholicism alone is the church Christ founded.[1] Every other Christian group lacks some essential qualities; at the very least every other group rejects the papacy (*code*).

Participational thinking uses the categories of "more and less" rather than "either/or." This approach assumes that the reality upon which one is reflecting is realized to different degrees in different situations but is nevertheless present in each situation. People employ participational thinking all the time. Notice how we think about what it means for something to live. A person lives, an animal lives, a plant lives, and—to make matters more complex—God lives. What it means to be alive differs in each case, and with God there is an infinite difference, but there is something similar about each instance, and our language captures that similarity through the same verb, *to live*. Being alive is not an either/or concept for these four realities; it is a more/less concept.

Using participational thinking, the recent council was able to teach that Roman Catholicism is the church of Christ, but that Eastern Orthodox communities, for example, are really and genuinely churches of Christ,[2] even if they realize ecclesiality to a lesser degree.

Newman thought in an essentialist way about other Christian

groups, and that kind of thinking caused him to decide against their reality as churches. He was out of step with post-Tridentine ecclesiologists in many ways, but not in this matter. Admittedly Newman's essentialism was not nearly as juridical as their approaches were. The *creed* of the church was not viewed as if one could itemize all its doctrinal statements into something like a Denzinger handbook. Creeds and the principle of dogma are crucial—recall Newman's abhorrence of liberalism—but revelation was viewed organically as the inner principle constituting a community of truth; thus the laity were not reduced to being those in the church who were there to be taught (*Ecclesia discens*) by the hierarchy (*Ecclesia docens*). In terms of *code,* Newman acknowledged the legitimacy of authority in the church, but authorities were not beyond criticism, nor were all expressions of authority divinely founded (e.g., the pope's temporal powers). Concerning *cult,* Newman rejoiced in the means of holiness found outside Roman Catholicism, and one must remember that these means were his first nurture and remained those of his family and old friends. He just could not see that the validity of Anglican baptism gave Anglicanism a share in the reality of being the church of Christ.

2. THE ROLE OF THE CHURCH'S NOTES. Primarily for apologetical purposes, Newman made use of the church's four notes or marks: one, holy, catholic, apostolic, to which he added the mark of visibility. The use of notes to identify the church of Christ did not solidify until the post-Reformation period. Before then, the number and purpose of notes varied. St. Augustine wrote of the distinctive characteristics of perfect wisdom, general accord in faith, and simply being called, by others, "the Catholic church." The notes used by Newman and by all post-Reformation Catholic writers came from the creed of the Council of Constantinople.[3] Newman called the notes "tokens" that point out Christ's church. Tokens were to be clear enough for simple and unsophisticated people to assess. As a result, Newman's description of the notes was based upon the church's external features because notes were supposed to be convincing on the basis of visible evidence.

Recent ecclesiology has returned to the richer biblical and patristic understanding of the church's unity, holiness, catholicity, and apostolicity.[4] Although the notes have some applicability to the church's external features, they cannot be recognized for what they are except through the eyes of faith. Gregory Baum writes, "It is generally recognized today that the credibility of the faith—however understood—is acknowledged by the same *élan* of a man's mind by which he opens himself to God's word and his saving wisdom."[5] Because the notes are God's gifts, being graced characteristics of the church as it were, they are not recognized by reason alone; they must encounter a searching *faith*, just as God's presence in Jesus of Galilee was only recognizable to the eyes of faith. Thomas Aquinas's understanding of the notes captures this spiritual and more interior viewpoint. The church is *one* through the common love uniting everyone; it is *holy*, being washed by the blood of Christ; it is *catholic*, excluding no person in principle; it is *lasting* (i.e., apostolic) since it has Christ and the apostles as its sure foundation.[6]

Understood in this way, the notes have a limited apologetical force as *rational* arguments. Instead of inviting an inquirer to view the external assets of the church, they direct one's gaze to its inner richness. If someone is led to accept the church because of its graced features, the decision is governed by a power to "see" where reason and the testimony of the external senses cannot fully reach. Such a decision is in accord with Newman's doctrine of the illative case, but it uses the sacramental property of notes rather than their institutional and juridical features.

The notes of the church, as understood within contemporary theology, function evocatively. They call the church to be more intensely the reality they describe. German writers express this call by a play on words. The notes are not only God's gifts (*Gabe*) to the community but are also goals (*Aufgabe*) to be pursued.[7] Seen within this current perspective, Newman's apologetical use of notes would be judged as too externalistic. He himself admitted that an argument from them is necessarily an external view, but he thought it served a purpose for some people. In describing Newman as a controversialist writer, I indicated that he framed his writing in relationship to his audience and to those things calculated to engender real assent in the reader. To one kind of audience, which I suspect he took to be theologically unsophisticated, he chose those perceptible features of Catholicism that struck the imagination: the unity of the community under the papacy, its worldwide presence, its fervor of devotion.

These were features that could be easily grasped and weighed. On the other hand, Newman was aware of more intellectual and less externalistic aspects of the notes, and this awareness dictated how he wrote to more literate and theologically reflective people. Take, for example, the note of apostolicity. The *Essay on Development* argued the substantial identity between current Roman doctrines and the apostolic doctrines. Newman's conclusion is fundamentally in accord with the emphasis Hans Küng advances; the teaching of the church, and not just its ecclesiastical officers, continues in the apostolic succession.[8] Although Newman's *Essay on Development* included the hypothesis of an infallible teaching office, something to which Küng would not agree, it nevertheless put attention on how the faith is understood by the whole church. It is only meant for those readers who can follow a rather subtle historical argument.

3. THE DEFENSE OF INSTITUTIONAL RELIGION. The next sounding comes from the contemporary concern to justify *ecclesial* Christianity (i.e., why belonging to a church matters). For an increasing number of Christians, the church seems incidental to their religious needs. They either stop being active or they continue membership in the most superficial way. The phrase, "the institutional church," carries a lot of dissatisfaction, and it prompts the frequent question: "Why do I need the institutional church in order to believe in God or to follow Jesus?" The question is really not addressed to this or that facet of the church *as institution* but rather expresses a deeper malaise touching the meaning of *social* religion as such. There is a growing privatized sense of religion, especially in the industrialized Western nations, and belief is becoming more of a private affair of the heart. The spirit of individualism that began with the Enlightenment has worked its way into a vast Christian consciousness. (Television evangelism in America plays to this spirit; the sacred liturgical space is now the room where the TV is.)

If Christianity is meant to be ecclesial, how do church 'apologists' talk to people who claim to be Christian but want no part of an organized church? One way might be called the approach "from above." One might argue from *tradition* that Christianity has always understood itself to be a socially organized group of Jesus' followers, or one might argue from the Bible that the New

Testament authors had a church in mind when they described the words and deeds of Jesus, an understanding very clear in Matthew 18, for example. In either case the starting point hovers, as an alleged axiom, above the person questioning institutional religion; in either case it usually does not work.

Other approaches are "from below." They begin from an experience with which most people can identify, that is to say, an experience of human life. Reflections on this experience then push toward its implications for socially organized religion. These approaches have more chance at success since they do not assume that which needs to be made meaningful. For three decades Karl Rahner wrote countless articles on the church. In his last writings one can perceive a shift in style from "above" (beginning from a doctrine) to "below" (beginning with the experience of human freedom); one can also perceive his increasing concern to justify ecclesial Christianity in the face of the devaluation of institutional religion in contemporary culture.[9]

Newman is with those who begin "from below." He reflects on the experience of moral conscience. We feel guilt, or well-being, in conjunction with certain free choices. Unable to shake the experience or to reduce it to emotional projections, we feel ourselves in the presence of a moral force, a horizon of truth, face to face in some vague way with a personal *other* that appears to speak to us, to prompt us. The morally sensitive person must then wonder if this voice has spoken more clearly and distinctly. Using this foundational approach, Newman then makes the case for the *meaningfulness* of the church not only from a human experience with which many can identify (the feeling of moral accountability) but especially from an individualized and keenly private experience (one's own conscience). He moves to the social value of revealed religion by refusing to let "my conscience" remain equated with "what I alone decide" but rather with seeking insight into "What does God ask of me?" Ecclesial Christianity then becomes the moral environment in which God, whose Word became part of human history in Christ, continues to provide a word of life in and through a group of people, a church people. Newman's idea of the church serves those people who *feel* the urgency of conscientious living, and that group may indeed include many who seek God and yet have wondered about the value of traditional churches for their search.

Newman's defense of ecclesial Christianity also tries to keep people in it. Some people quit the church because a particular incident or teaching has come to present an insurmountable difficulty. In his analysis of the nature of conviction (real assent), Newman reminds us first of all that a difficulty is not a doubt, and many difficulties do not add up to doubt, i.e., to the suspension of conviction. But difficulties are not trifling matters. All genuine faith has moments of confusion, and faith does not always assuage one's hurts or hungers. Belief in God is a good example. It does not ward off evil from one's life, nor does it inoculate one from experiencing the (seeming) absence of God. Believing does not always come easy.

To deal with difficulties about the church in the serious way they deserve, Newman would remind us of the manner the illative sense brings someone to belief in the church in the first place, and hence remind us of the things about which to think when someone ponders whether he or she needs in conscience to "stop going." From many stands of evidence that might have pointed a person toward the church, each inconclusive in itself, some power of the mind enables that person to gauge the cumulus of them and to see their upshot, especially in view of the antecedent probabilities that weigh in. Not every difficulty would have been resolved, however, when someone *decides* to believe, and it is important to underline this contention of Newman.[10] The illative sense enables someone to overcome all doubts—the things that are incompatible with assent—but not necessarily all difficulties.

Just as assent does not flow from a single strand of evidence, so also the evaporation of assent is not, or rather, should not, be caused by singled out difficulties. Newman's frequent contention is that great truths keep their ground against particular difficulties. Believing in the church is what Newman likes to term a "broad truth." It is the impression on us of the whole concrete reality and is not, to speak the fashion of modern bureaucracy, the "bottom line" after the many aspects of the church have been sifted through and calculated. A particular doctrine or a particular positive impression does not alone make people into ecclesial Christians; likewise the difficulties resulting from a souring experience ought not undo their commitment to church membership. Newman does not mean that bad experiences should not be unsettling; they obviously are, and one must deal with them in a healthy fashion, but they should not discredit the broad truth of the church's divinity where the full range of faith is lived out.

4. THE ROLE OF ECCLESIAL RECEPTION. Newman had described the Augustinian *securus judicat* (i.e., the whole community is a secure and unerring judge) as the principle on which everything depended. Contemporary theology has turned its attention to the phenomenon of *ecclesial reception,* as Newman's principle is called, because of its increasing importance in our time.[11]

The history of ecumenical councils affords a classic illustration of reception. Why is it that certain synods were received as ecumenical and hence normative for the whole church, while others that sometimes had a wider representation of bishops were not? Reception is not a case of simple obedience in which church members accept the teachings of a council because the church's authorities impose them on everyone. According to Yves Congar, it is rather a *process* of consent, and eventually of judgment, where the life of the church expresses itself as a spiritual discerning power.[12] Fifty-six years of excommunications and general uproar passed before the Council of Nicea was 'received' by Constantinople I (A.D. 381), and this council, from which the Western episcopate was absent, was itself not 'received' until the Council of Chalcedon (A.D. 451) accepted its teachings as a faithful development of Nicea's. In the meantime other synods had met, yet their teachings never took hold in the universal church, for example, the Council of Ephesus in 449. Furthermore, some decrees of territorial synods have achieved churchwide force because the larger church 'received' their formulations.[13] The Synod of Carthage in 418 on Pelagian matters and the Second Council of Orange in 529 dealing with grace and original sin took on greater teaching importance through reception, leading Congar to claim that these local councils were practically ecumenical in their eventual effects.[14]

What is the basis for reception? Since the late fourth century, the popes have claimed that their own approbation was necessary. While it is true that reception did not occur when the patriarch of the West explicitly rejected a synod, it does not explain how reception does occur. The Eastern Orthodox churches do not receive any of the papally approved medieval councils, and yet they have accepted the eight earliest councils.

Some common themes have emerged from contemporary studies of ecclesial reception. The church is portrayed as a Spirit-filled community possessing an ability to discern its own faith. It can sense in a particular teaching the faith it possesses, or it can reject an erroneous teaching in the manner in which the human body expels foreign materials entering it. In whatever case, the general membership of the church is not a passive subject awaiting the commands of authority. Finally, as Congar points out, the process of reception is not a *juridical* judgment by the wider church in the manner of a supreme court of appeal. "Reception does not confer validity but rather recognizes and attests that the *content* of the teaching answers to the well-being of the Church (*au bien de l'Église*)."[15]

These recent developments very much accord with Newman's own contentions, but he provided a *broad view* in which they might be more clearly understood. The Christian faith is the life of the Holy Spirit itself within the community, constituting it and animating it; in this respect the faith is revelation. The community remains in the truth because it not only has but is the unerring life of the Spirit. Newman is simply making *faith* to mean not only the content of one's belief (Thomas Aquinas's *faith which*) but primarily the believer's possession of God (Aquinas's *faith by which*). This understanding led Newman to attribute infallibility primarily to the whole church, and no other instance of infallibility can be appreciated if one does not begin with the total community being empowered to remain in the truth. The understanding also permitted Newman to describe the teachings of the church as a process having three moments: (1) The first is the period of *articulation*. The community attempts to put into linguistic form some aspect of the inner faith constituting it. (2) The second moment is a period of *pedagogy*. Those in the church charged with the office of public (i.e., official) teaching must discern what is to be taught. They can only look within the community (its Scriptures, its traditions, its theological developments, the laity's *sensus fidelium*) for the meaning of a doctrine, since church teaching is not the prophetic inspiration of new truths. Teachers, be they a council, a pope, a diocesan bishop, or the more recent national conferences of bishops, pray for the guidance of the Spirit in order to discern the *mind* of the church faithfully. When it is a moment of the highest teaching authority, that is, the defining of a dogma, the Holy

Spirit is called upon to assist in an unerring (infallible) statement of the faith. (3) The third moment is the period of *reception* during which the teaching reenters the community. We have seen that the reception process is both judgmental (the community recognizes or does not recognize its own faith in some particular teaching) and interpretive (the teaching reenters the mind of the community by being understood in a certain way). It was one thing for the Council of Chalcedon to teach that Jesus is divine; it was and is another thing for the community to understand the teaching in the right way. By giving reception an interpretive phase, Newman returned the process to its starting point, to the Spirit of truth within the community who keeps it faithful to the original revelation. By giving reception a judgmental phase, he emphasized the instinct that the church has to recognize its own well-being.

At the present time there is a struggle going on in Roman Catholicism about authoritative noninfallible teachings and whether any Catholic, and especially Catholic theologians, can dissent publicly from them. In the prologue I mentioned the birth control encyclical, *Humanae Vitae*, as creating a situation demonstrating this tension. The question of the theologian's position *vis-à-vis* noninfallible but nevertheless 'authoritative' teachings of the church is likely to continue for a long time, and we have seen principles in Newman's thought that suggest the tension never fully goes away. To that very sensitive issue I would add that the Augustinian-Newmanian *securus judicat* is likely to rule on the matter ultimately. If the magisterium, in its noninfallible teaching, is being faithful to the truth of revelation, it will possess the mind of the church in an even deeper way than the "religious submission" Vatican II teaches is owed to such teaching. If the noninfallible teaching is not capturing the demands of revelation, the teaching will gather dust in the lives of the people, ultimately.

5. THE PLACE OF DIALECTICS. A final perspective for sounding Newman comes from contemporary theological consciousness. An inescapable pluralism of interpretations has arisen in this century about what the church believes.[16] The contemporary pluralism is quite different from the diversity of theological schools (*scholae*) that existed in times past. Formerly, the differ-

ent tendencies were either unsuspected because of vast geographical separations, or they were recognized as different emphases within a wider context of shared presuppositions. The new pluralism is qualitatively different for many reasons: Historical data have become too enormous for any individual theologian to master; the methodologies which people use are at variance; philosophy and biblical exegesis no longer provide materials about which theologians agree, let alone the philosophers and exegetes themselves. Is the resulting inescapable pluralism the death of a unified faith?

Although Newman was not aware of the complexities of the issue as it is appreciated today, he was sensitive to the radically different ways people think. He thought that such different intellectual perspectives were a value, and consequently he argued for legitimate theological pluralism (chapter 3). The dialectics of multiple perspectives, furthermore, fitted quite compatibly with his sacramental notion of the church (chapter 4). The question to consider now is whether the unity of faith is ensured primarily by linguistic formulations (e.g., commonly accepted creeds) or by some other parameter.

Thomas Aquinas long ago noted that the object of faith is the *reality* behind doctrinal formulations and toward which they point. Could it be that the contemporary pluralism is reminding us how elusive is the task of formulating an understanding of the divine reality in a wording suitable to everyone's understanding? Might not distinct and tensive formulations of the Christian faith be a *desideratum*? Let us take, as an example, the belief in the Incarnation. No one aspect of the human life of Jesus adequately reveals to us his divine nature. We must deal with the entire range of ways he experienced human life and, consequently, the range of ways we experience him. The various expressions of his Galilean ministry, the self-emptying on the Cross, the exaltation of that human life in the Resurrection, and many other features, all together and each needing the others, are for us the one self-revealing image of the divinity. A Christology based on his preaching ministry alone, for instance, gives an incomplete picture of who Jesus is. On the other hand, when the multiple human experiences of Jesus are taken together in order to get the fullest picture, a dialectical tension is set in motion: the birth and death (of God), his *doxa* (acts of power) and *kenosis* (self-emptying), his divine knowledge and his growth in knowledge. Only by taking all of these experiences together, and by not retreating intellectually from any of the tensions, can we come to deal with the question he asked: "Who do you say I am?" And if the responses of Jesus' first followers are to be a guide for us—the responses preserved in the entire New Testament—then the dialectical tension ought to be kept. For Paul, Jesus is revealed as Lord in the Resurrection; for Matthew, he is Lord in his virginal birth; for Mark, he is revealed as Lord already in the ministry. We are richer today because the Christology of the New Testament does not present a single synthetic view but a multiplicity of views. Nevertheless, in all cases the object of scriptural witness is the one Jesus who posed the question.

For Newman, the revelation that the church is always attempting to fathom is the reality of the one self-revealing God. The fact that people bring such different viewpoints to the faith, and express themselves so variously, is a recognition of the inexhaustible mystery lying behind our understanding of the faith. Newman was not content to leave it there, however. These viewpoints must interact in what I have called a "dialectics of discourse," so that extravagances in one or another direction can be avoided. The end result, however, cannot hope to achieve what the New Testament itself did not achieve: a single synthetic formulation. As Mark's Gospel is in dialectical tension with John's, so also the pluralistic interpretations of the faith can be accepted as a healthy tension in Newman's idea of the church. The dialectics are not just a path to a goal beyond themselves, but they are already, in and of themselves, an experience of the ever-elusive nature of the divine.[17]

Newman urged the dialogical process in the church of his day, and he would press for it today if he could. This process is all the more important when one notes the growing sense of retrenchment in Roman Catholicism. The Second Vatican Council, as mentioned earlier, did open up the church, and some church authorities fear that too much chaos (i.e., doctrinal deviations, local innovations) has come in the door. The danger is that a new kind of ultramontanism might emerge. Newman would resist that possibility, not because the loss of order is good or because an open dialogue needs another chance to get it right this time, but because the experience of dialogue itself is already the engagement of the elusive Truth. There will come a time, not here below, when God will be known directly and in full light. During the present pilgrimage of the church, however, and in the world as we know it, the truth is experienced in the dialogue, in shadows and images as it were, recalling the epitaph Newman chose for himself, *ex umbris et imaginibus in veritatem.*[18]

Abbreviations

Apol.	*Apologia pro Vita Sua*
Ari.	*The Arians of the Fourth Century*
Ath.	*Select Treatises of St. Athanasius*, 2 vols.
AW	*Autobiographical Writings*
Bibl.	*The Theological Papers of John Henry Newman on Biblical Inspiration and on Infallibility*
Call.	*Callista*
CF	*On Consulting the Faithful in Matters of Doctrine*
DA	*Discussions and Arguments*
Dev.	*An Essay on the Development of Christian Doctrine*
Diff.	*Certain Difficulties Felt by Anglicans in Catholic Teaching*
	Volume 1: *Twelve Lectures Addressed to the Anglican Party of 1833*
	Volume 2: *Letter to Pusey* and *Letter to the Duke of Norfolk*
Ess.	*Essays Critical and Historical*, 2 vols.
Faith	*The Theological Papers of John Henry Newman on Faith and Certainty*
GA	*An Essay in Aid of a Grammar of Assent*
HS	*Historical Sketches*, 3 vols.
Idea	*The Idea of a University, Defined and Illustrated*
JHN	John Henry Newman
Letters	*The Letters and Diaries of John Henry Newman*
OS	*Sermons Preached on Various Occasions*
Prepos.	*Lectures on the Present Position of Catholics in England*
PS	*Parochial and Plain Sermons*, 8 vols.
US	*Fifteen Sermons Preached before the University of Oxford*
VM	*The Via Media of the Anglican Church*
	Volume 1: *Lectures on the Prophetical Office of the Church*
	Volume 2: *Occasional Letters and Tracts*

Notes

PROLOGUE

1. Henri Bergson, *The Two Sources of Morality and Religion* (London: Macmillan and Co., 1935).
2. Leonard and Arlene Swidler, eds., *Women Priests: A Catholic Commentary on the Vatican Declaration* (New York: Paulist, 1977). For the Vatican Declaration's use of Thomas Aquinas, see Edward Jeremy Miller, "Aquinas and the Ordination of Women," *New Blackfriars* 61 (1980): 185–90.
3. Volumes 11–31 of *The Letters and Diaries of John Henry Newman* (London: Thomas Nelson and Sons, and Oxford: Clarendon Press, 1961–), covering Newman's Roman Catholic period, were completed under the editorship of C. S. Dessain. Of the first ten volumes, covering the Anglican period, six have been completed. My own review of a segment of the series may be found in *Thomist* 38 (1974): 372–75.
4. *DA*, p. 295.
5. See David DeLaura, ed., *Victorian Prose: A Guide to Research* (New York: Modern Language Association of America, 1973). The continuing series, *Newman Studien* (Nuremberg: Glock and Lutz), compiled by Werner Becker and Heinrich Fries et al., provides listings of recent scholarship.
6. See W. H. van de Pol, *De Kerk in het Leven en Denken van Newman* (Nijkerk: Callenbach, 1936); Norbert Schiffers, *Die Einheit der Kirche nach Newman* (Düsseldorf: Patmos, 1956). Stanislas Jaki, *Les Tendances Nouvelle de l'Ecclésiologie* (Rome: Herder, 1957), devotes a section to Newman, as does Louis Bouyer, *L'Église de Dieu* (Paris: Editions du Cerf, 1970). Jan Walgrave has a short essay, "Le sens ecclésial du Newman," *Dictionnaire de Spiritualité Ascétique et Mystique* IV/1:433–36. See also Edward Jeremy Miller, "Newman's Dialogical Vision of the Church," *Louvain Studies* 8 (1981): 318–31.
7. See *Letters and Correspondence of John Henry Newman during His Life in the English Church,* ed. Anne Mozley, 2 vols. (London: Longmans, Green, and Co., 1903); *Correspondence of John Henry Newman with John Keble and Others,* ed. at the Birmingham Oratory (London: Longmans, Green, and Co., 1917); *Letters of John Henry Newman,* ed. Derek Stanford and Muriel Spark (London: Peter Owen, 1957).
8. In the present study Newman's spelling has been retained as well as his punctuation, except when the punctuation might confuse a modern

reader. The initial word of a quotation has been capitalized or not in accordance with current conventions of style. Unusual usages have been acknowledged with *sic.*

CHAPTER ONE

1. John Coulson, *Newman and the Common Tradition* (Oxford: Clarendon Press, 1970).
2. Wilfrid Ward, *The Life of John Henry Cardinal Newman*, 2 vols. (London: Longmans, Green, and Co., 1912); Meriol Trevor, *Newman: Light in Winter* and *Newman: The Pillar of the Cloud* (London: Macmillan and Co., 1962). Trevor's abridgment of these two volumes, *Newman's Journey* (Glasgow: Collins, 1974; reprint, Huntingdon, Ind.: Our Sunday Visitor, 1985), is the best "short" introduction to Newman.
3. JHN to Richard William Church, 16 June 1872, *Letters,* 26:115.
4. *Prepos.,* p. 278.
5. JHN, memorandum, 28 December 1834, *Letters and Correspondence,* ed. Mozley, 1:366.
6. *GA,* p. 65.
7. *GA,* p. 62.
8. *Prepos.,* p. 283.
9. *GA,* p. 269.
10. *Prepos.,* p. 284.
11. Some critics of Newman's conversion have focused on the final chapter of the *Apologia,* wherein he describes infallible teaching in Catholicism. They charge that he accepted Catholic authority merely to overcome his dread of religious skepticism. W. B. Selbie, *The Life of A. M. Fairbairn* (London: Hodder and Stoughton, 1914) is representative. The final chapter of the *Apologia,* however, presupposes the earlier discussion of first principles that characterized Newman's Anglican period and remained with him. Catholic authority was not a deflection from these principles but rather their logical extension. See Newman's notes in *The Theological Papers of John Henry Newman on Faith and Certainty,* ed. Hugo de Achaval and J. Derek Holmes (Oxford: Clarendon Press, 1976), pp. 140–57.
12. *Apol.,* p. 4.
13. *GA,* p. 63.
14. The first half of the *Grammar of Assent* could be subtitled: Can I believe as if I saw? As sight fills the imagination with vivid notice of objects, so conscience fills the imagination with its vivid and duty-bound images. Assents follow on apprehensions and are stronger as the apprehensions are the more vivid. When one believes in God through "real apprehension," it is as if God "is seen." See *GA,* p. 102. Edward Caswall wrote in the flyleaf of his copy of the book this summary from Newman: "Object of the book is twofold. In the first part shows [*sic*] that you can believe what you cannot understand. In the second part that you can believe what you cannot absolutely prove." Caswall's book is in the Archives of the Birmingham Oratory, Birmingham, England.

15. *GA*, p. 117.

16. *Apol.*, p. 27.

17. Newman describes style as a "thinking out into language," and a writer's mental attitudes and force of logic "are imaged in the tenderness, or energy, or richness of his language." See *Idea*, pp. 276, 278.

18. *Dev.*, p. 325.

19. *Apol.*, p. 48.

20. *John Henry Newman: Commemorative Essays on the Occasion of the Centenary of His Cardinalate*, ed. M. K. Stolz (Rome: Tipografia Guerra, 1979), p. 101. Newman's full acceptance speech upon receiving the ceremonial letter of nomination for the cardinalate, the so-called Biglietto speech, is given on pp. 99–105.

21. Newman claimed as a false assumption "that whatever can be thought can be adequately expressed in words." *GA*, p. 264.

22. *GA*, p. 34.

23. On the role of apprehension and the decision to act, which is all-important in religion, Newman notes, "Not that real apprehension, as such, impels to action, any more than notional; but it excites and stimulates the affections and passions by bringing home facts to them as motive causes." *GA*, p. 12.

24. *GA*, p. 35.

25. *GA*, p. 36.

26. Bernard Lonergan, *Insight* (San Francisco: Harper and Row, 1978), p. x. In *A Second Collection*, ed. William Ryan and Bernard Tyrrell (Philadelphia: Westminster, 1974), Lonergan acknowledges Newman's influence. See pp. 38, 263. Newman calls firmness of assent the work of the illative sense. Lonergan calls it a virtually unconditioned judgment, i.e., there are no further pertinent questions to pose, such that the conclusion is no longer conditioned by a prior supposition needing response. See also Lonergan's *Method in Theology* (New York: Herder and Herder, 1972), p. 162.

27. *GA*, pp. 92–93.

28. *GA*, p. 94.

29. *Prepos.*, p. 224.

30. *GA*, p. 160.

31. JHN to William Froude, 29 April 1879, *Letters*, 29:115. A correspondence over many years with Froude led Newman to formulate the positions presented systematically in the book. The Froude materials, as well as Newman's contrast with John Locke's philosophy, have been analyzed by William Fey, *Faith and Doubt: The Unfolding of Newman's Thought on Certainty* (Shepherdstown, W. Va.: Patmos Press, 1976).

32. *GA*, p. 278.

33. *GA*, p. 282.

34. *GA*, p. 293.

35. *GA*, p. 345.

36. JHN to W. Froude, 29 April 1879, *Letters*, 29:116. The entire letter to Froude, pp. 112–20, is one of Newman's best commentaries on his own *Grammar of Assent*.

37. Newman goes so far as to claim that "the antecedent probability is even found to triumph over contrary evidence, as well as to sustain what agrees with it." See *Dev.*, p. 114.

38. *Apol.*, p. 20.
39. *GA*, p. 317.
40. JHN to Henry James Coleridge, 5 February 1871, *Letters*, 25:280.
41. Newman describes conscience as being "so constituted that, if obeyed, it becomes clearer in its injunctions, and wider in their range, and corrects and completes the accidental feebleness of its initial teachings. See *GA*, p. 390. The same theme is met twenty-five years earlier in *Dev.*: "Obedience to conscience, even supposing conscience ill-informed, tends to the improvement of our moral nature, and ultimately of our knowledge" (p. 87).
42. *Apol.*, p. 119.
43. *Apol.*, p. 186. Newman's Anglican contemporary, Dean Richard W. Church, corroborated Newman's description of his patient deliberations. See *The Oxford Movement* (London: Macmillan, 1891; reprint, Chicago: Univ. of Chicago Press, 1970), p. 147.
44. Jan Walgrave, *Le Développement du Dogme* (Paris: Casterman, 1957), p. 11.
45. *AW*, p. 272.
46. Walgrave, *Le Dévelop.*, p. 14.
47. Notice the way Newman has contrasted science and literature. "Science is universal, literature is personal; science uses words merely as symbols, but literature uses language in its full compass, as including phraseology, idiom, style, composition, rhythm, eloquence, and whatever other properties are included in it." *Dev.*, p. 275.

CHAPTER TWO

1. For a biblical approach, see Hans Küng, *The Church* (London: Burns and Oates, 1967). A more philosophical method is followed by Karl Rahner, *Foundations of Christian Faith* (New York: Seabury, 1978).
2. *Apol.*, p. 241.
3. Many of Newman's early sermons stress self-reflection as the keenest perception of evil's extent. See *PS*, 1:173.
4. *Faith*, p. 139.
5. *GA*, p. 109.
6. *GA*, p. 110.
7. Friedrich von Schlegel, *Philosophie des Lebens*, ed. Jean-Jacques Anstett, Ernst Behler, and Hans Eichner (Munich: Verlag Ferdinand Schoningh, 1969), 10:47. See Jan Walgrave, "La Conscience Morale et la Specificité de la Morale Chrétienne selon J. H. Newman," *Studia Moralia* 14 (1976): 105–19.
8. *PS*, 1:216.
9. *PS*, 1:42.
10. *PS*, 2:105.
11. *PS*, 5:17, 241.
12. *Faith*, p. 154.
13. *Faith*, p. 87.
14. "I begin by assuming . . . the world . . . totus in maligno positus est." JHN to William Samuel Lilly, 25 July 1876, *Letters*, 28:95.
15. See Lonergan, *Method*, pp. 76–81.

16. *GA*, p. 423.
17. *GA*, p. 431.
18. JHN to Canon John Walker, 6 July 1864, *Letters*, 21:146.
19. *GA*, p. 429. Note Newman's letter of 12 October 1848 to Catherine Ward on the roles of reason and will, *Letters*, 12: 289–90.
20. JHN to Frederic Rogers (Lord Blachford), 6 July 1872, *Letters*, 26:131.
21. JHN to Henry Arthur Woodgate, 22 August 1872, *Letters*, 26:152.
22. JHN to Eliza Margaret (Izy) Froude, 9 April 1873, *Letters*, 26:287–88.
23. JHN to Arthur Arnold, 20 September 1872, *Letters*, 26:173.
24. JHN to Richard Holt Hutton, 18 June 1864, *Letters*, 21:121.
25. *Ari.*, p. 76.
26. *Dev.*, p. 87.
27. JHN to an unknown correspondent, 10 September 1875, *Letters*, 27:353. The letter quotes *Apol.*, p. 9.
28. JHN to an unknown correspondent, 19 September 1875, *Letters*, 27:357–58.
29. JHN to Hutton, 18 June 1864, *Letters*, 21:122.
30. JHN to an unknown correspondent, 4 February 1867, *Letters*, 23:49.
31. *Dev.*, p. 90. Newman gives an extended argument from the notion of prophet in his letter to William Pope, 15 April 1853, *Letters*, 15:349.
32. JHN to J. H. Willis Nevins, 19 June 1874, *Letters*, 27:79.
33. *Dev.*, p. 92.
34. *Dev.*, p. 78.
35. The tests are theological instruments, controversial and debatable; they do not have the practical character needed to keep a church united, nor are they warrants for correct churchwide decisions. Newman describes the seven tests in *Dev.*, pp. 171–206.
36. The judgment on the *broad issue* is similarly the strategy of the *Essay on Development*, even though it tracks particular doctrines as it works out the seven tests (notes) of genuine developments. Nicholas Lash faults psychological readings of the *Essay on Development*, such as Jan Walgrave's *Le Développement du Dogme*. Newman "built up a powerful case for trusting that [the Roman Catholic] Church's authoritative judgments but this is not the same thing for claiming that those judgments are automatically justified because they are the judgment of church authority, whatever be the evidence of exegesis, history and theology." Lash, "Second Thoughts on Walgrave's 'Newman,' " *Downside Review* 87 (1969): 343. For those aspects of doctrine that were still open questions, it is true that Newman gave priority to historical investigation and theological reasoning. Few championed theological debate and intellectual freedom as much as he. Lash's contention that this is Newman's constant method, however, is not supported by Newman's letters. In them Newman contends that church teaching is true because it is an infallible oracle, and that hypothesis alone answers to the need of personal conscience for a sure hold on revealed doctrine. See *Letters*, 18:333–36, 18:438, 22:160, 25:30–32, 27:79. See also *Dev.*, p. 86.
37. Newman's position that the church is able to speak unerringly, at a time of crisis, is exactly Karl Rahner's argument against Hans Küng's concept of indefectibility. See Küng's position in *Infallible? An Inquiry* (Garden City:

Doubleday, 1971). Rahner's response to Küng's German text first appeared in *Stimmen der Zeit* 95 (1970): 361–77, and was reprinted in English in *Homiletic and Pastoral Review* 71 (1971):11–27.

38. Newman thought that Edward Pusey's *Eirenicon* carried the attitude, "Enumerate the doctrines I must believe and I will say if I can become one of you." JHN to Pusey, 23 March 1867 and 16 August 1868, *Letters*, 23:105, 24:125. Newman gives a clear instance of his own situation in relation to the doctrine of transubstantiation. "I did not believe the doctrine till I was a Catholic. I had no difficulty in believing it, as soon as I believed that the Catholic Roman Church was the oracle of God." *Apol.*, p. 239.

39. The *Apologia* will guide the account. For other accounts of the Tractarian movement, Newman's role in it, and his conversion to Roman Catholicism, see Church, *Oxford Movement;* Sidney Leslie Ollard, *A Short History of the Oxford Movement* (London: Mowbray and Co., 1915); Christopher Dawson, *The Spirit of the Oxford Movement* (London: Sheed and Ward, 1933); Eugene Fairweather, ed., *The Oxford Movement* (New York: Oxford Univ. Press, 1964); M. R. O'Connell, *The Oxford Conspirators* (London: Macmillan, 1969). The following reviews appeared when the *Apologia* was first published: *American Quarterly Church Review* 17 (1865): 661–85; *British and Foreign Evangelical Review* 13 (1864): 771–803; *Christian Examiner* 79 (1865): 343–63; *Christian Observer* 63 (1864): 661–85; *Christian Remembrancer* 3 (1864): 162–93; *Fraser's Magazine* 70 (1864): 265–303; *Union Review* 2 (1864): 379–401, 481–505, 506–17.

40. *Apol.*, p. 70.

41. *VM*, 1:16.

42. *Apol.*, p. 106.

43. *Apol.*, p. 114.

44. *Apol.*, p. 117.

45. Newman's rejection of the Via Media construct was reconfirmed in 1841 when he was translating St. Athanasius. Here he perceived that the full Arian position was the Protestant position, the semi-Arian party was in a Via Media location, and Rome was then where it is now. See *Apol.*, p. 139.

46. "*It is not written to prove the truth* of Catholicism, as it distinctily observes (e.g., in the first 4 pages) but to answer an *objection against* Catholicism. The historical *fact* that the present Roman Church is the continuation of the Primitive, is so luminous, that there would be nothing left but for a man to enter it at once, *except* for certain objections. Those objections the Book professes to answer, and they are these: that portions of the doctrine of the present Roman Church are not taught in the Primitive." JHN to Catherine Ward, 18 November 1848, *Letters*, 12:332.

47. See JHN to Catherine Ward, 18 November 1848, *Letters*, 12:335–36; JHN to Miss Rowe, 16 September 1873, *Letters*, 26:366.

48. John Henry Newman Papers, vol. 4 (1845–50), Birmingham Oratory Archives.

49. See *Dev.*, p. 252; *Ari.*, pp. 392–93.

50. The Anglican Branch Theory considered the Greek church a living continuation, but Newman remarked that it had not held a general council in a thousand years, and he thought it in a state of suspended animation. See

Letters, 24:390. A more extended treatment of the Greek church is given in *Diff.*, 1:330–62.

51. JHN to Henry Wilberforce, 7 March 1849, *Letters*, 13:78–79.

52. The literature on doctrinal development is vast. See Jan Walgrave, *Unfolding Revelation* (Philadelphia: Westminster, 1972); Nicholas Lash, *Newman on Development: The Search for an Explanation in History* (Shepherdstown, W. Va.: Patmos Press, 1975); Jaroslav Pelikan, *Development of Christian Doctrine* (New Haven: Yale Univ. Press, 1969); George Lindbeck, "The Problem of Doctrinal Development and Contemporary Protestant Theology," *Concilium* 21 (1967): 133–49; Karl Rahner, "The Development of Dogma," *Theological Investigations* (Baltimore: Helicon, 1961), 1:39–77.

53. JHN to F. R. Wegg-Prosser, 22 February 1852, *Letters*, 15:42.

54. JHN to Anthony John Hanmer, 18 November 1849, *Letters*, 13:296.

55. The lure of this world and the competition it poses to spiritual values is a theme that runs through the eight volumes of the *Parochial and Plain Sermons*. Note, in particular, the sermons "The Church, A Home for the Lonely" and "The Invisible World" in volume 4. The sway of the world over the intellect is also a theme of the *Idea of a University*.

56. *PS*, 4:186.

57. *PS*, 6:288.

58. *PS*, 6:195.

59. *PS*, 6:280.

60. *PS*, 6:289.

61. The sermon, "Encouragement to Faith," develops the need of supports for one's faith. *PS*, 3:236.

62. *PS*, 4:209–10.

63. *PS*, 3:222.

64. The question can be posed to the New Testament canon itself whether the "early Catholicism" of the later writings, e.g., Timothy and Titus, is a legitimate development or a corruption from Corinthians. See Rudolf Schnackenburg, *The Church in the New Testament* (New York: Herder and Herder, 1965). What Newman means by the patristic church expressing the meaning of the New Testament, Lonergan intends by "doctrine" having a constitutive function of meaning. See Lonergan, *Method*, p. 298.

65. JHN to Robert Charles Jenkins, 4 December 1870, *Letters*, 25:239.

66. JHN to Lord Charles Thynne, 3 February 1852, *Letters*, 15:27.

67. JHN to Daniel Radford, 15 October 1862, *Letters*, 20:306.

68. Practically every sermon in the *Parochial and Plain Sermons* exhibits the theme of holiness. After he became a Roman Catholic, Newman did not write out his Sunday sermons, only those for special occasions; they are contained in *Sermons Preached on Various Occasions*.

69. JHN to John Rickards Mozley, 19 April 1874, *Letters*, 27:55.

70. JHN to Miss Bristowe, 15 April 1866, *Letters*, 22:212–13.

71. See *Prepos.*, p. 54, 62, 75. Newman describes the "cure of souls" (the classic term for spiritual ministry) in the Anglican church as an engagement with no means to carry it to effect. See JHN to Mrs. William Froude, 15 February 1846, *Letters*, 11:113.

72. JHN to Wilberforce, 8 June 1846, *Letters*, 11:175. See also *Diff.*, 1:16. New-

man's strongest condemnation of Anglicanism came in his letter to the *Globe* newapaper, 28 June 1862, written to deny the rumor he was leaving Roman Catholicism; he called Protestantism the "dreariest of possible religions" and said the Anglican service made him shiver. *Letters*, 20:215–6. But in a letter of 21 July 1862 to a friend, Charles Crawley, he said his harsh language was calculated to show not only his reason for being opposed to reconversion but also his *feelings*. *Letters*, 20:242.

73. JHN to Robert Ornsby, 8 March 1861, *Letters*, 19:480. For Newman's observations on other Anglican authorities, see JHN to William Gowan Todd, 12 August 1850, *Letters*, 14:39.

74. *Diff.*, 1:6. See also pp. 8, 22.

75. These lectures were subsequently published as volume 1 of *Certain Difficulties Felt by Anglicans in Catholic Teaching*.

76. *Diff.*, vol. 1, lecture 3. The entire lecture considers this question, drawing upon the distinction, *ex opere operato* and *ex opere operantis*.

77. *Apol.*, n. E, pp. 339–42.

78. Edward Bouverie Pusey, *Legal Force of the Judgment of the Privy Council in re Fendall v. Wilson* (London: Parker, 1864), p. 36.

79. H. E. Manning, *The Working of the Holy Spirit in the Church of England: A Letter to the Rev. E. B. Pusey, D. D.* (London, 1864), reprinted in *England and Christendom* (London: Longmans, Green, and Co., 1867), pp. 83–103. See Newman's letter of 21 December 1866 to Charlotte Wood, *Letters*, 22:328.

80. *Diff.*, 2:11.

81. JHN to Isaac Williams, 7 June 1863, *Letters*, 20:460.

82. JHN to John Cowley Fisher, 22 April 1875, *Letters*, 27:284.

83. JHN to an unknown correspondent, 1 May 1870, *Letters*, 25:118–19. See also JHN to Frederick George Lee, 21 November 1869, *Letters*, 24:380.

84. *Ess.*, 2:87.

85. *Apol.*, p. 341; *Ess.*, 2:77.

86. Louis Bouyer, *Newman: His Life and Spirituality*, trans. J. Lewis May (New York: Kenedy and Sons, 1958), p. 280, incorrectly notes that Newman was ordained by Cardinal Giacomo Fransoni *sub conditione*. See John J. Hughes, "Two English Cardinals on Anglican Orders," *Journal of Ecumenical Studies* 4 (1964): 1–26.

87. See JHN to Simeon Wilberforce O'Neill, 11 August 1865, *Letters*, 22:30.

88. JHN to Coleridge, 6 Februrary 1868, *Letters*, 24:29. See also *Ess.*, 2:80.

89. JHN to Thomas Wimberley Mossman, 17 September 1868, *Letters*, 24:147–48. See also *Ess.*, 2:80, 83.

90. JHN to Mrs. W. Froude, 30 November 1856, *Letters*, 17:467. Pusey had always hoped that Newman's conversion would make Roman Catholics see what is good in Anglicans. See Pusey's letter to Keble in H. P. Liddon, *Life of Edward Bouverie Pusey* (London: Longmans, Green, and Co., 1893), pp. 460–63.

91. JHN to Ambrose Phillipps de Lisle, 3 March 1866, *Letters*, 22:170. See also 12:234.

92. JHN to Wilberforce, 24 August 1864, *Letters*, 21:210.

93. Coulson, *Common Tradition*, p. 162.

94. JHN to John Campbell Shairp, 18 December 1870, *Letters*, 25:250.

95. JHN to J. P. Taylor, 15 December 1869, *Letters*, 24:391.

CHAPTER THREE

1. David Tracy, *The Analogical Imagination* (New York: Crossroad, 1981), p. 69. Tracy wishes to establish warrants for truth claims. He argues that all good theological discourse is a drive from and to its "publics," i.e., society, the church, and the academy. The warrants are worked out with these three publics in mind. Fundamental theology primarily relates to the academy, systematic theology to the church, and practical theology to the public of society.

2. Yves Congar, *Lay People in the Church* (Westminster, Md.: Newman Press, 1967), p. xi.

3. Quoted in Trevor, *Newman: The Light in Winter*, p. 408, and in *CF*, p. 41.

4. Quoted in Congar, *Lay People*, p. 12.

5. *In Sent.* VI (editio Quaracci), p. 1, art. unicus, q. 4.

6. Congar, *Lay People*, pp. 17–18.

7. JHN, memorandum, 22 May 1859, *Letters*, 19:140–41. This memorandum notes that these were not the verbatim words but did capture the sense of Ullathorne's and Newman's comments.

8. Congar, *Lay People*, p. 41.

9. Ibid., p. 45.

10. *AW*, p. 259.

11. *Prepos.*, pp. 389–90.

12. Congar, *Lay People*, passim.

13. Edward Schillebeeckx, *Layman in the Church* (New York: Alba, 1963), p. 36.

14. Edward Jeremy Miller, "Confirmation as Ecclesial Commissioning," *Louvain Studies* 10 (1984): 106–21. Extensive bibliography is provided by Aiden Kavanagh, *The Shape of Baptism* (New York: Pueblo, 1978), and by Murphy Center, ed., *Made Not Born* (Notre Dame: University Press, 1976).

15. *Prepos.*, p. 381.

16. For his views on Archbishop Paul Cullen of Dublin, see Newman's three letters to Ornsby of 1 July 1860, 23 July 1862, and 2 December 1864, *Letters*, 19:379, 20:241, 21:331. See also JHN to Bartholomew Woodlock, 4 March 1868, *Letters*, 24:46.

17. JHN to William Monsell, 6 September 1863, *Letters*, 20:518.

18. JHN to Sir John Simeon, 29 January 1865, *Letters*, 21:398.

19. JHN to Monsell, 12 January 1865, *Letters*, 21:384–85.

20. JHN to Thomas William Allies, 30 November 1864, *Letters*, 21:327.

21. Newman once remarked about Manning, "I am inclined to think that the Archbishop considers only an ignorant laity to be manageable." JHN to J. Spencer Northcote, 17 April 1872, *Letters*, 26:66.

22. JHN to Edward Healy Thompson, 5 January 1865, *Letters*, 21:374.

23. JHN to Ornsby, 2 December 1864, *Letters*, 21:331.

24. JHN to Thomas Harper, 10 February 1869, *Letters*, 24:213.

25. JHN to Emily Bowles, 30 April 1871, *Letters*, 25:327.

26. *Ari.*, p. 445. Portions of the *Rambler* article are reprinted as n. 5 in the appendix of the 1871 edition of the *Arians of the Fourth Century*.

27. Acton's review of Pierre-Adolphe Chéruel, *Marie Stuart and Catherine de Medici*, appeared in the *Rambler* 22 (1858): 135. For a listing of every article to appear in the *Rambler* as well as an informative essay about the

magazine, see *Wellesley Index to Victorian Periodicals: 1824–1900*, ed. Walter Houghton (Toronto: Univ. of Toronto Press, 1972) 2:732–84.

28. Sir. John Acton wrote to Richard Simpson of Newman's real feelings: "I had a 3 hours' talk with the venerable Noggs who came out at last with his real sentiments to an extent which startled me, with respect both to things and persons, as H E [the cardinal], Ward, Dalgairns, etc., etc., natural inclination of men in power to tyrannise, ignorance and presumption of our would-be theologians, in short, what you or I would comfortably say over a glass of whiskey. . . . He thinks the move provoked both by the hope of breaking down the R. [*Rambler*] and by jealousy of Döllinger." *Letters*, 18:559, n. 3.

29. Quoted in *Letters*, 19:129–30, n. 3.

30. Dr. John Gillow to JHN, 15 May 1859, *Letters*, 19:134, n. 3.

31. Pope Pius IX, in his encyclical of 2 February 1847, *Ubi Primum*, asked local bishops to assess the "devotion" of their clergy and laity to the Immaculate Conception. In a letter to W. G. Ward, 11 March 1849, Newman gives his sense of the request; see *Letters*, 13:81–82. For his recollection during the *Rambler* affair, see JHN to Gillow, 16 May 1859, *Letters*, 19:135.

32. See JHN to Gillow, 16 May 1859, *Letters*, 19:136.

33. JHN to Bishop William Bernard Ullathorne, 16 May 1859, *Letters*, 19:137. Ullathorne held that the only value in consulting the laity was to prove that a doctrine preexisted in the mind of the magisterium.

34. Newman's 22 May 1859 memorandum of the meeting is in *Letters*, 19:141. See also JHN to Thompson, 29 May 1859, *Letters*, 19:150.

35. V. F. Blehl, "Newman's Delation," *Dublin Review* 234 (1960–61): 296–305. Newman's memorandum of 14 January 1860 about the delation is in *Letters*, 19:279–83.

36. The only complete English text is *On Consulting the Faithful in Matters of Doctrine*, ed. John Coulson (London: Chapman, 1961). It is no longer in print. In German, see "Über das Zeugnis der Laien in Fragen des Blaubens," *Ausgewählte Werke Newmans*, ed. Matthias Laros and Werner Becker (Mainz: Grünewald, 1959), 4:255–92. See also the introduction and translation by Otto Karrer, "Uber die Befragung der Glaubigen in Dingen der christlichen Lehre," *Hochland* 40 (1947–48): 401–14, 549–57.

37. *CF*, p. 55.

38. *CF*, p. 63.

39. *Ari.*, p. 467, n. 5. Giovanni Perrone is quoted as numbering "sensus fidelium" among the "instruments of tradition."

40. *CF*, pp. 75–76.

41. *CF*, p. 77.

42. *CF*, p. 76.

43. *Ari.*, p. 467.

44. *CF*, p. 106.

45. JHN to William John Copeland, 20 April 1873, *Letters*, 26:294.

46. Ignaz von Döllinger, *Der Papst und das Concil* (Leipzig: Steinacker, 1869), originally a series of articles in the *Augsburger Allgemeine Zeitung* under the pseudonym of Janus; also published in English as *The Pope and the Council* (London: Rivingtons, 1869).

47. JHN to Pusey, 4 August 1867, *Letters*, 23:284. Pusey sought an "irenic ecumenism."

48. JHN to Acton, 17 September 1862, *Letters*, 20:271.

49. JHN to William Maskell, 12 February 1871, *Letters*, 25:284.

50. JHN to an unknown correspondent, 13 March 1866, *Letters*, 22:181.

51. "I am opposed to laymen writing Theology, on the same principle that I am against amateur doctors and still more lawyers—not because they are laymen, but because they are *autodidaktoi*." JHN to John Moore Capes, 19 January 1857, *Letters*, 17:504. From this statement one can conclude Newman would support lay theologians if they had the requisite training. See his 17 April 1857 letter to W. G. Ward and Ward's teaching of dogmatic theology at St. Edmunds, Ware, *Letters*, 18:18.

52. JHN to Mrs. F. R. Ward, 8 May 1859, *Letters*, 19:128.

53. The advertisement is given in *Letters*, 19:88.

54. JHN to Bowles, 19 May 1863, *Letters*, 20:447.

55. JHN, memorandum, 4 March 1868, *Letters*, 24:45–46.

56. JHN to Acton, 31 December 1858, *Letters*, 18:562.

57. JHN to Peter Gallwey, 26 February 1865, *Letters*, 21:422–23.

58. JHN to Coleridge, 16 June 1865, *Letters*, 21:496.

59. JHN to Wilberforce, 12 August 1868, *Letters*, 24:120.

60. For good analyses of ultramontanism, see Roger Aubert, ed., *History of the Church*, vol. 8, *The Church in the Age of Liberalism* (New York: Crossroad, 1981), pp. 304–15; and J. Derek Holmes, *More Roman Than Rome: English Catholicism in the Nineteenth Century* (Shephardstown, W. Va.: Patmos Press, 1978).

61. Regarding Anglican writings included in the Uniform Edition, Newman added corrective footnotes and appendixes on matters he viewed differently as a Roman Catholic. Charles Stephen Dessain, *John Henry Newman* (London: Adam and Charles Black, 1971), pp. 170–74, gives the full listing; Dessain's book is the best introduction to the intellectual content of Newman's writings.

62. *Dev.*, p. 90.

63. *Diff.*, 1:315.

64. *Idea*, p. 47.

65. W. G. Ward collected into book format a series of his *Dublin Review* articles and published them as *The Authority of Doctrinal Decisions Which Are Not Definitions of Faith, Considered in a Short Series of Essays* (London: Burns and Oates, 1866).

66. JHN to W. G. Ward, 9 May 1867, *Letters*, 23:217.

67. Ignatius Ryder, *Idealism in Theology: A Review of Dr. Ward's Scheme of Dogmatic Authority* (London: Longmans, Green, and Co., 1867). Ryder's mother was a sister-in-law of Archbishop Edward Manning, the close ally of Ward. The Ryder-Ward debate has been ably treated by Damian McElrath in *The Syllabus of Pius IX: Some Reactions in England* (Louvain: Publications Universitaires, 1964).

68. JHN to W. G. Ward, 30 April 1867, *Letters*, 23:197; see also 23:189–90. Pope John XXIII's encyclical letter convoking the Second Vatican Council, *Ad Petri Cathedram*, refers this famous phrase to Newman and quotes with

approval his argument in *Diff.*, vol. 1, lecture 10, that legitimate diversity can exist within Catholic thinking. *Acta Apostolicae Sedis* 51 (1959): 513. Vatican II's pastoral constitution, *Gaudium et Spes*, 92, quotes in turn the pope's use of Newman's phrase. The Latin phrase itself comes from an unknown patristic source.

69. JHN to Maskell, 12 February 1876, *Letters*, 28:24–25. Note Newman's words of 25 February 1875 to Jenkins regarding papal infallibility: "There are many open questions; and partizans of the Pope, as if to compensate for his temporal loses, wish to close them in favor of the extremest sense of them." *Letters*, 27:235.

70. *Diff.*, 2:79.

71. Conserving the past does not mean a simplistic repetition of classical texts. The Arian party argued that the *homoousios* of the Nicean party was not in the Bible. Athanasius admitted it was not there, but that its meaning captured the sense and direction of the New Testament texts.

72. *Idea*, p. 469. Certain Thomistic positions were condemned by the archbishop of Paris in 1277.

73. *Idea*, p. 470.

74. JHN to W. G. Ward, 18 February 1866, *Letters*, 22:157.

75. *Diff.*, 1:303.

76. *Idea*, p. 467.

77. *Idea*, p. 478.

78. JHN to Coleridge, 29 April 1869, *Letters*, 24:247. Newman drafted but never sent this letter.

79. JHN to Monsell, 13 January 1863, *Letters*, 20:391.

80. *Apol.*, p. 267.

81. JHN to Henry Nutcombe Oxenham, 9 November 1865, *Letters*, 22:99.

82. *Dev.*, p. 140.

83. Walgrave, *Unfolding Revelation*, p. 41. An extended précis of his book may be found in Edward Jeremy Miller, *Thomist* 37 (1973):378–83.

84. JHN to Wilberforce, 20 August 1869, *Letters*, 24:316.

85. JHN to John Wallis, 23 April 1867, *Letters*, 23:187.

86. JHN to Bishop David Moriarty, 1 November 1870, *Letters*, 25:223. Moriarty, ordinary of Kerry, was one of the few bishops not in the ultramontane camp.

87. "Old Catholics" refers to a loosely associated group of small communities that broke from Rome and in 1889 were brought together in the Union of Utretch. A number of Catholic priests and laity in Germany and the Netherlands refused to accept the decrees of Vatican I, thinking them innovations. Hence the description, *Old* Catholics.

88. JHN to Maskell, 12 February 1871, *Letters*, 25:283.

89. JHN to Matthew Arnold, 3 December 1871, *Letters*, 25:442.

90. Henry Edward Manning, "Caesarism and Ultramontanism," *Weekly Register*, 3 January 1874, pp. 5–7. This short newspaper essay led Manning into a debate with J. F. Stephen in the pages of the *Contemporary Review* (hereafter *CR*). See J. F. Stephen, "Caesarism and Untramontanism," *CR* 23 (March 1874): 497–527; H. E. Manning, "Ultramontanism and Christianity," *CR* 23 (April 1874): 683–702; J. F. Stephen, "Christianity and Ultra-

montanism," *CR* 23 (May 1874): 989–1017; H. E. Manning, "Christianity and Antichristianism," *CR* 24 (June 1874): 149–74. William E. Gladstone took his cue from the interpretations of papal prerogatives that Manning advanced.

91. The full title of Gladstone's expostulation was *The Vatican Decrees in Their Bearing on Civil Allegiance: A Political Expostulation* (London: Murray, 1874), reprinted in *Newman and Gladstone: The Vatican Decrees*, introd. Alvan S. Ryan (South Bend: Univ. of Notre Dame Press, 1962), pp. 1–72.

92. *Diff.*, 2:177.

93. JHN to Rogers, 2 October 1874, *Letters*, 27:123; see also 27:198, 27:383. Even Newman's choice to address his letter to the duke of Norfolk is instructive. The House of Norfolk was the symbol of the "Old Catholic Religion," i.e., the English Catholic tradition that endured through penal times and was put off by the ultramontane tendencies of recent converts. See JHN to duke of Norfolk, 8 April 1881, *Letters*, 29:361.

94. Bishop Moriarty to JHN, 24 February 1875, *Letters*, 27:237, n. 1.

95. JHN to Northcote, 17 April 1872, *Letters*, 26:65.

96. Newman's shadow over Vatican Council II has been widely discussed. See Charles Stephen Dessain, "Cardinal Newman as Prophet," *Concilium* 37 (1968): 79–98.

CHAPTER FOUR

1. *Diff.*, 2:261.

2. The notion of submission is explained in JHN to William Robert Brownlow, 25 October 1863, *Letters*, 20:545.

3. JHN to Pusey, 23 March 1867, *Letters*, 23:104.

4. JHN to Pusey, 22 March 1867, *Letters*, 23:99.

5. See *Letters*, 12:40, 15:165, 17:281.

6. JHN to Pusey, 23 March 1867, *Letters*, 23:105. See Edward Jeremy Miller, "The Galileo Affair," *Dominicana* 50 (1965): 258–73.

7. JHN to Acton, 30 June 1861, *Letters*, 19:523.

8. See JHN to Ullathorne, 30 December 1862, *Letters*, 20:378–79.

9. JHN, memorandum, December 1862, *Letters*, 20:369, n. 1.

10. Ibid. Note his treatment in *Diff.*, 2:341.

11. See JHN to fellow Oratorian Henry Bittleston, 28 October 1862, *Letters*, 20:331; and JHN to Mrs. John Simeon, 10 November 1867, *Letters*, 23:365.

12. JHN to Archbishop Georges Darboy, n.d., *Letters*, 25:259.

13. *Diff.*, 2:248.

14. JHN to Pusey, 21 July 1867, *Letters*, 23:272.

15. JHN to J. R. Bloxam, 22 February 1870, *Letters*, 25:37.

16. Ibid.

17. There has been some confusion whether Newman was an "Inopportunist," the name for the minority party at the Vatican Council. In the *Letter to Norfolk* he clearly states that he does not think a definition would be inopportune. Inopportunity to him means something uncharitable and a

false step, whereas a truth might well be inexpedient at a particular time. See *Diff.*, 2:193; JHN, memorandum, 27 June 1870, *Letters*, 25:151.

18. JHN to Moriarty, 28 January 1870, *Letters*, 25:17.

19. JHN to Ullathorne, 28 January 1870, *Letters*, 25:18–19. A portion of the letter is in Cuthbert Butler, *The Vatican Council: 1869–1870* (London: Collins and Harvill, 1962), pp. 182–83. The four publications Newman listed were strongly ultramontane.

20. See Newman's reflections on the Old Catholics in his letter to Malcolm Maccoll, 6 March 1875, *Letters*, 27:240.

21. See the lengthy explanation sent to Robert Whitty, 12 April 1870, *Letters*, 25:92–96.

22. Ibid.

23. Ibid.

24. Ibid.

25. JHN to Nevins, 25 June 1874, *Letters*, 27:84.

26. In the *Letter to Norfolk*, Newman answers Gladstone's charge that papal infallibility is a novelty not supported by ancient doctrines and Scripture; he argues that historical scholarship neither proves nor disproves the dogma. The centuries' long discussion about papal infallibility, moreover, has been a growing insight into the Petrine scriptural texts, ending with a "definitive recognition of the doctrine thus gradually manifested to [the Church]." *Diff.*, 2:319.

27. *Diff.*, 2:300; *Letters*, 25:31, 82.

28. See *Letters*, 25:185, 26:139. As instances, Newman mentions *Essay on Development* (1845), pp. 75–92; Birmingham Lectures of 1850, in *Prepos.*, pp. 334–35, 338; and an 1856 preface to *The Church of the Fathers*, in *HS*, 2:xiii. Numerous letters before 1870 affirm Newman's belief in papal infallibility.

29. *Diff.*, 2:312.

30. The phrase is Newman's own; see *Diff.*, 2:339. See also Charles Stephen Dessain, "Infallibility: What Newman Taught in Manning's Church," in *Infallibility in the Church: An Anglican-Catholic Dialogue*, ed. Austin Ferrer et al. (London: Darton, Longman and Todd, 1968), pp. 59–80. A recent article arguing a thesis-antithesis-synthesis reltionship between theologians and magisterium is Ian Ker, "Newman's visie op de verhouding van leergezag en theologien," *Tijdschrift voor Theologie* 21 (1981): 132–45.

31. *Diff.*, 2:328.

32. JHN to Alfred Plummer, 3 April 1871, *Letters*, 25:309. This letter contains Newman's objections to Döllinger's position. Bishop Vinzenz Gasser, the official Relator of the Schema dealing with papal infallibility, commented: "We do not exclude cooperation with the Church because infallibility is given to the Roman Pontiff not by way of inspiration or revelation but by way of divine assistance. Hence, the Pope must take the right means . . . to find the truth." There is no absolute necessity to consult the Church, but there is "a *relative* necessity or opportuneness." Mansi 52:1213, 1215.

33. See *Diff.*, 2:316.

34. *Diff.*, 2:325.

35. JHN to the editor of the London *Times*, 9 September 1872, *Letters*, 26:163.

That popes have moral faults is even an argument for the true nature of infallibility. See JHN to Mrs. Magdalene Helbert, 10 September 1869, *Letters*, 24:328–31.

36. The most blatant case seems to have been Pope Honorius. In order to quell a dispute, Honorius sent a letter to the patriarch of Constantinople using the formula of "one will" in Christ. Years later, the Monothelites utilized his formula. The Third Council of Constantinople (A.D. 681) formally anathematized Honorius. Newman's analysis of the Honorius case may be found in his 16 June 1872 letter to Nevins, *Letters*, 26:117–18.

37. *Bibl.*, p. 118.

38. *Diff.*, 2:329.

39. *Diff.*, 2:334.

40. JHN to Ryder, 16 July 1866, *Letters*, 22:262.

41. Ibid. See also *Bibl.*, p. 113.

42. *Diff.*, 2:320.

43. The council never officially ended. 1 September 1870 turned out to be the last meeting day. A week later troops of the new Italian government invaded the Papal States, and on 20 October the pope suspended the council indefinitely.

44. JHN to Margaret A. Wilson, 24 October 1870, *Letters*, 25:220. Newman also translates Augustine's phrase as "the Christian commonwealth judges without misgiving." See JHN to Helbert, 20 October 1869, *Letters*, 24:354.

45. Bishops Luigi Riccio of Naples and Edward Fitzgerald of Little Rock (United States) voted "no." See Butler, *Vatican Council*, p. 414. At a trial ballot on 13 July, 451 conciliars voted "yes," 88 voted "no," and 62 votes "yes, with reservations." See Mansi 52:1243.

46. JHN to Ullathorne, 6 June 1870, *Letters*, 25:138–39.

47. See JHN to de Lisle, 24 July 1870, *Letters*, 25:165.

48. JHN to Ambrose St. John, 27 July 1870, *Letters*, 25:167.

49. JHN to Helbert, 20 October 1869, *Letters*, 24:354.

50. Ibid., p. 355.

51. Butler, *Vatican Council*, pp. 417–38, provides a moving account of this period and the various struggles of conscience.

52. JHN to Walker, 17 June 1867, *Letters*, 23:254.

53. JHN to Izy Froude, 28 July 1875, *Letters*, 27:337–38.

54. Ibid.

55. Besides a preface, Newman added corrective footnotes to the 1837 text. In a letter of 18 December 1877 to H. P. Liddon, Newman explained his choice of the new title, *The Via Media*. "The Volumes are directed against myself, against my defence of the Church of E, against my assault upon the Church of Rome. Via Media is my own term. Of course I had chosen it, not as original with me, but as Hall's and many others'. . . . And my argument founded on the term 'Via Media' did not lie so much in Anglicanism as being in the middle, as in 'Romanism' being in the extreme. I did not argue, nor fancy Hall etc. to argue, 'That which is in the middle must be right, Anglicanism is in the middle, Ergo,' but 'Rome is wrong, because it is so extreme.'" *Letters*, 28:283.

56. JHN to Lilly, 25 July 1876, *Letters*, 28:95.

57. Charles Stephen Dessain, *The Spirituality of John Henry Newman* (Minneapolis: Winston, 1980), chap. 4, describes Newman's retrieval of resurrection theology. For a treatment of models describing Christ's redemptive work, see Edward Jeremy Miller, "Inclusivist and Exclusivist Issues in Soteriology: To Whom Does Jesus' Saving Power Extend?" *Perspectives in Religious Studies* 12 (1985): 123–39.

58. JHN to de Lisle, 12 March 1875, *Letters*, 27:248.

59. JHN to Elizabeth Anstice, 18 December 1845, *Letters*, 11:69.

60. A detailed analysis of the preface is found in Richard Bergeron, *Les Abus de L'Église d'après Newman* (Tournai: Desclée et Cie, 1971). Maurice Nédoncelle has a very short analysis in "Newman, théologien des abus de l'Église," *Oecumenia: Jahrbuch für ökumenische Forschung* (Gütersloh: Mohn, 1967), pp. 116–34. Volume 1 of the *Via Media* appeared in June 1877 and was reviewed by a number of magazines: *Contemporary Review* 30 (1877): 1093–98; *Church Quarterly Review* 5 (1877): 232–36; *Dublin Review* 29 (1877): 511–17; *Month* 12 (1877): 368–73; *Westminster Review* 52 (1877): 495–97.

61. *VM*, 1:xxxvii.

62. *VM*, 1:xxxviii.

63. Vatican II's *Dogmatic Constitution on the Church* uses the models of prophet, priest, and king to describe the "people of God" (chap. 2), the hierarchy (chap. 3), and the laity (chap. 4). The basis for applying these models to the laity, especially in their prophetic role, is found in Newman's writings.

64. *VM*, 1:xli.

65. Ibid.

66. *VM*, 1:xlvii.

67. *VM*, 1:xlviii.

68. *VM*, 1:lxxv.

69. *VM*, 1;l.

70. *VM*, 1:lxiv.

71. *VM*, 1:xciv.

72. John Rickards Mozley published the entire correspondence years later in the *Contemporary Review* 76 (1899): 357–70. In the introduction he blamed himself for the termination of the correspondence because of his inability to understand the drift of his uncle's fifth letter. Newman's letters are in volume 27 of *Letters*, dated 1, 4, and 21 April, 16 May, and 3 December 1875.

73. Baron Friedrich von Hügel, 30 June 1877, *Letters*, 28:215.

74. JHN to J. R. Mozley, 1 April 1875, *Letters*, 27:260–61. Newman developed other themes with his nephew. The goodness of the church is slowly dispelling the evils that afflict it. Abuses do not arise from the church's formally professed principles but from a neglect of them. The church of the New Testament had abuses, so to quarrel with the present church because it is not faultless is to quarrel with the apostolic church.

75. JHN to James L. Molloy, 11 September 1859, *Letters*, 19:212.

76. Edward Schillebeeckx, *Christ the Sacrament of the Encounter with God* (New York: Sheed and Ward, 1963); Schillebeeckx, *The Mission of the Church*

(New York: Seabury, 1977); Karl Rahner, *The Church and the Sacraments* (New York: Herder and Herder, 1963); Otto Semmelroth, *Die Kirche als Ursakrament* (Frankfurt a.M.: Knecht, 1953); Avery Dulles, *Models of the Church* (Garden City: Doubleday, 1974).

77. Dulles, *Models*, p. 58.
78. Coulson, *Common Tradition*, p. 31.
79. Church, *Oxford Movement*, p. 59.
80. See *US*, p. 330.
81. *Apol.*, pp. 10, 18.
82. *Apol.*, p. 10.
83. John Keble, *The Christian Year* (London: Parker and Co., 1883). The Tractarian series, *Church of the Fathers*, contained sketches of patristic Christianity, the spirit of which was practically forgotten in the early nineteenth century.
84. *US*, p. 75.
85. *Call.*, p. 327.
86. *Call.*, p. 314.
87. *OS*, p. 64.
88. *PS*, 1:19–20.
89. *Dev.*, p. 325.
90. *Ath.*, 2:327.
91. *PS*, 3:169.
92. *PS*, 3:221.
93. Schillebeeckx, *Christ the Sacrament*, passim.
94. *PS*, 4:228.
95. *PS*, 4:205.
96. *PS*, 4:289.
97. *PS*, 5:10.
98. Before the Resurrection, Jesus was not "imperfect" in the sense of being a sinner or in the sense of lacking anything integral to being fully human and fully divine. But the Jesus of the Ministry experienced the "limitations" of a nonresurrected humanity; he prayed in faith that his prayer be heard, he wanted companions for support the night before he died, etc.
99. Peter Berger, *The Sacred Canopy* (Garden City: Doubleday Anchor, 1969).
100. Jan Walgrave, "The Idea of the Church: Reflections on John Coulson's *Newman and the Common Tradition*," *Louvain Studies* 4 (1973): 265–78.
101. *Dev.*, p. 40.

EPILOGUE

1. As recently as 1950, Pope Pius XII wrote in the encyclical, *Humani Generis,* that "the Mystical Body of Christ and the Roman Catholic church are one and the same." *Acta Apostolicae Sedis* 42 (1950): 571.
2. The council's decree, *On Ecumenism,* par. 3, left vague its use of the phrase, "churches or ecclesial communities of the West," to describe non-Orthodox Christian communities. A strong case can be made that Anglicanism,

Lutheranism, etc., are churches of Christ in terms of the council's participational thinking. See Yves Congar, *Dialogue between Christians* (Westminster, Md.: Newman Press, 1966), pp. 184–213.

3. The fullest study of the notes of the church, in this context, is Gustave Thils, *Les Notes de l'Éqlise dans l'Apologétique Catholique dupuis le Réforme* (Gemblous: Duculot, 1937).

4. Küng, *The Church;* Michael Schmaus, *Katholische Dogmatik,* vol. 3/1, *Die Lehre von der Kirche* (Munich: Hueber, 1958); Gregory Baum, *The Credibility of the Church* (London: Burns and Oates, 1968).

5. Baum, *Credibility,* p. 105.

6. Aquinas, *Expositio in Symbolum Apostolorum,* art. 9.

7. Küng, *The Church,* p. 268; German text in *Die Kirche* (Freiburg: Herder, 1967), p. 319.

8. Küng, *The Church,* p. 355.

9. Anne Carr, *The Theological Method of Karl Rahner,* American Academy of Religion Dissertation Series 19 (Missoula: Univ. of Montana Press, 1977).

10. For the importance of the human will in Newman's doctrine of the illative sense, see M. Jamie Ferreira, *Doubt and Religious Commitment* (Oxford: Clarendon Press, 1980). For a synopsis and analysis, see the review by Edward Jeremy Miller, *Thomist* 48 (1984): 309–14.

11. Alois Grillmeier, "Konzil und Rezeption: Methodische Bemerkungen zu einem Thema der oekumenischen Diskussion der Gegenwart," *Theologie und Philosophie* 45 (1970): 321–52; Yves Congar, "La 'réception' comme réalité ecclésiologique," *Revue des Sciences Philosophiques et Théologiques* 56 (1972): 369–403; *Ecumenical Review* 22 (1970); John T. Ford, "Newman on Reception of Doctrine," *Proceedings of the Catholic Theological Society of America* 36 (1981): 187–89.

12. Congar, "La 'réception'," p. 370.

13. See Piet Fransen, "L'autorité des Conciles," *Unam Scantam,* vol. 38, *Problémes de l' Autorité* (Paris: Editions du Cerf, 1962), pp. 59–100.

14. Congar, "La 'réception'," p. 379.

15. Ibid., p. 399. See also Gustave Thils, *L'infaillibilité du peuple chrétien "in credendo": Notes de théologie post-tridentine* (Louvain: Warny, 1963).

16. See Karl Rahner, "Pluralism in Theology and the Oneness of the Church's Profession of Faith," *Concilium* 46 (1969): 103–23; Piet Fransen, "Unity and Confessional Statement," *Bijdragen* 33 (1972): 2–38.

17. Karl Rahner has called dialogue in the church "a sacrament of initiation into the nameless mystery." "A Small Fragment on the Collective Finding of Truth," *Theological Investigations* (Baltimore: Helicon, 1969), 6:86.

18. Newman's epitaph, which he composed himself, can be translated as, "from out of shadows and images into the truth," or, more loosely, "no more shadows and pictures, only the truth now."

Select Bibliography

ewman bibliographies can easily march on for pages. To avoid a lengthy list, I would direct readers to the articles by Dessain and Svaglic in *Victorian Prose* below, which are the best introductions to the literature. These can be supplemented by the Griffin survey of secondary studies, the articles by John Ford, and the ongoing series *Newman Studien*. The Centre of Newman Friends, Via Aurelia 257, 00165 Roma, Italy, provides bibliographical updating through a newsletter. The best "short" introduction to Newman's life is Trevor's *Newman's Journey*, and the best introduction to the intellectual context of his writings is Dessain's *John Henry Newman*, listed below.

PRIMARY SOURCES

1. Primary materials in the Uniform Edition, published by Longmans, Green, and Co., London, New York, Bombay. Date in ⟨⟩ indicates year of composition; date in [] indicates year of incorporation into the Uniform Edition; date in () indicates edition used here.

Apologia pro Vita Sua. ⟨1864⟩ [1873] (1905).

The Arians of the Fourth Century. ⟨1833⟩ [1871] (1908).

Callista, A Tale of the Third Century. ⟨1855⟩ [1876] (1910).

Certain Difficulties Felt by Anglicans in Catholic Teaching. Vol. 1: *Twelve Lectures Addressed to the Anglican Party of 1833* ⟨1850⟩ [1879] (1908); Vol. 2: *Letter to Pusey* ⟨1866⟩ [1876] (1910) and *Letter to the Duke of Norfolk* ⟨1875⟩ [1876] (1910).

Discourses Addressed to Mixed Congregations. ⟨1849⟩ [1871] (1913).

Discussions and Arguments on Various Subjects. ⟨1836–55⟩ [1872] (1911).

An Essay in Aid of a Grammar of Assent. ⟨1870⟩ [1870] (1913).

An Essay on the Development of Christian Doctrine. ⟨1845⟩ [1878] (1909).

Essays Critical and Historical. 2 vols. ⟨1828–46⟩ [1871] (1910).

Fifteen Sermons Preached before the University of Oxford. ⟨1826–43⟩ [1871] (1909).

Historical Sketches. 3 vols. ⟨1853, 1833, 1854⟩ [1872] (1909).

The Idea of a University, Defined and Illustrated. ⟨1852–59⟩ [1873] (1912).

Lectures on the Doctrine of Justification. ⟨1838⟩ [1874] (1908).

Lectures on the Present Position of Catholics in England. ⟨1851⟩ [1872] (1913).

Loss and Gain: The Story of a Convert. ⟨1848⟩ [1874] (1911).

Parochial and Plain Sermons. 8 vols. ⟨1834–43⟩ [1868] (1907–11).

Select Treatises of St. Athanasius. 2 vols. ⟨1842⟩ [1881] (1920).

Sermons Bearing on Subjects of the Day. ⟨1843⟩ [1869] (1909).

Sermons Preached on Various Occasions. ⟨1857⟩ [1870] (1913).

Tracts Theological and Ecclesiastical. ⟨1874⟩ [1874] (1913).

Two Essays on Biblical and Ecclesiastical Miracles. ⟨1826, 1842⟩ [1870] (1911).

Verses on Various Occasions. ⟨1867⟩ [1874] (1900).

The Via Media of the Anglican Church. Vol. 1: *Lectures on the Prophetical Office of the Church* ⟨1837⟩ [1877] (1911); Vol. 2: *Occasional Letters and Tracts* ⟨1830–41⟩ [1877] (1908).

2. Other primary materials.

Addresses to Cardinal Newman with His Replies. Edited by William P. Neville. London: Longmans, Green, and Co., 1905.

Correspondence of John Henry Newman with John Keble and Others. Edited at the Birmingham Oratory. London: Longmans, Green, and Co., 1917.

Faith and Prejudice and Other Unpublished Sermons of Cardinal Newman. Edited by Charles Stephen Dessain. New York: Sheed and Ward, 1956.

John Henry Newman, Autobiographical Writings. Edited with Introductions by Henry Tristram. London: Sheed and Ward, 1956.

Letters and Correspondence of John Henry Newman during His Life in the English Church. Edited by Anne Mozley. 2 vols. London: Longmans, Green, and Co., 1903.

The Letters and Diaries of John Henry Newman. Edited by Charles Stephen Dessain et al. 31 volumes when completed. London: Thomas Nelson and Sons, and Oxford: Clarendon Press, 1961–.

Letters of John Henry Newman. Edited by Derek Stanford and Muriel Spark. London: Peter Owen, 1957.

Meditations and Devotions of the Late Cardinal Newman. Edited by W. F. Neville. London: Longmans, Green, and Co., 1901.

My Campaign in Ireland. Aberdeen: A. King and Co., 1896.

The Mystery of the Church. Edited by M. K. Strolz. Rome: Centre of Newman Friends, 1981.

Newman the Oratorian: His Unpublished Oratory Papers. Edited by Placid Murray. Dublin: Gill and Macmillan, 1969.

On Consulting the Faithful in Matters of Doctrine. Edited with an Introduction by John Coulson. London: Chapman, 1961.

On the Inspiration of Scripture. Edited with an Introduction by J. Derek Holmes and Robert Murray. London: Chapman, 1967.

The Philosophical Notebooks of John Henry Newman. Edited with an Introduction by Edward Sillem. 2 vols. Louvain: Nauwelaerts, 1969.

Sermon Notes of John Henry Cardinal Newman: 1849–1878. Edited by the Fathers of the Birmingham Oratory. London: Longmans, Green, and Co., 1913.

Stray Essays on Controversial Points, Variously Illustrated. Private Printing of the Birmingham Oratory, 1890.

The Theological Papers of John Henry Newman on Biblical Inspiration and on Infallibility. Edited by J. Derek Holmes. Oxford: Clarendon Press, 1979.

The Theological Papers of John Henry Newman on Faith and Certainty. Edited by Hugo de Achaval and J. Derek Holmes. Oxford: Clarendon Press, 1976.

GENERAL BIBLIOGRAPHIES AND REVIEWS
OF THE LITERATURE

Benard, Edmond Darvil. "Newman Centennial Literature: A Bibliography." In *American Essays for the Newman Centennial,* edited by John K. Ryan and Edmond Benard, pp. 211–27. Washington: Catholic Univ. Press, 1947.

Blehl, Vincent. *John Henry Newman: A Bibliographical Catalogue of His Writings.* Charlottesville: Univ. Press of Virginia, 1978.

Dessain, Charles Stephen. "Newman's Philosophy and Theology." In *Victorian Prose: A Guide to Research,* edited by David DeLaura, pp. 166–84. New York: Modern Language Association of America, 1973.

Dupuy, Bernard-Dominique. "Bulletin d'Histoire des Doctrines: Newman." *Revue des Sciences Philosophiques et Théologiques* 45 (1961): 125–76; 56 (1972): 78–126.

Earnest, James David, and Gerard Gracey. *John Henry Newman: An Annotated Bibliography of His Tract and Pamphlet Collection.* New York: Garland, 1984.

Ford, John T. "Newman Studies: Recent Resources and Research." *Thomist* 46 (1982): 283–306.

———. "Recent Studies on Newman: Two Review Articles." *Thomist* 41 (1977): 424–440.

Fries, Heinrich, and Werner Becker, eds. *Newman Studien.* 11 vols. to date. Nuremberg: Glock and Lutz, 1948–.

Griffin, John R. *Newman: A Bibliography of Secondary Sources.* Front Royal, Va.: Christendom College Press, 1980.

Svaglic, Martin J. "Man and Humanist." In *Victorian Prose: A Guide to Research,* edited by David DeLaura, pp. 113–65. New York: Modern Language Association of America, 1973.

Tristram, Henry, and Francis Bacchus. "Newman (John Henry)." *Dictionnaire de théologie catholique,* cols. 353–98. 11th ed. Paris: Letouzey, 1931.

SELECTED SECONDARY TEXTS CITED IN NOTES

Aubert, Roger, ed. *History of the Church.* Vol. 8, *The Church in the Age of Liberalism.* New York: Crossroad, 1981.

Baum, Gregory. *The Credibility of the Church.* London: Burns and Oates, 1968.

Berger, Peter. *The Sacred Canopy*. Garden City: Doubleday Anchor, 1969.

Bergeron, Richard. *Les Abus de L'Église d'après Newman*. Tournai: Desclée et Cie, 1971.

Bergson, Henri. *The Two Sources of Morality and Religion*. London: Macmillan and Co., 1935.

Bouyer, Louis. *L'Église de Dieu*. Paris: Editions du Cerf, 1970.

————. *Newman: His Life and Spirituality*. Translated by J. Lewis May. New York: Kenedy and Sons, 1958.

Butler, Cuthbert. *The Vatican Council: 1869–1870*. London: Collins and Harvill, 1962.

Carr, Anne. *The Theological Method of Karl Rahner*. American Academy of Religion Dissertation Series 19. Missoula: Univ. of Montana Press, 1977.

Church, Richard W. *The Oxford Movement*. London: Macmillan, 1891. Reprint. Chicago: Univ. of Chicago Press, 1970.

Congar, Yves. *Dialogue between Christians*. Westminster, Md.: Newman Press, 1966.

————. *Lay People in the Church*. Westminster, Md.: Newman Press, 1967.

Coulson, John. *Newman and the Common Tradition*. Oxford: Clarendon Press, 1970.

Dessain, Charles Stephen. *John Henry Newman*. London: Adam and Charles Black, 1971.

————. *The Spirituality of John Henry Newman*. Minneapolis: Winston, 1980.

Dulles, Avery. *Models of the Church*. Garden City: Doubleday, 1974.

Ferreira, M. Jamie. *Doubt and Religious Commitment*. Oxford: Clarendon Press, 1980.

Fey, William. *Faith and Doubt: The Unfolding of Newman's Thought on Certainty*. Shepherdstown, W. Va.: Patmos Press, 1976.

Holmes, J. Derek. *More Roman than Rome: English Catholicism in the Nineteenth Century*. Shepherdstown, W. Va.: Patmos Press, 1978.

Jaki, Stanislas. *Les Tendances Nouvelle de l'Ecclésiologie*. Rome: Herder, 1957.

Kavanagh, Aiden. *The Shape of Baptism*. New York: Pueblo, 1978.

Küng, Hans. *The Church*. London: Burns and Oates, 1967.

————. *Infallible? An Inquiry*. Garden City: Doubleday, 1971.

Lash, Nicholas. *Newman on Development: The Search for an Explanation in History.* Shepherdstown, W. Va.: Patmos Press, 1975.

Liddon, H. P. *Life of Edward Bouverie Pusey.* London: Longmans, Green, and Co., 1893.

Lonergan, Bernard. *Insight.* San Francisco: Harper and Row, 1978.

―――. *Method in Theology.* New York: Herder and Herder, 1972.

―――. *A Second Collection.* Edited by William Ryan and Bernard Tyrrell. Philadelphia: Westminster, 1974.

McElrath, Damian. *The Syllabus of Pius IX: Some Reactions in England.* Louvain: Publications Universitaires, 1964.

Pol, W. H. van de. *De Kerk in het Leven en Denken van Newman.* Nijkerk: Callenbach, 1936.

Rahner, Karl. *The Church and the Sacraments.* New York: Herder and Herder, 1963.

―――. *Foundations of Christian Faith.* New York: Seabury, 1978.

Schiffers, Norbert. *Die Einheit der Kirche nach Newman.* Düsseldorf: Patmos, 1956.

Schillebeeckx, Edward. *Christ the Sacrament of the Encounter with God.* New York: Sheed and Ward, 1963.

―――. *Layman in the Church.* New York: Alba, 1963.

Schlegel, Friedrich von. *Philosophie des Lebens.* Edited by Jean-Jacques Anstett, Ernst Behler, and Hans Eichner. Munich: Verlag Ferdinand Schoningh, 1969.

Schnackenburg, Rudolf. *The Church in the New Testament.* New York: Herder and Herder, 1965.

Semmelroth, Otto. *Die Kirche als Ursakrament.* Frankfurt a.M.: Knecht, 1953.

Strolz, M. K., ed. *John Henry Newman: Commemorative Essays on the Occasion of the Centenary of His Cardinalate.* Rome: Tipografia Gurerra, 1979.

Swidler, Leonard, and Arlene Swidler, eds. *Women Priests: A Catholic Commentary on the Vatican Declaration.* New York: Paulist, 1977.

Thils, Gustave. *L'infaillibilité du peuple chrétien "in credendo": Notes de théologie post-tridentine.* Louvain: Warny, 1963.

―――. *Les Notes de l'Église dans l'Apologétique Catholique depuis le Réforme.* Gemblous: Duculot, 1937.

Tracy, David. *The Analogical Imagination.* New York: Crossroad, 1981.

Trevor, Meriol. *Newman: Light in Winter* and *Newman: The Pillar of the Cloud.* London: Macmillan and Co., 1962.

———. *Newman's Journey.* Glasgow: Collins, 1974. Reprint. Huntingdon, Ind.: Our Sunday Visitor, 1985.

Walgrave, Jan. *Le Développement du Dogme.* Paris: Casterman, 1957.

———. *Unfolding Revelation.* Philadelphia: Westminster, 1972.

Ward, Wilfrid. *The Life of John Henry Cardinal Newman.* 2 vols. London: Longmans, Green, and Co., 1912.

Index of Names

(Persons are indexed if they are mentioned in the narrative, if they wrote to or received letters from Newman, or if the endnote mentioning them is more than simply a bibliographical resource.)